CHILDREN IN URBAN SOCIETY

THE URBAN LIFE IN AMERICA SERIES
RICHARD C. WADE, GENERAL EDITOR

STANLEY BUDER
PULLMAN: An Experiment in Industrial Order
and Community Planning, 1880–1930

ALLEN F. DAVIS
SPEARHEADS FOR REFORM: The Social Settlements
and the Progressive Movement, 1890–1914

LYLE W. DORSETT
THE PENDERGAST MACHINE

JOSEPH M. HAWES
CHILDREN IN URBAN SOCIETY: Juvenile Delinquency in
Nineteenth-Century America

MELVIN G. HOLLI
REFORM IN DETROIT: Hazen S. Pingree and Urban Politics

KENNETH T. JACKSON
THE KU KLUX KLAN IN THE CITY, 1915–1930

ZANE L. MILLER
BOSS COX'S CINCINNATI: Urban Politics in the Progressive Era

RAYMOND A. MOHL
POVERTY IN NEW YORK, 1783–1825

HUMBERT S. NELLI
ITALIANS IN CHICAGO, 1880–1930: A Study in Ethnic Mobility

JAMES F. RICHARDSON
THE NEW YORK POLICE: Colonial Times to 1901

PETER J. SCHMITT
BACK TO NATURE: The Arcadian Myth in Urban America,
1900–1930

CHILDREN
IN URBAN SOCIETY

Juvenile Delinquency
in Nineteenth-Century America

JOSEPH M. HAWES

NEW YORK
OXFORD UNIVERSITY PRESS
1971

To Kay and Lyda

Foreword

Americans have always shown a special fondness for youth. Perhaps it is because as a nation we were the offspring of Europe, a young Republic among older countries, that we have managed to think of ourselves as permanently young. Even though we face our 200th birthday in 1976, most Americans persist in this illusion of youth. And when new countries are born—especially in the case of Israel—the tendency is to think of them as somehow part of our historical generation, distinct from the older societies of Europe and Asia. And every year the extraordinary investment in universal education is simply an annual reminder of this commitment to our children.

Thus the recent estrangement between generations has brought particular pain to most Americans, throwing in doubt the conventional view of family relationships. For our fascination with youth has always carried with it the belief that every child is essentially good, that with care and affection and education he would grow up to be a virtuous and useful citizen. There were, to be sure, "bad" children, but they were few and their presence did not disturb the basic assumption. Deviant behavior could be explained away by individual problems, by special circumstances, or even by unnatural causes.

Scholars have long known this popular view to be at least shallow and mistaken—when it was not a mask for deep anxiety. Behind every Tom Sawyer there lurked a Huckleberry Finn; even Horatio Alger paired off Robert Rushton and James Leech. In this volume Joseph Hawes examines another strain of American childhood—the juvenile delinquent. What did society do when its expectations about the young were upset, when cherished values seemed challenged by significant numbers even if they were only children? In examining this troublesome thread the author begins when the question was first raised, in the colonial period, and brings it down into modern times. Out of this continuing concern, he finds the roots of contemporary attitudes and policies.

Mr. Hawes begins with the changing legal framework of American society which increasingly separated young offenders from older criminals. Once viewed simply as miniature adults, children were handled without special consideration. By the mid-nineteenth century, both judicial procedures and agency practices treated young lawbreakers, at least for first and minor offenses, as wayward youngsters rather than dangerous criminals. The object of public policy was prevention and reformation rather than punishment and revenge. The author starts with the establishment of the first separate institution for juvenile delinquents in the United States, the New York House of Refuge; the story culminates with the establishment of the Juvenile Court in Chicago in 1899. By the twentieth century, children brought before Judge Ben Lindsay in Denver found the experience more like a conversation with a kindly, if stern, uncle rather than the forbidding confrontation characteristic of courtrooms in the previous century.

Indeed, Mr. Hawes sees the American movement toward a more humane treatment of juvenile delinquency as part of a general concern in Western countries. The crusade was transatlantic, with Americans members of a kind of interlocking directorate of reform. Most of the ideas, he points out, originated in Europe, but they found their widest adoption in the United States. "The New World," he asserts, "served as a kind of laboratory for the thinkers of the Old World." Oliver Twist was, of course, the West's most famous delinquent, and Dickens's novel had a profound impact here as well as in Great Britain. But equally important was the work of the more obscure Mary Carpenter, who pioneered in free day schools, industrial feeding schools, and reform schools. Johann Wichern's *Rauhe Haus* near Hamburg attracted a stream of American visitors as did its French counterpart, the *Colonie Agricole*.

And the lively debate between Italian and French anthropologists and sociologists had their analogue in this country. The author knows it is both mistaken and unwise to pull this national movement out of its broad Western context.

Part of that broader context, of course, was the rise of the modern city, which sharpened the question. There had always been "bad" children on the countryside, but scattered populations and generous space both isolated and diluted the damage done by youthful offenders. In cities, on the other hand, the problem was more concentrated and more visible and the consequences more easily understood. Every city had its "dangerous class," as contemporaries called the large numbers of wayward and vagrant youngsters. Untouched by family discipline or the restraints of schooling, their presence was one of persistent concern and fear. In fact the connection between urbanization and juvenile delinquency was so close that every generation of reformers proposed as one solution the sending of city children to farms or remote reformatories. As an Illinois judge of the Juvenile Court put it: "I can authoratively [sic] declare that there is nothing so enchanting to a boy as country life." Yet as urban growth continued, so did the number of children who needed care and help.

But Mr. Hawes sees the development of new institutions as a reflection of changed attitudes as well as laws and agencies, and he skillfully weaves together the activities of pioneers in reforming the public's perception of children with the work of agencies and institutions entrusted with their care. This technique gives a concreteness and persuasiveness often lacking in books dealing with only the commanding figure of a movement or its most famous institutional embodiment. Readers will find here a wide range of well known figures seen in a new light; Mark Twain and Horatio Alger; G. Stanley Hall and John Dewey; Lester Ward and William Graham Sumner; Jane Addams and Anthony Comstock. They will also discover people who should never have been forgotten like Charles Loring Brace, Theodore Lyman, Zebulon Brockway, and John Griscom. In short, this is no narrow monograph, but a study which ranges across a broad segment of our national experience.

Indeed, there is a curious contemporary ring to this historical study. Almost all the vexing present problems are here. As early as 1904 G. Stanley Hall could write that "there is a marked increase of crime at ages twelve to fourteen, not in crimes of one kind, but all kinds," and "adolescence is preeminently the crucial age when most first commitments occur and the most vicious careers begin." There was concern with the collapse of family structure ("God's reformatory" in Charles Loring Brace's felicitous phrase) and the inability of parents to exercise control over children. Nor were the schools any help, for as one contemporary confided, "much in our present education is artificial, mechanical, arbitrary; and the product is only too frequently a living conventional lie." In seeking solutions reformers suggested job training, regular employment, individual counseling and care, lenient (or stern) probationary supervision, and wide-scale changes in urban institutions. Hence, like other volumes in the *Urban Life in America* series, *Children in Urban Society* illumines an important, if neglected, historical topic while it provides a useful perspective for the understanding of an urgent problem of our time.

RICHARD C. WADE
GENERAL EDITOR
URBAN LIFE IN AMERICA

New York, N.Y.
April 1971

Preface

Until recently scholars have all but ignored the history of juvenile delinquency in the United States. The growing numbers of troubled young people in the United States had so captured the interests and energies of writers and scholars that they concentrated their efforts on explaining or attempting to solve the problem of juvenile delinquency in contemporary America. Rarely did these writers acknowledge the fact that the youthful offenders, like the poor, have always been with us and that nineteenth-century Americans also faced the challenges of wild and undisciplined children on city streets. Now, however, scholars like Richard S. Pickett and Anthony Platt have helped to show that juvenile delinquency existed in earlier times and to explain some of the methods society used in the nineteenth century to try to solve the problem of juvenile delinquency.

My purpose is to bridge the gap between Pickett's book on the New York House of Refuge and Platt's work on The Cook County Juvenile Court,[1] while at the same time presenting a complete narrative of American responses to the challenge of juvenile delinquency. For the most part, the institutions and methods which are used today to "treat" juvenile delinquents in the United States first appeared during the nineteenth century. Thus, this study provides background and perspective for today's efforts to solve the problem of juvenile delinquency. I hope that sociologists, social reformers, and people who work with juvenile delinquents would find it interesting and perhaps useful.

A history of juvenile delinquency in nineteenth-century America is basically a chapter in the history of the city in the United States.

Such a study reveals one of the great number of social problems which resulted from the concentration of population in American cities in the nineteenth century. An investigation of a problem such as juvenile delinquency also reveals the inadequacy of governmental agencies and institutions designed to handle urban social problems and thus also reveals some of the deficiencies of city government as a whole. Just as informal responses would be needed to meet the growing problem of juvenile delinquency in nineteenth-century America, so would informal and private means be found to offset the lack of an adequate administrative structure for the nineteenth-century American city.

My basic approach to the problem of wayward children in nineteenth-century America has been historical, although one of the main methods of analysis I have used is based on Emile Durkheim's theory that crime is functional. Nevertheless, I want to emphasize that present utility is not my chief concern. I am not trying to explain juvenile delinquency or to discuss possible solutions to this continuing problem. In order to avoid distorting the evolution of juvenile delinquency and its treatment in the last century, I have tried not to apply today's attitudes and theories to nineteenth-century children. I have tried to present the problem of juvenile delinquency as nineteenth-century Americans saw it and trace their reactions and responses to that problem.

The story has many sub-plots, but there are two fairly clear lines of descent, one for institutions and the other for the main ideas in the history of juvenile delinquency in nineteenth-century America. If the story has a theme, it is that of an increasing individualization of the treatment of juvenile delinquents and a growing awareness on society's part that young offenders were individuals in need of help rather than members of a stereotyped group which merited society's condemnation.

I could not have begun this effort without the help and guidance of a number of people. First, I must express my appreciation to Professor William H. Goetzmann who encouraged me to undertake this task and who has been of immeasurable help to me in its completion. Others who read the entire manuscript and provided help and criticism are Professors David D. Van Tassel, H. Wayne Morgan, Robert A. Divine, and Ivan Belknap of the University of Texas, and Mrs. Mary Margaret Albright of Austin, Texas. In addition, I owe a special debt to those who read portions of the manuscript: Professors Barnes F. Lathrop, Michael G. Hall, and Robert Crunden of the University of Texas, and Mrs. Virginia Noelke of Austin, Texas. The errors that remain, however, are my own responsibility.

Special thanks go to Mr. Charles Dwyer and Mrs. Jean Herold of the Inter-Library Borrowing Service of the University of Texas at Austin. Without their assistance this study literally could not have been written. Mrs. Michelle Aldrich, whose husband has already acknowledged her as "a frighteningly efficient research assistant," helped immensely by chasing down several fugitive items in the Library of Congress. I wish to thank also the unfailingly courteous and efficient staffs of the Manuscript Division of the Library of Congress, the Manuscript Division of the Carnegie Library of Syracuse University, the Manuscript Division of the University of Chicago Library, and the Schlesinger Library at Radcliffe College. A special word of gratitude goes to Mr. Francis J. Ordway, the Superintendent of the Lyman School for Boys at Westborough, Massachusetts and the boys in Lyman Hall at the school for their enthusiastic interest in my study. Thanks are also due to Sharon Cunningham and Anne C. Rowland who helped to compile the index. To my wife's relatives, Mr. and Mr. John Schnell of Crownsville, Maryland, who provided food and shelter during a summer's work at the Library of Congress, goes a full vote of thanks. Finally, this study was supported by University Fellowships in 1967–68 and 1968–69 and travel grants from the Graduate School of the University of Texas at Austin, for which thanks are due.

J.M.H.

Austin, Texas
January 1971

Acknowledgments

I wish to thank Mrs. Charlotte Olmsted Kursh for permission to quote from the papers of her father, Frederick Law Olmsted; Mrs. Albert Mellinkopf for permission to quote from the papers of Judge Ben Lindsey; Mrs. S. Rae Logan for permission to quote from the papers of her mother, Mrs. Ethel Sturges Dummer; and the George Arents Research Library of Syracuse University for permission to use the records of the New York House of Refuge.

Contents

CHILDREN IN URBAN SOCIETY

1

The Awful Tragedy of Jesse Pomeroy, Nineteenth-Century America's Most Notorious Juvenile Delinquent

On a Saturday afternoon in July, 1874, workmen were clearing the cellar of a house at 327 Broadway Street in South Boston, Massachusetts, so that the new owner, James Nash, could open a grocery store. One of the workmen, a man named McGuiness, moved a large stone resting on a pile of ashes and discovered a human skeleton. As McGuiness brushed the ashes away, tattered bits of clothing indicated that he had found the remains of a small girl. The workmen called the police, and soon Captain Dyer and two other officers from Station VI, only a short distance away, arrived on the scene.

Dyer knew that four months before, Katie Curran, a ten-year-old girl from the neighborhood, had mysteriously disappeared. There seemed to be little doubt that McGuiness had found her skeleton. Dyer took the scraps of clothing to the station house and compared them with a swatch of material the Currans had given the police. The pieces matched in color and design, and the distraught mother identified the clothing as having belonged to her daughter.

Neighbors recalled that the house had been formerly occupied by a Mrs. Pomeroy and her two sons, Charles and Jesse. Jesse, the younger of the two boys, was at fifteen brought to trial for the brutal murder of a little boy. Even before he had been accused of the murder of the little boy, Jesse Pomeroy had acquired a notorious reputation as a bully in the neighborhood. Earlier he had gone to the State Reform School at Westborough for torturing some of the little boys in the neighborhood, but he had recently been released as reformed. When the Curran girl had been reported missing, suspicion immediately fell on young Pomeroy, but questioning and a search of the cellar of the house at 327 Broadway turned up nothing. Nevertheless, the neighbors had continued to mutter about Jesse.[1]

In 1872 Jesse Pomeroy had enticed several—at least six—small boys into isolated spots where he systematically tortured them. In September of that year young Pomeroy was arrested and tried before the court for juvenile offenders in Suffolk County[2] and sentenced to the State Reform School. At Westborough his behavior was apparently good, for in less than two years he was released.

Mrs. Ruth Ann Pomeroy lived apart from her husband and worked as a dressmaker. She maintained a shop in the house at 327 Broadway and lived nearby at 312 Broadway. On the morning of March 18, 1874, she sent Jesse over to open the shop. Meanwhile, ten-year-old Katie Curran left home a little early for school and wandered into the Pomeroy shop looking for papers. Jesse told her that he had some in the cellar. Later he gave the following account: "I followed her, put my arm about her neck, my hand over her mouth, and with my knife in my right hand, cut her throat." He dragged the body over behind a water closet and piled ashes and stones on it. He then washed off his cheap pocket knife and returned to the shop.

No one missed Katie until late afternoon. When she failed to return home as expected, her mother went to the police. Captain Dyer began a routine investigation for a child he believed to be playing somewhere in the neighborhood. A newsboy had seen Katie go into the Pomeroy shop and told Mrs. Curran about it.

She told Captain Dyer, but he only laughed at her. A detective at the police station told her that there was no way into the cellar of the Pomeroy shop and that she had no reason to be alarmed. At Mrs. Curran's insistence, Dyer questioned the newsboy and had his men search the cellar.

Shortly over a month later, on April 22, Jesse left to go to "the city," Boston. As he walked along Dorchester Avenue, he saw a little boy, Horace Millen, playing in the street. He offered to show the boy "the steamer" and together they wandered into a marsh. Pomeroy carefully lifted the boy over a small stream, and then he attacked him with the same knife he had used on Katie Curran. The boy put up quite a struggle, and Pomeroy stabbed him repeatedly. Again, Pomeroy carefully washed off the knife. Then he went on his way to Boston. Two boys playing in the marsh had seen Pomeroy lift the Millen boy across the stream. Later they came across the body and sent for the police.

Jesse Pomeroy confessed to the murder of Horace Millen, and when asked why he did it, replied: "I do not know; I couldn't help it," and pointing to his head, added "it is here." While Pomeroy was awaiting trial, the workmen discovered the remains of Katie Curran. "The boy fiend," as the newspapers referred to Pomeroy, confessed to her killing as well. When the news of Jesse Pomeroy's implication in the Curran case spread, Mrs. Pomeroy and Charles had to be placed in protective custody. To allow the uproar to die down, the trial was delayed until December. Meanwhile, reporters treated their readers to a fantastic account of the reasons for young Pomeroy's brutal actions.

The *Boston Daily Globe* of July 21, 1874, claimed that "three well-known physicians" had visited Mrs. Pomeroy to find out all they could about the boy and perhaps learn the reasons for his crimes. Mrs. Pomeroy, its account went on, told the doctors that her husband—from whom she was then separated—had been a butcher. During the time she was pregnant with Jesse she often went to the slaughter-house to witness the killing of the animals, taking a particular delight in watching the process and sometimes assisting her husband. When Jesse was a little boy, he often spent a great deal of time in his father's butcher shop and amused himself by plunging knives into raw meat. The facts were enough, the article concluded, to say that Jesse was "simply marked by his mother, as other children have been, only in a different way."

In a later interview, however, Mrs. Pomeroy denied this story. The "three prominent physicians" had not visited her, and her husband had not been working as a butcher when she was expecting Jesse. In fact, said Mrs. Pomeroy, she had never seen an animal slaughtered. Furthermore, Jesse's father only carried carcasses around the city market; he did not own a butcher shop. Mrs. Pomeroy thought that her son's mania had been caused by an illness that developed soon after he had been vaccinated for smallpox.

The trial of Jesse Pomeroy for the murder of Horace Millen began on December 8, 1874. Although Pomeroy had confessed to this crime and the murder of Katie Curran, both the Attorney General and the District Attorney for Suffolk County represented the Commonwealth of Massachusetts against him. The prosecution contended that Pomeroy was guilty of murder in the first degree and set forth a careful, although circumstantial, chain of evidence linking him to the crime. The defense did not dispute the fact of the killing, but claimed that Jesse Pomeroy was insane. The defense showed that his behavior had been consistently unusual since early childhood. Former neighbors testified that he had once tortured and killed a cat, and that he was "strange" and sometimes violent. Several little boys described how Pomeroy had lured them to isolated spots and tortured them. One of the boys described how Jesse had beaten him repeatedly and had stuck pins into him. Following the little boys on the stand, two employees of the State Reform School testified to Pomeroy's good behavior as an inmate. Mrs. Pomeroy then took the stand and recalled that her son often had severe headaches and violent nightmares. A former teacher testified that Jesse had been a good student, but added that he annoyed other children and would not take punishment. When reproved he would say, "I could not help it." After a challenge from the Attorney General, which was over-ruled, the defense counsel introduced Pomeroy's confession of the murder of Katie Curran.

To conclude its case the defense called two experts in insanity. The first, Dr. John C. Tyler, was a specialist in the treatment of the insane. He had visited Pomeroy in his cell several times and had followed, he claimed, the evidence given in the trial. What struck him about the boy's actions was the lack of a motive. Taken together with the strange, violent behavior, the bloodthirstiness, and the headaches, his actions indicated that Jesse Pomeroy was insane. Another factor pointing to the boy's insanity, Dr. Tyler added, was his "insensibility to the consequences of his acts." Finally, the Doctor concluded, the fact that Pomeroy had felt strong pressure in his head before each of his terrible deeds, indicated epilepsy. In the cross-examination the Attorney General developed the view that the acts of Jesse Pomeroy accessory to the murder were those of a sane person. He had chosen a secluded spot, had tried to avoid observation and detection, and had thrown away the weapon. Dr. Tyler also admitted that a love of cruelty for its own sake might constitute a motive for committing acts of cruelty.

The second expert witness for the defense was Dr. Clement A. Walker, who had been the superintendent of the Boston Lunatic Hospital for twenty-three years. Dr. Walker thought that the evidence presented in the trial indicated that Pomeroy was "la-boring under a mental disorder." As Dr. Tyler had done, Dr. Walker cited Pomeroy's lack of motive. Dr. Walker had also ex-amined the boy in his cell. During these examinations Pomeroy had not shown any remorse for his actions, and as a result Dr. Walker concluded that he was insane. Walker also agreed with Tyler's diagnosis of epilepsy. In the cross-examination the At-torney General established that Dr. Walker did not think that the evidence presented during the trial showed Pomeroy to be insane. It did indicate, however, that the boy was "wholly irresponsible on account of mental aberration." Furthermore, the fact that the boy had run away after committing his crime was proof that he knew right from wrong.

Now the Commonwealth called its own expert witness, Dr. George T. Choate, who was in private practice in New York. Dr. Choate, who had been the superintendent of the Massachusetts State Lunatic Hospital at Taunton, had treated Horace Greely. Dr. Choate said that he was unable to decide whether Pomeroy was insane or not from the evidence given at the trial. As the other experts had done, Dr. Choate had visited Pomeroy in his cell. In those interviews, Choate said, the boy indicated that he knew the consequences of his acts. Consequently, Dr. Choate believed that Pomeroy was sane when he murdered the Millen boy. After Dr. Choate's testimony the court adjourned, with only the attorneys' final arguments remaining before the case went to the jury.

Charles Robinson, the chief counsel for the defense, asked the jury to return a verdict of not guilty by reason of insanity. In his summation Robinson reviewed the evidence and contended that it clearly showed Jesse Pomeroy to be insane. He charged that Dr. Choate's testimony had been biased in favor of the prosecution and closed by characterizing Pomeroy as "an unfortunate boy, whose mind was impelled to evil by an unseen and inexplicable power."

The prosecution's case, the Attorney General claimed, rested on three clear facts: Horace Millen had been killed; Jesse Pomeroy killed him, and Jesse Pomeroy had acted with premeditation. On the question of premeditation the Attorney General said that time was not an important factor. What mattered was whether or not Pomeroy had acted as a free agent. The circumstances surrounding the crime, he argued, indicated that the boy knew right from wrong and that he had not been insane. The testimony of the experts, he reminded the jury, was only evidence, and he stressed the fact that under cross-examination the experts called by the defense had admitted that the circumstances surrounding the crime indicated that Jesse Pomeroy was sane.

In his charge to the jury the judge told them that they had to decide two questions: Whether Jesse Pomeroy had murdered Horace Millen, and if he had, what degree of murder it was. Jesse Pomeroy was over fourteen, and if he was of sound mind, he was responsible for his acts. The judge reminded the jury of its duty to weigh all evidence, including the expert testimony, before rendering its verdict.

After deliberating for over two hours the jury sent out two questions. If Pomeroy had taken the Millen boy to the marsh only to torture him and later decided to kill him, was this premeditated murder? Second, they wanted to know if homicide committed under circumstances of extreme atrocity was murder in the first degree. The court ruled that premeditation did not require any specified amount of time, so long as the malice aforethought had been formed before the crime was committed. The second question was answered by a statute which stated that a homicide committed under such circumstances was murder in the first degree. In a little more than an hour the jury returned with a verdict of guilty of murder in the first degree. The foreman of the jury then handed two documents to the judge. The first indicated that the jury had found its verdict because of the atrocity of the crime. In the second the jury requested that the usual penalty of death for first degree murder be commuted to life imprisonment.

Despite two escape attempts, Jesse Pomeroy spent the rest of his life in jail. The impact of his crimes and the questions they raised was felt throughout the country, and Pomeroy became the best-known juvenile delinquent in nineteenth-century America.

The case of Jesse Pomeroy represents the challenge of juvenile delinquency to nineteenth-century America. Every vagrant or homeless child and every youthful offender seemed to the essentially conservative men at the top of American society a potential Jesse Pomeroy, and a threat to the orderly progress of American civilization.

Juvenile delinquency, the involvement of children with law-enforcement officials, was necessarily an urban problem. This was true because urban society offered more opportunities for juvenile misbehavior, and because a city environment imposed more constraints on youthful activities than a rural setting. One of the main causes of juvenile delinquency was the dislocation or disruption of family life. The pressures and rigors of city living often caused the break-up of families and forced children to shift for themselves in the unfriendly streets of the city. Finally, when children did misbehave, city dwellers relied on public officials to deal with them. In the country and in small towns, each family saw itself as a vital member of the community. Consequently, youthful misbehavior in a rural environment rarely led to official action; instead small-town dwellers accepted the problems presented by youthful trouble-makers with a "boys will be boys" attitude.[3]

The purpose of this study is to delineate, discuss, and analyze the major institutional responses to the challenge of juvenile delinquency in nineteenth-century America. As such it presents a series of such institutions, ranging chronologically from the establishment of the New York House of Refuge in 1825 to the creation of the juvenile court in 1899. By no means are all such institutions discussed; rather the study focuses on those that represented a departure from the established traditions of treating juvenile delinquents. The chief goal is to tell the story of how Americans changed the methods they used to try to solve the continuing problem of juvenile delinquency. Such a story, however, is more than a discussion of changing institutions; it also reveals some of the basic patterns of American culture—particularly the process through which that culture was transmitted during the nineteenth century. Society regards a youthful law-breaker or trouble-maker —a juvenile delinquent—as somewhat uncivilized. He does not behave according to society's expectations; that is, he does not conform to society's values and norms. He has not, in short, fully absorbed the culture of his society. What he needs, then, is treatment that will inculcate the values and norms of society. Thus, the story of how American society responded to the challenge of juvenile delinquency in the nineteenth century reveals some of the basic values of American culture.

Those essential values are further revealed by the study of the changing definitions of juvenile delinquency. According to the well-known sociologist, Emile Durkheim, "crime is . . . necessary." It

> brings together upright consciences and concentrates them. We have only to notice what happens, particularly in a small town, when some moral scandal has just been committed. They stop each other on the street, they visit each other, they seek to come together to talk of the event and to wax indignant in common. From all the similar impressions which are exchanged, from all the temper that gets itself expressed, there emerges a unique temper, more or less determinate according to the circumstances, which is everybody's without being anybody's in particular.

Aside from its destructiveness and the concern it causes, crime has a use in society. It provides the chief means by which a society identifies its essential values. What a given society regards as a crime indicates what that society holds most dear.[4]

But the main purpose of this study remains that of tracing the changing institutional responses to the continuing challenges of juvenile delinquency. The men who worked to create the New York House of Refuge in 1825, the first institution for juvenile delinquents in the United States, carried with them certain basic assumptions about children and about crime. Those assumptions were rooted in colonial America's ways of dealing with misbehaving children and in the ideals and writings of some of the leading thinkers of the enlightenment—men like Voltaire, Montesquieu, Beccaria, and John Howard.

2

Background: The Heritage of Colonial America and the Eighteenth-Century World

The community may respond to the challenge of juvenile delinquency in several ways: it may take a negative approach and prescribe special punishments for children's delinquent acts, or it may make its expectations for children quite explicit and exhort parents and teachers to see that children live up to these ideals. In colonial America the Virginians preferred a more positive approach to the problem of youthful behavior; the only references to children in their statutes provided for the religious and vocational education of young Virginians. Like the Virginians, the Puritans passed laws calling for the religious and vocational education of their children, but they also had statutes which provided strict punishments for the transgressions of the young. The Quakers of Pennsylvania also stressed the need for vocational education of children to keep them from being idle, but unlike the Puritans, they had no statutes describing specific punishments for children who broke the law. There was, however, a measure of community response to juvenile misbehavior among the Quakers, since their meetings often dealt with the minor offenses of children.

II

In the early years of the English settlements in North America, the colonists, conscious of their unusual situation, developed a "rude, untechnical popular law." But as lawyers came over from the mother country and as the study of law became fashionable, the settlements gradually adopted the English common law. At times, however, the settlers completely ignored the common law or departed from some of its essential pirnciples.[1]

When Massachusetts adopted the *Body of Liberties* in 1641 after six years of deliberation, it was "the first attempt at a comprehensive reduction into one form of a body of legislation of an English-speaking country," and it represented a substantial departure from the common law. One of the provisions regarding children explained that

> If any child, or children, above sixteen years old, and of sufficient understanding, shall CURSE or SMITE their natural FATHER, or MOTHER, he or they shall be putt to death, unless it can be sufficiently testifyed that the Parents have been very unchristianly negligent in the education of such children: so provoked them by extreme and cruel correction, that they have been forced thereunto, to preserve themselves from death or maiming: *Exod* 21:17, *Lev* 20:9, *Exod* 21:15.

Although it was not applied, this passage illustrates the severity of the Puritan moral laws. Most of the material contained in the early Massachusetts laws came from the English common law, but the sections dealing with religious or moral conduct were based on the Old Testament. Colonial Virginia, on the other hand, while it modified the common law to some extent, did not base its moral law on the Old Testament.[2]

The Puritans regarded children as miniature adults who required some special consideration because they were small and ignorant. There was much work to be done in colonial Massachusetts, and even children could not be idle. The Puritans regarded play as sinful and a waste of time. As a student of colonial children points out, "the very desire for recreation was deemed another evidence of the child's 'corrupt nature.'" Since the child was ignorant and corrupt, he had to learn to be a righteous adult. In 1642 the General Court of Massachusetts required parents and masters of indentured servants to teach their children to read and to understand the capital laws of the country and the principles of religion. In addition Puritan parents had to see that their children learned a trade or "calling." Usually a boy chose his calling between the ages of ten and fourteen. After he made his choice, his parents apprenticed him to a master to learn his trade. The Puritans believed that children were born and continued to be sinners just like unredeemed adults, as the following selection from Anne Bradstreet's "Childhood" illustrates:

> Stained from birth with *Adams* sinfull fact,
> Thence I began to sin as soon as act:
> A perverse will, a love to what's forbid,
> A serpent's sting in pleasing face lay hid:
> A lying tongue as soon as it could speak,
> And fifth commandment do daily break.

In spite of this attitude, however, the Puritans made special provisions in their laws for misbehaving youth. The section on children and youth in the 1660 edition of Massachusetts laws ordered the selectmen of each town to see that parents educated their children. If the parents failed to do this, the selectmen also had the authority to take the children away from their parents and place them out as apprentices. The 1660 laws also contained a new penalty for disobedient children. The preamble to this section sounded like a present-day complaint: "It appeareth, by too much experience, that diverse children and servants doe behave themselves disobediently & disorderly, towards their parents, masters, & Governors." The law gave a magistrate the power to summon before him "any such offender, & upon conviction of such misdemeanors, . . . sentence him to endure such corporal punishment, by whipping or otherwise, as in his judgment the merit of the fact shall deserve, not exceeding ten stripes for one offense." [3]

The laws of 1660 also regarded lying as a punishable offense;

for a person fourteen or over the fine was ten shillings, with higher fines for repeated offenses. For children under fourteen the laws provided that "their parents or masters shall give them correction" in the presence of "some officer if any magistrate shall so appoint." Another common offense of young people which the 1660 statutes covered was failure to observe the Sabbath. The preamble to the section concerning Sabbath transgressions complained of "sundry abuses and misdemeanors committed by divers persons on the Lordsday, not only by children playing in the streets, and other places, [but also] by youths, mayds, and other persons, both strangers and others, uncivilly walking in the streets and fields." The law ordered that "no children, youths, maids or other persons, shall transgress in the like kind on penalty of being reputed great provokers of the high displeasure of the Almighty God." If after this dire warning, a child between seven and fourteen should profane the Sabbath, the law provided that the proper officials should admonish the parents or masters of the offending youth for a first offense and fine them for later offenses. The law made an exception for children under seven, but added in parentheses: "not that we approve younger children in evil." Those over fourteen were admonished in person and were expected to pay their own fines. Another evil which children in Massachusetts were supposed to avoid was "excess apparel"—wearing clothes "unbecoming a wilderness condition." The law warned that such children were in danger of being "corrupted and effeminated" by such finery. Puritans were supposed to dress according to the "quality and condition of their persons or estate." [4]

Since idleness was clearly a sin, the General Court in 1672 added a law making it an offense to lure young people from their studies or work. "Whosoever shall any wayes cause or suffer any young people, or persons whatsoever, whether children, servants, apprentices, schollars belonging to the colledg, or any latin school, to spend any of their time or estate, by night or by day, in his or their company," the law said, "shall forfeit the summ of forty shillings." The law was particularly directed at the shopkeepers, ship masters, and tavern-keepers. This was probably the first law

to approach the concept of contributing to the delinquency of a
minor.

Children always seem to try the patience of their elders, and
Puritan children were no exception. In 1675 the Massachusetts
General Court complained that "there is a woful breach of the
fifth commandment to be found among us, in contempt of authority, civil, ecclesiastical and domestical." The General Court
instructed "all county courts, magistrates, commissioners, selectmen, and grand-jurors" to "take strict care that the laws already
made and provided in this cause be duley executed, and [to note]
particularly, that evil inferiours [were] absenting themselves out
of the families whereunto they belong." The officials were supposed to prevent children and servants from "meeting with corrupt
company without leave . . . which evil practice is of a very peril-
ous nature, and the root of much disorder." [5]

The Puritans did not specifically define juvenile delinquency,
but many aspects of their life in the New World, taken together,
indicate that they did have some reasonably coherent ideas about
youthful misbehavior. In the first place, they had a strong sense
of community. The Puritans had not come to North America to
make their fortunes; they came as on a great mission. They came,
as Perry Miller so aptly phrased it, on "an errand into the wilderness." Because of their goal to establish a model society, they
were peculiarly sensitive to the actions of every member of their
community. They felt—or hoped that the eyes of the world were
on them, and they could not permit the slightest misstep—even
the naturally mischievous actions of small children. But the Puritan
attitude toward children was ambivalent. They saw the child as a
sinner from birth. Like an adult, he was supposed to work hard
in order to avoid idleness and temptation, and yet the Puritans
made special provisions in their laws for children under fourteen.

The Puritans also tried to prevent youthful misbehavior by
giving their children a thorough moral education. As Cotton
Mather said, "tis very pleasing to our Lord Jesus Christ, that our
children should be well formed with, and well-informed in the
rules of civility, and not be left a clownish, and sottish and ill-bred

sort of creatures." He thought that children "should read and write and cyphar, and be put into some agreeable calling." In 1642 the Massachusetts General Court had required parents and masters of indentured servants to teach their children or servants to read. Five years later, the General Court ordered towns with a population of fifty or more to provide a school where children could learn to read, write, and do simple arithmetic. Towns having a hundred or more people had to support a master who could teach Latin and Greek. One of the main purposes of these education laws was to prevent idleness—to make sure that every young Puritan knew enough to support himself and to keep himself from becoming a public charge. School was like work; by keeping children busy, it kept them out of mischief.[6]

For all practical purposes the first laws in colonial New York and Pennsylvania were the laws of New England. In 1665 not long after the English had captured the New Netherlands from the Dutch, the New English governor, Richard Nicolls, summoned delegates to ratify a code of laws which he had drawn up. Nicolls based his draft on the statutes of New England, but this code was popularly known as the "Duke's Laws" because the governor was acting for the Duke of York.[7]

The Duke of York's laws applied both to New York and to Pennsylvania until 1682, when William Penn arranged for an assembly to draft a set of laws for his proprietorship. This assembly met in December, 1682 and passed the "Great Law." According to the "Great Law," families with children were to "cause such to be instructed in reading and writing; so that they may be able to read the Scriptures; and to write by that time they attain twelve years." This legislation also directed parents and guardians of orphans to teach the children in their care "some useful trade or skill, that the poor may work to live, and the rich, if they become poor, may not want."

In many respects the Puritans and the Quakers held similar views of children. Both agreed that parents should teach their children to read and write, and they also agreed that everyone should learn a trade. The Quakers, however, were far less ex-

plicit in their statutes about the behavior of children than the
Puritans were. Certainly children in colonial Pennsylvania misbehaved, but in doing so they did not break a law which applied
specifically to them. When a child misbehaved, either his family
took care of his discipline or the Quaker meeting dispensed a
mild and paternalistic correction.[8]

In general, there were fewer laws and restrictions governing
the behavior of children in colonial Virginia than there were in
Massachusetts. In spite of this, however, there were some striking
similarities between the two colonies. The first code in Virginia,
the "Articles, Lawes, and Orders, Divine, Politique, and Martiall,"
which were introduced by Sir Thomas Gates in 1610, did not mention children at all, but in 1619, Virginia's first General Assembly
met to replace them with a code closer to the common law.[9]

In the meantime children came to Virginia. In the estimation of
the settlers, the population of Virginia was dangerously low. Accordingly, the Virginia Company made arrangements with the
Common Council of London to have 100 young vagrants collected
from the streets of London and sent to Virginia in 1618. The
Virginians were glad to have the children, and in 1619 they
persuaded the Common Council to send a hundred more. Apparently the city fathers of London were only too happy to help
the Virginia Company, since they were able to get rid of the
tougher young characters on their streets. In a letter to Sir Robert
Nauton, Sir Edwin Sandys, then treasurer of the Virginia Company, asked for help in completing the arrangements for the
second group of young vagrants. Some of the children did not
want to go to Virginia: "Now it falleth out," Sandys wrote, "that
among these children being illdisposed & fitter for any remote
place than for this city [some] declare their unwillingness to go
to Virginia." These were the very ones "of whom the city is
especially desirous to be disburdened," and Sandys added, "in
Virginia under severe masters they may be brought to goodness."

Like the Puritans of Massachusetts, the early settlers of Virginia
explained their activities in theological terms—although the Virginians added an economic rationale to the religious justifications

for their colony. Virginia's early statutes reflected the religious tone of the colony, and they provided for the religious instruction of the colony's children. In 1636 the General Assembly ordered the ministers of the colony to spend "halfe an hower or more . . . to instruct the youth and ignorant persons of his parrish in the ten commandments[,] the articles of the beliefe[,] and the Lord's prayer." The Assembly also ordered "all fathers, mothers, maysters and mistresses" to send their children to the church at "the tyme appoynted, obediente to heare." Those who did not observe this act were to be "censured by the corts."

Neither the Virginians nor the Puritans condoned idleness on the part of children. In 1646 the Virginia General Assembly passed an act designed to prevent the "sloath and idleness wherewith young children are easily corrupted." The act provided for "the educating of youth in honest and profitable trades and manufactures" and criticized those parents who, "either through fond indulgence or perverse obstinacy," were unwilling to part with their children for apprenticeship and training.

In spite of their law on religious instruction for young people and the statute advocating apprenticeship for all children, the Virginians did not make any specific provisions concerning juvenile misbehavior. Instead, the common law prevailed. The Virginians, in comparison with the Puritans, were more indulgent toward their children and placed less emphasis on standards of conduct for young people. They were also less concerned about education. Wealthy planters sometimes sent their children to England for schooling, but more often they hired tutors. Only the well-to-do could afford tutors, and although the common people occasionally established schools for their children, most of the young people in Virginia did not go to school at all.[10]

In colonial times children usually learned a trade when their parents bound them out or apprenticed them. The indenture or contract between an apprentice and his master provides another insight into the behavior expected of young people at that time. A typical indenture required the apprentice to keep his master's secrets, obey his commands, and protect his property. The con-

tract also prohibited certain kinds if conduct on the part of the
apprentice: "he shall not commit fornication nor contract matri-
mony within said term," read one indenture. "At cards, dice or any
other unlawful game," it continued, "he shall not play." Often,
especially in New England, masters called on the courts to discipline wayward young indentured servants and apprentices. Sometimes the court ordered the offending youth whipped, but if the
offense were serious—and particularly if the master had to pay a
fine—the court might order an extension of the servant's term.
Thus colonial Americans had a certain amount of experience in
dealing with juvenile delinquents, but they provided no specialized
treatment for them and entertained no thought of reforming
youthful wrongdoers.[11]

III

The penal system of colonial America, with its emphasis on
corporal and capital punishment, was very much like that of the
rest of the Western world. During the eighteenth century, however, Europeans began to question the values and institutions of
the society in which they lived. The "enlightened men" of that
century saw their world as corrupt and full of evil; they sought to
remake society along rational lines and according to the dictates
of natural law. Men like Voltaire, Montesquieu, and Cesare
Beccaria wrote about the inequities and wrongs of laws made by
men and advocated a new, rational law.

Voltaire struck the first blow for reform of the criminal law by
drawing attention to its abuses. Montesquieu followed him and
argued that the punishments were too harsh. "The severity of
punishments," he wrote, "is fitter for despotic governments, whose
principle is terror, than for a monarchy or a republic, whose spring
is honor and virtue." He also contended "that there should be a
certain proportion in punishments, because it is essential that a
great crime should be avoided rather than a smaller, and that
which is more pernicious to society rather than that which is less."

To paraphrase Montesquieu, "the punishment should fit the crime." [12]

Voltaire had shown that the system of criminal justice in eighteenth-century Europe was wrong, and Montesquieu had indicated the direction for reform to take, but an obscure Italian, Cesare Beccaria, indicated exactly what was wrong and explained how the system should be modified. Beccaria's *Tratto dei delitti e delle pene* (*An Essay on Crimes and Punishments*), published in 1764, argued for a rational relationship between crime and punishment. The prevailing theory concerning that relationship held that the severity of punishment deterred would-be criminals. Beccaria, however, believed that "crimes are more effectually prevented by the certainty [rather] than the severity of punishment." He also thought that the laws should apply to all citizens equally, that the authorities should apply punishments as quickly as possible, and that punishments should be determined by laws and not by men.[13] The *Essay on Crimes and Punishments* was an enlightened document which attacked the absurdities and abuses of the criminal law in Europe in the eighteenth century. More than any other book, it transformed the penal practices of modern Europe, and it had profound influences on American penology as well. It was a blueprint for the reformer who would rationalize a penal system, and it soon became the textbook for the "classical" school of penology and criminology.

After Beccaria's essay and Jeremy Bentham's similar views in the *Introduction to Politics and Morals*, England still suffered from one of Western society's cruelest penal codes. The criminal who committed a felony there counted himself lucky if he escaped death. There were four basic punishments in English criminal law: death, whipping, fines, and transportation. The English did not imprison criminals (except when they were awaiting trial). Prisons and jails were primarily for debtors, but a sentence to one was little better than execution, for, as one twentieth-century student of the period has noted: "more men died from fever in gaols in the eighteenth century, after a few months of stifling, hungry life, than were ever legally put to death each year on the scaffold."

The prisons were in private hands for the most part, and many were none too secure—making it necessary for the keeper to chain the prisoners. The prison-keeper received only a small allowance for each prisoner, but he often made his business pay by pocketing the allowance and charging the prisoners for various amenities. There were cases where men died in prison even though they had been acquitted—because they were in debt to the prison-keeper.

In 1773 John Howard became Sheriff of Bedford and, unlike most of his colleagues, he took his responsibilities seriously. He was appalled at the conditions he found in the jails and prisons of his own jurisdiction and journeyed throughout England, finding conditions equally bad wherever he went. To find examples of better prison management and to develop a plan for reform, Howard went to Europe in 1775. The system used in the prison at Amsterdam particularly impressed him; there the authorities had put the prisoners to work—not just to occupy or discipline them, but in the hope of reforming them.[14]

After returning to England, Howard published *The State of Prisons*, in which he described the prisons of England and the Continent and recommended reforms. The book was a sensation—in part because of the shocking state of the jails and prisons, but also because Howard recommended a complete change in English penal theory. Of the English prisons in particular, Howard wrote: "Debtors crowd the gaols (especially those in London) with their wives and children. There are often by this means, ten or twelve people in a middle-sized room; increasing the danger of infection, and corrupting the morals of the children." Howard's book reminds a modern reader of the muckrackers of the early twentieth century in the United States and of some of the reports of parliamentary select committees in the nineteenth century. These are pages of dry, workmanlike prose describing the horrible physical conditions in the places of confinement and equally graphic and unemotional descriptions of the inmates. Howard painted a picture of filth and squalor almost beyond imagination, but he also recommended a series of reforms. He called for the separation of the inmates by

age, sex, and in accordance with the reasons for their imprisonment. He also asked for confinement in cells, salaried prison
workers, chaplains, and medical officers. Furthermore, he believed
that prison officials should be held responsible for the condition
of the inmates in their charge.[15]

In Pennsylvania John Howard's ideas found receptive minds.
When the first Quakers had settled in the New World, they had
adopted a criminal code much milder than that of England. They
had to give up this code, however, and until the American Revolution the English colonies in North America followed the mother
country in penal practices. One significant difference was that in
the colonies the death penalty was assigned to a much smaller
number of offenses than in the mother country. In 1776 a group
of Quakers founded the Philadelphia Society for Assisting Dis-
tressed Prisoners—the first organization of its kind in North America. It collapsed, however, when the British occupied Philadelphia
during the Revolutionary War. In 1787 the prison reformers
founded the Philadelphia Society for Alleviating the Miseries of
Public Prisoners. The members of this organization, because of
their Quaker beliefs, and because of the writings of John Howard,
Becarria, Montesquieu, and Jeremy Bentham, sought to establish
a penal system whose main purpose would be to reform criminals.
In January, 1788, they wrote to John Howard and expressed their
gratitude for his efforts: "The society heartily concur with the
friends of humanity in Europe, in expressing their obligations to
you for having rendered the miserable tenants of prisons the objects of more general attention and compassion, and for having
pointed out some of the means of not only alleviating their miseries,
but of preventing their crimes and misfortunes which are the
cause of them."

In 1787 the jail in Philadelphia was like those John Howard had
been visiting. The young, the old, criminals awaiting trial, debtors,
men and women, were indiscriminately herded together. One of
the prison officers kept a bar in the jail and sold liquor to anyone
who had the money to buy it. Before an inmate could leave, he
had to pay his accumulated jail fees. Following the ideas of

Howard and other reformers, the society persuaded the state of Pennsylvania to erect the Walnut Street Prison where the prisoners would be classified according to age, sex, and the nature of their offense. The inmates who had committed serious offenses were confined in solitary cells and permitted no work. The other prisoners were supposed to work in shops during the day, and the proceeds of their labor were to be used to help defray prison expenses. Debtors were confined separately. But this scheme never worked properly. Before the system could be given a fair trial, the Walnut Street Prison became too crowded.[16]

If the Quakers of Pennsylvania were going to reform criminals, something had to be done about the state's criminal code. Since 1718, Pennsylvania had been using a set of criminal laws which were considerably harsher than the original Quaker code. As early as 1783 a group of men led by Benjamin Franklin, William Bradford, and Benjamin Rush, had begun a movement to change the state's criminal law. In 1786 they persuaded the legislature to pass a law substituting imprisonment for capital punishment. They worked with the Society for Alleviating the Miseries of Public Prisoners after its creation, and by 1794 William Bradford had written, and the legislature had adopted, a systematic revision of the criminal laws. This revised code provided for imprisonment for most criminal offenses and prescribed regulations for a penitentiary system based on the procedures that were supposed to have been used at the Walnut Street Prison.[17]

IV

In 1794, Thomas Eddy, a Quaker who lived in New York, traveled to Philadelphia to visit the Walnut Street Prison and also to talk with the members of the Society for Alleviating the Miseries of Public Prisoners. Eddy returned to New York and immediately began working for the reform of the criminal code of his state. Together with Philip John Schuyler, De Witt Clinton, and John Jay, he convinced the New York legislature to adopt a new criminal code in 1796. The revised laws provided for two state prisons and reduced the number of crimes for which capital punishment was prescribed. The first of the new prisons, Newgate, was built in Greenwich Village in 1797, but it soon proved too small. Many prisoners were pardoned after only a short period in order to make room for new convicts. This was hardly the system envisioned by John Howard or Beccaria, and in 1801 Thomas Eddy wrote *An Account of State Prisons* in which he presented a comprehensive and specific plan for the reformation of criminals. Like the Quakers of Pennsylvania he advocated cellular confinement and believed the reformation of criminals would take place through a process of reflection or penitence during their long and lonely incarceration.

New York's growing population soon made another penal institution necessary, and in 1816 the legislature authorized the construction of two new prisons. The first, at Auburn, was begun on the group-confinement plan which had been typical of the prisons John Howard had investigated. However, a group of reformers persuaded the New York legislature to institute the cell system in a part of the prison in 1819. The cells were three feet wide and seven feet in height and depth. There were no outside windows; ventilation was from the roof. The inmates convicted of minor offenses were expected to work, but the prison authorities confined the hardened felons in these small cells without any labor or exercise of any kind. The health of the men thus confined soon deteriorated and some of them went insane. In 1823 the New York prison officials worked out a compromise, known as the "Auburn System," which consisted of solitary confinement at night, congregate work by day, and silence at all times.

In Philadelphia the Society for Alleviating the Miseries of Public Prisoners, long dissatisfied with the overcrowded conditions at the Walnut Street Prison, petitioned the legislature year after year to construct a new prison on the solitary system. Finally, in 1829 the solons rewarded their efforts and ordered construction to begin on a new institution at Cherry Hill, just outside Philadelphia. When completed it was a curious structure; seven cell blocks radiated from a central tower. Each cell had its own courtyard and toilet facilities. The inmates were supposed to live and work in these cells, seeing no one except the chaplain and other prison officials. In his solitude the convict would have time to reflect on his past wrongdoings and repent of his sins. He would emerge from prison—or the "penitentiary"—as a new man, reformed and redeemed.[18]

Thus by the 1830's there were two rival penal systems in the United States, both of which claimed to be reforming their inmates. Distinguished visitors, like Alexis de Tocqueville and Charles Dickens, came to America expressly to see these new systems and to report on them to their governments. A brief glance at the period of penal reform which ended with the creation of the Auburn and Pennsylvania systems indicates that this movement, like so many other reform movements, was not bound by national or geographical barriers. It was, indeed, a transatlantic crusade. Significantly, most of the ideas for penal reform came from Europe, but Americans built the institutions which put these ideas into practice. In effect, the New World served as a kind of laboratory for the thinkers of the Old World.

The new penitentiaries, however, did not live up to their founders' expectations. They did not prevent crime, and often supposedly "reformed" men returned to prison for second and third offenses. In time the penitentiaries would lose their reforming character and become primarily custodial institutions, but the reformers who had founded them did not give up. Instead of trying to reform hardened offenders, they turned their attention to the younger criminals and potential criminals and shifted their emphasis from the reformation of the adult criminal to the prevention of crime by means of the reformation of juvenile delinquents.

3

The New York House of Refuge: The First Institution for Juvenile Delinquents in the United States

In the fall of 1822 two men met in one of New York City's parks. They were James W. Gerard, a young lawyer, and Isaac Collins, a Quaker, and both were members of the Society for the Prevention of Pauperism. Every year this Society presented a public report to suggest ways of carrying out its purposes. Usually, one man, with the assistance of two others "for form's sake," wrote this report. Gerard was talking to Collins about the street children of New York because he was going to write the report for 1822 on "the reformation of juvenile delinquents." Collins, whose father was a Philadelphia printer, became interested in the treatment of juvenile delinquents after reading the annual report of an English institution for young offenders. Gerard had become interested in juvenile crime as a result of the very first case he tried, that of a fourteen-year-old boy accused of stealing a bird. The young lawyer won acquittal for his client by arguing that prison would corrupt the boy. The case so interested Gerard that he began to investigate the facilities for detaining prisoners in New York. He also decided to join the Society for the Prevention of Pauperism.

Gerard presented his report at a public meeting held in the ballroom of the City Hotel in February, 1823. "Those who are in the habit of attending our criminal courts, as jurors or otherwise," Gerard said,

> must be convinced of the very great increase of juvenile delinquency within these few years past, and of the necessity of immediate measures to arrest so great an evil. . . . Those whose walks are limited to the fairer parts of our city know nothing of the habits, the propensities and criminal courses, of a large population in its remote and obscure parts. . . . it is with pain we state that, in five or six years past, and until the last few months, the number of youth under fourteen years of age, charged with offenses against the law, has doubled; and that the same boys are again and again brought up for examination, some of whom are committed, and some tried; and that imprisonment by its frequency renders them hardened and fearless.

This was hardly surprising, Gerard said, if one knew the conditions of the prisons and the Bridewell. (A Bridewell then had about the same functions as a county jail in twentieth-century America.) At the Bridewell persons awaiting trial because they could not afford to pay bail were all packed into one large room, "the young and the old . . . promiscuously crowded together. . . . Boys who have been charged with picking pockets, stealing watches, and the like crimes," Gerard continued, "have declared before the police when [asked] how they came to such things, that they learned the art from the experienced offenders they met in [the] Bridewell. . . ."

Every year one to two hundred children between the ages of seven and fourteen appeared in the criminal courts of New York City. Some were homeless and most of them were "the children of poor and abandoned parents" whose "debased character and vicious habits" caused them to be "brought up in perfect ignorance and idleness, and what is worse in street begging and pilfering." Gerard concluded with a recommendation that a "house of refuge" for young convicts be established where juvenile delinquents might be reformed. "Unless the heart is corrupt indeed, and sunk deep in guilt," Gerard said, "the youth would undergo a change of feeling and character, and he would look on crime with greater abhorrence, because he himself had been a cr__ _al." [1] Gerard's report led to the creation of the first separate institution for juvenile delinquents in the United States, the New York House of Refuge.

II

Even before the end of the second decade of the nineteenth century, the City of New York was well on its way to becoming the largest and most prosperous city in the United States. But as the city increased in wealth and size, some of its most prominent citizens worried about the depressing conditions of the city's poor.[2] The nationally known chemistry teacher, John Griscom, his neighbor, Thomas Eddy, and a set of like-minded friends began meeting to discuss what they called "the perishing and dangerous classes," the impoverished and criminal elements among the city's population. Somehow, it did not seem right that an American city should have the same kind of discouraging problems which beset the cities of the Old World. The informal gatherings at Griscom's house set the stage for the creation of a formal organization to do something about the problems of the lowest classes of society.

On December 16, 1817, Griscom's friends and other philanthropic citizens formed the Society for the Prevention of Pauperism in the City of New York. They elected a veteran of the Revolutionary War, General Matthew Clarkson, as chairman and appointed a committee to draw up a constitution, to study the "causes" of pauperism and continual and hereditary poverty, and to suggest remedies. The Society met again in February of the following year to hear the committee report on the causes of pauperism. The committee listed "juvenile delinquency" as one of the major causes of pauperism. To alleviate the threat of youthful crime the committee suggested that child convicts be confined in a building separate from the regular prison for adult criminals. For the next three years the Society for the Prevention of Pauperism continued to recommend the complete separation of youthful offenders from older convicts in prisons and jails.[3]

In the meantime John Griscom had gone to Europe to visit the Continent's charitable institutions, particularly those devoted to children. One of the most important of the institutions Griscom saw was that maintained by the Philanthropic Society at Hoxton, England. The Society had been organized in London in 1788 as a means of preventing the children of convicts from growing up in idleness and crime. In 1804 the directors moved their Society's operation to Hoxton and began accepting other children, especially juvenile offenders, who seemed likely to grow up into a criminal life. Griscom noted that "it is the peculiar distinction of this society, to seek for children in the nurseries of vice and iniquity, in order to draw them away from further contamination, and to bring them up to the useful purposes of life." The Society received both boys and girls, although it kept them separated "by a high wall which prevents all intercourse." The chemistry teacher from New York thought that the boys received "a sufficient share of school learning," and described the various trades which master workmen taught the boys: printing, bookbinding, shoemaking, tailoring, rope-making, and twine spinning. The girls learned domestic skills, "so as to qualify . . . for useful and respectable service." In passing through the workshops of this beneficent institution, "where industry and skill were apparent," Griscom concluded, "it was cheering to find that so many wretched children were 'snatched as fire brands' from criminality and ruin, and restored to the prospects of respectable and honourable life." [4]

On the Continent Griscom was especially impressed by "Hofwyl," an institution in Switzerland devoted to "problem" children. M. Philip Emanuel Fellenberg had founded this complex of schools only a few years earlier. Fellenberg and Heinrich Pestalozzi, one of the seminal minds in the history of education, had worked together in an effort to teach the orphans, the homeless, and the delinquent children of Switzerland how to make a living for themselves. In 1774, Pestalozzi, who had been brooding about the failures of the institutions society had developed to aid the poor—orphan asylums, poor-houses, prisons, and the like—brought a group of vagrant children to his farm at Neuhof. He treated the children as if they were members of his own family, worked with them in the fields, and tried to give them the rudiments of an education. But Pestalozzi was a poor manager and, despite a number of appeals to the public for funds, was forced to abandon the project in 1780. In one of his appeals he had written: "I have for a long time thought it probable that, under favorable circumstances, young children might be able to earn their own living without undue labor, provided that enough capital were advanced to organize an establishment, in which they would not only live, but at the same time receive a certain elementary education." Pestalozzi tried in vain to attract the necessary finances to promote his ideas until Fellenberg invited him early in the nineteenth century to help at the experimental establishment at Hofwyl, Fellenberg's estate. In 1807 Fellenberg had founded the "Literary Institution" for the sons of the nobility and upper classes. The next year he founded the "Agricultural Institution," or "Poor School" for the children of the common people. Pestalozzi's gentle and abstract ways led to conflict with the stricter and more business-like Fellenberg and they soon parted, but the teacher of the poor school, Joseph Vehrly, conducted his school on Pestalozzi's principles.[5]

Soon after he arrived at Hofwyl, Griscom had a brief interview with Fellenberg, who discussed the principles of his institution and his own particular philosophy of education. Briefly he explained that Hofwyl's two schools were designed to give the two extreme classes of society a better understanding of each other. The rich, observing the poor, would learn to respect their industry and skill; the poor would regard the rich as benefactors by experiencing their kindly influence. All of this would be accomplished without any mingling of the classes, since the two schools—though conducted in close proximity—were separate.

The school for the poor boys particularly impressed Griscom. "Their teacher [Vehrly]," he wrote, "is a young man of very extraordinary qualifications. . . . He lives with them, eats, sleeps, and works with them, dresses as they do, and makes himself their friend and companion, as well as their instructor." Vehrly had

clearly borrowed his principles from Pestalozzi: "Much pains are
taken to impress on the minds of the pupils, a deep sense of the
importance of time, and of habits of industry," Griscom recalled,
"and from the reports that have been published by commissioners
appointed to examine the establishments, it is evident that the
most favourable results had attended these endeavors." Vehrly
taught his young charges traditional and vocational matter. He
concentrated on agriculture, and each boy had his own plot to
cultivate. Those who wished could also learn a trade in one of the
several workshops on the grounds. Both Vehrly and Fellenberg
were "strongly imbued with a sense of religious obligation, and
unremittingly attentive to awaken those sentiments in the minds
of the pupils." The New York philanthropist was so impressed
with what he had seen at Hofwyl that he recommended that the
United States adopt a similar approach: "The greatest recommendation of the Pestalozzian and Fellenberg plan of education is
the moral charm which is diffused throughout all its operations."
Griscom knew that many of Fellenberg's notions—especially those
of his upper-class school—were alien to American traditions, but
he argued that poor schools like the one Vehrly taught "would
soon impart to a large and populous district . . . a moral tone of
incalculable importance to its highest interests and welfare." If
white children could not be induced to attend such a school, he
suggested that the school accept Negro children. "Such an experiment, with persons of this description, would be highly interesting," he added, for "it would put to flight the ridiculous theory
of those who contend for an organic inferiority on the part of
the blacks." Finally, he noted that to succeed such an institution
needed a man of unusual talents to run it—a man like Vehrly.[6]

When Griscom returned to New York, he found that the Society
for the Prevention of Pauperism was still discussing the causes of
pauperism, although the members of the Society found their attention turning increasingly to the question of juvenile delinquency.
To them a juvenile delinquent was a young person (under twenty-
one) who had broken the law, or who wandered about the streets,
neither in school nor at work and who obviously lacked a "good"

home and family. Such a criminal or vagrant youth would probably lack the skills of a trade and would be illiterate as well. Most such children would certainly grow up to be paupers or criminals, persons which the community would have to maintain with charity or tax money. By the second decade of the nineteenth century this dependent class had grown large enough to disturb the prosperous middle-class members of the Society for the Prevention of Pauperism. The members reasoned that adult paupers and criminals had been delinquents in their youth and that the best way to eliminate pauperism was to reform juvenile delinquents. The Society's *Annual Report* for 1819 discussed conditions in the New York penitentiary—particularly the fact that there were many children confined there—and asked: "Shall we send convicts in the morning of life, while the youthful mind is ardent and open to vivid and durable imlpressions, to this unhallowed abode, to be taught in all the requisites that will enable them to come forth when their terms of imprisonment expire, more prepared to invade the peace of cities and communities?" No, the report concluded, "to say that this is not a great source of pauperism and nursery of crime and outrage, is denying the fairest deductions of reason." [7]

Meanwhile, the problem of wayward and criminal children had been taken up by other groups and individuals in New York. In 1803 Edward Livingston, the Mayor of the city who later became one of the country's leading penal reformers, attempted to form a society to help young ex-convicts, but he was unable to find enough people interested to initiate his project. On August 14, 1809, the Common Council of New York City designated the Almshouse as "an asylum for lost children." But the Almshouse and the penitentiary seemed inappropriate places for children, and in March, 1812, the Council reported that it had received "a communication of John Stanton on the subject of erecting an asylum for the protection of profligate orphans of the city." "Stanton" in this case was undoubtedly the Reverend John Standford, chaplain of the Almshouse, who asked the Council to "make an attempt to rescue from indolence, vice, and danger, the hundreds of vagrant children and youth, who day and night infest our streets." He recommended the creation of "an asylum for vagrant youth," but beyond noting the receipt of his letter, the Council took no action on his request.[8]

Seven years later, in June, 1819, Mayor Cadwallader Colden, Jr., who was also a member of the Society for the Prevention of Pauperism, and the Recorder, Peter Augustus Jay, went on an inspection tour of the city's charitable institutions and reported their findings to the board in charge of the prison and the Bridewell. They complained about the mixing of young and old convicts in the penal institutions and noted that young criminals posed a difficult problem. "The members of the board, who are judges of the Criminal Court," the Mayor and the Recorder said, "must often have felt how difficult it is, satisfactorily to dispose of these young culprits." If the judge turned them loose, they would soon be back on another charge, but if the judge sentenced them to prison, they would mingle with older convicts and be encouraged in a life of crime. "The jury, as well as the Court," the report continued, "feel a reluctance to convict and condemn them when it is believed that the infliction of punishment, by confinement in the Penitentiary, will tend to harden them in vice." In their conclusion Colden and Jay argued that if the boys could be effectively isolated from the other convicts and then taught a trade, "imprisonment would sometimes produce reformation."

In September of the same year, two more members of the Common Council, the Alderman for the Second Ward and his assistant, visited the Almshouse, the Bridewell, and the penitentiary, and found that conditions had slightly improved. The children were now kept separate from the older convicts, and "considerable attention" was devoted to teaching them "the common branches of education." But the Council members complained that the children were not learning a trade.

In February, 1820, the Grand Jury included among the presentments which it forwarded to the Common Council the recommendation that "all persons under 15 years of age who may be committed to Bridewell be confined in a separate apartment to preclude intercourse with persons of mature age." The following year, in June, the Reverend John Standford sent the Council another letter, again suggesting that it establish "an asylum for vagrant youth." The Council referred the letter to the Mayor and the Commissioners of the Almshouse, who endorsed the chaplain's recommendation and indicated that they had already ordered the boys in the penitentiary charged with vagrancy transferred to the Almshouse. Shortly after this step, the Commissioners of the Almshouse decided to take the remainder of the boys in the penitentiary into the Almshouse, even though more than half of the boys moved there originally had escaped. The boys could stay only for the summer, however, since the building usually filled up with adults during the winter months.

By the spring of 1823 several different efforts to create a separate institution for wayward and criminal children in New York had coalesced into a movement. The Mayor and Almshouse Commissioners had endorsed the Reverend John Standford's suggestion to establish an asylum for vagrant youth, and in June the members of the Society for the Prevention of Pauperism, probably in response to the paper James Gerard had given in February, established a committee "to prepare a report on the subject of establishing a House of Refuge, or prison for the reformation of juvenile delinquents." Among the committee members were John Griscom, Isaac Collins, and Gerard. As the committee prepared its report, Griscom's account of his travels in Europe appeared and probably helped to publicize the movement on behalf of an institution for juvenile delinquents.[9]

The Society called a public meeting in the ballroom of the City Hotel in December, 1823, and John Griscom read the committee's report. "It will be admitted by every person conversant with human nature, and with the great objects of political association," Griscom said, "that there are few judicial considerations of greater importance than the wise adaptation of punishment to crime." Then Griscom stressed the idea that punishment deters criminals and thereby protects property. One of the purposes of this public meeting, then, was to find new, better, and possibly cheaper ways of defending society against the threat of crime—including juvenile crime.[10]

Griscom went on to charge that most penitentiaries had not lived up to their original promise, because their officers now lacked "the same intelligent and disinterested zeal" which their founders had possessed. The greatest deficiency in the penitentiaries was inadequate classification, the separation of prisoners by offenses and ages. Consequently, convicts "of all ages and degrees of guilt" found themselves thrown together and the penitentiaries were fast becoming "schools and colleges of crime." Perhaps, Griscom continued, the old system of "whipping posts, pillories, and croppings" would be better. In some states, however, there were penal institutions, "where classification is an object of careful attention." These were penitentiaries "directed with a constant reference to the moral faculties" and "clothed in the spirit which seeks to restore, in order that it may safely forgive." Thus, Griscom argued, governments should recognize that "those who are guilty of crime should receive the chastisement due to their offenses," and that "no pains should be spared to remove the causes of offense, and to diminish, as far as possible, the sources of temptation and corruption." Such an approach was particularly appropriate for juvenile delinquents—"a class whose increasing numbers, and deplorable situation in this city, loudly call for the more effective interposition of its police, and the benevolent interference of our citizens in general."

Following Gerard's earlier report, Griscom turned to a discussion of the byways of the city where one could see "the ragged and uncleanly appearance, the vile language, and the idle and miserable habits of great numbers of children, most of whom were of school age or capable of some useful employment." Many of these children had no parents, and many had parents who were "too poor or too degenerate" to provide their children with the clothing necessary to go to school or to work. It was no surprise that many of these children turned to vagrancy and crime:

> Accustomed, in many instances, to witness at home, nothing in the way of an example, but what is degrading; early taught to observe intemperance, and to hear obscene and profane language without disgust; obliged to beg, and even encouraged to

acts of dishonesty, to satisfy the wants induced by the indolence of their parents—what can be expected, but that such children will, in due time, become responsible to the laws for crimes, which have thus, in a manner, been forced upon them? Can it be consistent with real justice, that delinquents of this character, should be consigned to the infamy and severity of punishments, which must inevitably tend to perfect the work of degradation, to sink them still deeper in corruption, to deprive them of their remaining sensibility to the shame of exposure, and establish them in all the hardihood of daring and desperate villainy?

To gain further evidence, the members of the committee had asked both the District Attorney and the keeper of the Bridewell about the treatment of juvenile offenders. The District Attorney gave them a list of "more than 450 persons" under twenty-five who had been sentenced either to the Bridewell or the penitentiary. "A very considerable number" of them were between nine and sixteen years old. These were vagrants; none of them had been charged with a specific offense. The list included "children who profess to have no home, or whose parents have turned them out of doors and take no care of them." The committee believed that children in such circumstances would "eventually have recourse to petty thefts." If they were girls, they would "descend to practices of infamy, in order to save themselves from the pinching assaults of cold and hunger." The members of the committee decided to visit the Bridewell themselves. There the keeper told them that the old and young spent a part of every day together, "because the prison is so constructed that it will not admit of keeping them otherwise." Two-thirds of the young people in the Bridewell had been there before. "It may well be submitted to the judgment of a discerning public," they wrote, "whether an exposure of a few days to such company and fare as here represented, is not sufficient to suppress, in youthful minds, all virtuous emotions." Having noted these facts, they concluded that it was "highly expedient" that a "house of refuge" for juvenile delinquents be established near the City of New York "as soon as practicable."

According to the committee, a house of refuge would be "an asylum in which boys under a certain age, who become subject to the notice of the Police, either as vagrants, or homeless, or charged with petty crimes, may be received, [and where they may be] judiciously classed according to their degrees of depravity or innocence, [and then] put to work at such employments as will tend to encourage industry and ingenuity." The committee also proposed to teach the boys "reading, writing, and arithmetic, and . . . the nature of their moral and religious obligations." The primary purpose of the treatment of the boys was "to afford a prompt and energetic corrective of their vicious propensities and hold out every possible inducement to reformation and good conduct."

The proposed house of refuge would also have a department for girls "either too young to have acquired habits of fixed depravity, or those whose lives have in general been virtuous, but who, having yielded to the seductive influence of corrupt associates, have suddenly to endure the bitterness of lost reputation, and are cast forlorn and destitute upon a cold and unfeeling public." The committee realized that this was a controversial proposal, but indicated that they thought a girls' department would be an "advantage to the institution." They also pointed out that "similar institutions in Europe" included departments for girls. The committee thought that the institution maintained by the Philanthropic Society near London appeared "to come nearest in its general system to that which we would recommend."

Griscom finished the report and turned the platform over to Mayor Colden. The assembly, probably at the committee's suggestion, then passed a series of resolutions. The first endorsed the creation of a house of refuge, and the second urged "that a society be now formed under the appelation of the 'Society for the Reformation of Juvenile Delinquents.'" Successive resolutions named the board of managers and the treasurer of the new society and outlined rules for membership. Once these resolutions passed, Peter Augustus Jay, the City Recorder, James W. Gerard, and others gave brief speeches in support of the proposed house of refuge. They touched themes which were now familiar: that prison corrupted young people who were sent there, that there were as many as four hundred boys under sixteen arrested annually, and that such an arrest almost always meant the beginning of another criminal career. The speakers also said that society now made it practically impossible for a criminal to reform, and claimed that the house of refuge might save as many as two hundred children a year from crime and infamy. At the conclusion of the meeting the officers of the new Society collected over $800 and announced that they would canvass the entire city for funds.

Shortly after this meeting the Reverend Mr. Standford wrote to the Common Council for the third time about the city's vagrant youth. He reminded the Council of his interest in an asylum for them and concluded: "If I may be permitted to name a permanent spot for such an establishment, it is the premises now occupied as the U.S. Arsenal, at the fork of the Bloomingdale Road. . . . In my estimation, it could not be appropriated to a more useful purpose, or prove more honourable to the city."

In February the newly formed Society for the Reformation of Juvenile Delinquents sent a memorial to the Common Council stating that they were "desirous of establishing an institution which shall serve at once as a refuge for neglected or depraved children . . . and praying the aid of the corporation in donations of lands or otherwise." The Council referred the request to a special committee, which wholeheartedly endorsed the proposal: "The committee believes that such an institution, properly regulated and conducted, would not only tend to improve the condition of society by lessening the commission of crime, and the number of convicts sent to our prisons, but would have a tendency to diminish the expences [sic] of the city incurred on that account." The Common Council arranged to have the land on which the Arsenal was located returned to the city's jurisdiction. The city then gave the land to the Society, and the Society paid the federal government $2000 for the buildings and the wall.[11]

The Society now sought state financial aid and sent a memorial to the New York legislature in Albany. John Griscom's report, read at the City Hotel in December, formed the main part of the memorial. The managers of the Society explained that they had obtained land and buildings for the proposed house of refuge, but they did not have enough money to keep the project going. While the members of the new Society waited to learn if the legislature would appropriate money for their institution, the Secretary of State for New York, J. V. N. Yates, in a report on pauperism in the state, noted that a great many paupers were children under fourteen, who might "at no distant day form a fruitful nursery for crime unless prevented by the watchful super-intendence of the legislature." [12]

Meanwhile, a select committee of the legislature met to draft a bill to charter the New York House of Refuge and place it under state supervision. The bill passed without a negative vote on March 29, 1824. The question of state financial aid remained unsettled, however, and the Society for the Reformation of Juvenile Delinquents asked the Common Council of New York to endorse a request for the proceeds of a tax on public amusements in the City of New York. The Common Council agreed and sent a memorial of their own to Albany along with the request from the Society. But the state granted no money to the House of Refuge in 1824, and it was not until 1829 that the Society received a substantial and steady income from public funds.[13]

III

The act incorporating the Society for the Reformation of Juvenile Delinquents in the City of New York outlined the procedures for membership in the Society and made the Board of Managers responsible for the operation of the House of Refuge. Thus, America's first institution for juvenile delinquents was a "mixed" institution. That is, a private philanthropic group established and operated it, but the state had chartered it and provided for the conditions of its operation. The act of incorporation also contained the first statutory definition of juvenile delinquency in the United States. It authorized the Managers "to receive and take into the house of refuge to be established by them, all such children who shall be taken up or committed as vagrants, or convicted of criminal offenses" if a judge thought they were "proper objects." The Managers could also "place the said children committed to their care, during the minority of such children at such employments, and cause them to be instructed in such branches of useful knowledge, as shall be suitable to their years and capacities." The Managers had the power to bind out children (with their consent) as apprentices until they reached legal maturity. The children remained under the control of the Managers until the boys were twenty-one and the girls were eighteen, or until the officials at the House of Refuge decided that they were "reformed" and agreed to their discharge. Thus, the New York House of Refuge began the use of the indeterminate sentence long before penal reformers advocated it in the late nineteenth century as a necessary innovation in American penology.[14]

The House of Refuge began its operations in the old arsenal building on January 1, 1825, with six boys and three girls. By the end of the first year, a total of seventy-three children had come to the Refuge, fifty-four boys and nineteen girls, and fifty-six remained in the institution. Of the seventeen children who left during the first year, nine had been indentured as apprentices or servants, four had been discharged, and four boys had "absconded."[15]

Most of the children who came to the House of Refuge that first year and most of the ones who came later were "very ignorant." Even those few who had learned to read "had acquired no relish for intellectual improvement. Their habits, as it [sic] respects skill and useful industry, were still more deplorable." Particularly surprising was the fact that the girls could not perform any of the standard feminine tasks; they could not cook, sew, or iron. For the first year the boys spent most of their time cleaning up the grounds and helping to erect a new building and make the wall higher. When they were not busy with their newly learned domestic tasks, the girls planted grass. Once the maintenance tasks were finished, the boys began to learn shoemaking and tailoring, and the girls found themselves doing all of the mending and laundry for the institution.

The schedule, which the superintendent had worked out, allowed two hours a day, one in the morning and one in the evening, for formal instruction. The curriculum included spelling, reading, writing, and cyphering (arithmetic). To some extent the inmates taught themselves, since the Lancastrian or monitorial system was used. Apparently, the combination of labor and instruction and the system of discipline at the House of Refuge were effective. The *Annual Report* for the first year noted that "of the whole number in the house, the superintendent reports that [only] eleven are still restless and refractory." Four of the boys had run away, but the Managers and the superintendent were apparently satisfied with the other children, who had been in the House of Refuge at one time or another in 1825.[16]

Methods of discipline varied; the superintendent sometimes put the "subjects" on a ball and chain. He also used handcuffs, legirons, and the "barrel." On January 28, 1825, Superintendent Curtis noted in his daily journal that six subjects, two of whom were girls, had been talking during a meal. He "took each of them to the barrel which supports them while the feet are tied on one side and the hands on the other. . . . With the pantaloons down [this device] gives a convenient surface for the operation of the 6 line cat." On that same day a boy wearing handcuffs made himself a key. The superintendent "put him in prison," locked his leg iron to the wall, and instructed the staff to feed him on bread and water. In spite of these restraints, however, the boy broke out of "prison," but the police soon recaptured him. Curtis refused to have this boy back at the House of Refuge, and so he went to the penitentiary. Corporal punishment was not confined to boys. On March 13, 1825, the superintendent put leg irons on a girl who "does not obey the orders of coming when called, and neglects her work for playing in the yard." Curtis also gave one "sullen, ill-natured and disobedient" girl "a dose of salts"—apparently aloes, a purgative. She came to the House of Refuge in March, 1825, and was "very trying." She did not "transgress in things of

importance" but she was "artful and sly" and told "many equiv-
ocating stories." Her conduct exasperated Superintendent Curtis
and he "gave her a ball and chain and confined her to the house."
She escaped twice; once the police recaptured her, and once she
returned on her own. She went out as a servant, but voluntarily
returned to the House of Refuge. Another indenture took the
girl to her majority, but on December 26, 1829, the superintendent
wrote that "she is said to be on the town." [17]

The situation at the Refuge made some of these punishments
necessary. The walls presented no real barrier, and the superintendent had to appoint some of the boys as guards. There were,
consequently, a number of escapes. On October 4, 1825, Superintendent Curtis noted in the daily journal that "this evening has
been spent in making confessions on the repeated attempts of
escaping." As a result,

> great freedom of speach [sic] and frankness appeared to our
> entire satisfaction, all the movements and plans as well as the
> persons who have manifested a desire to go has [sic] been fully
> exposed. . . . It tells us that the insecurity which we have daily
> felt on this subject has been well grounded; and that there is no
> security with our present encumbrances.

The fact that the magazine of the old arsenal still contained
powder also added to the superintendent's worries. In addition
many of the inmates in the House of Refuge were boys over
sixteen, for legally any boy under twenty-one could be sent there.
In September, 1826, the superintendent complained about the
"large notorious & hardened villains" who came to the Refuge.
"I fear," he said, "that our extended wish to do good will in
consequence of introducing these ill bred hardened boys among
the first and young offenders, will prove a curse rather than a
blessing." Since the old arsenal building was clearly inadequate,
the Acting Committee (which functioned as a board of trustees
for the House of Refuge) decided to erect a new building which
would provide "greater security." In April, 1825, the Committee
resolved to add workshops and small utility buildings to their
construction plans and decided that the new main building should

contain "cells and accommodations for a number of delinq'nts not exceeding one hundred." In that same month the United States Army sent a man to remove the powder from the magazine, which somewhat reduced the "insecurity." [18]

To pay for the new building the managers of the Society appealed to the public for more money. In May, 1825, they issued an *Address to Annual Subscribers* in which they claimed that "already the number of vagrant children who beg and steal in our streets is perceptibly diminished." There were thirty-five boys and eleven girls in the House of Refuge at that time "in a situation where there is no temptation to vice . . . and, where, instead of being left to prey on the public, they will be fitted to become valuable members of society." To continue this important work the managers felt compelled "to erect . . . an additional stone building with separate dormitories for each child, on a plan somewhat resembling the State Prison at Auburn. . . ." To be sure that their contributions were worthwhile "subscribers and the public" were invited "to call at the House of Refuge, and see that idleness has become changed to industry, filth and rags to cleanliness and comfortable appearance, [and] boisterous impudence to quiet submission. . . ."

The Acting Committee directed the superintendent to employ a foreman and four to six masons to erect the building with the assistance of the boys. The masons and the boys finished the new cell-house in April, 1826. It was a two-story stone building with barred windows and heavy doors. Inside were small "dormitories" —three feet, three inches wide—for each boy. The new building did make it more difficult to escape and brought about the complete separation of the male and female departments. "We find ourselves in possession and enjoyment of all the long wished advantages of the new building," Superintendent Curtis wrote, "and we also find (as we may allways [sic] expect) that our anticipations are not realised." The boys now had to do their own cooking, and for a time they proved less adept than the girls.[19]

From the first the House of Refuge attracted a stream of visitors, distinguished and otherwise. Soon after the Refuge opened, a father appeared and demanded the return of his son. Only after he had secured a writ of habeas corpus did the superintendent permit the man to take his boy. In May, 1826, Governor De Witt Clinton of New York, the Governor of Ohio, the Mayor of New York, "and various other dignitaries and their wives" came to the House of Refuge and left apparently "well-pleased." In July three men from Pennsylvania came to study the House of Refuge because they were planning to establish a similar institution in Philadelphia. "They left us highly gratified," the superintendent noted in the daily journal, "with a determined resolution to advance the same good cause they had witnessed. . . ." A week later, the sister of a former inmate came by to see some of her old friends. She was wanted by the police, however, and the superintendent arranged to have her detained. Such guests must have appeared frequently for on July 26, 1826, Superintendent N. C. Hart (Joseph Curtis had resigned on July 11, 1826) noted in the daily journal that "it is found that now and then improper persons get into our yard on visiting days. I have given direction to the gate-keeper not to permit any to enter (even on visiting days) Unless they are very respectable looking persons. . . ." [20]

On Sundays many of the Managers drove out to the House of Refuge to attend the worship services. Two of the most regular visitors were John Griscom and Isaac Collins, both of whom figured prominently in the founding of the refuge. Griscom sometimes talked to the boys about science. On August 13, 1826, for example, he spoke on "the creation of man and matter," and on New Year's Day, 1827, he illustrated his talk with a magic lantern. Collins gave some books for the library. Among the titles were *Essays on Virtue*, the *Life of Captain Cook*, a *Report* of the British and Foreign School Society, *Robinson Crusoe*, and *Wonderful Escapes*.[21]

At the end of the second year, in the *Annual Report* the Managers explained the theories which guided the efforts to reform juvenile delinquents at the House of Refuge. "The young offender," they said, "should, if possible, be subdued by kindness. His heart should first be addressed, and the language of confi-

dence, though undeserved, be used towards him." They added
that the young inmate should be taught that "his keepers were
his best friends and that the object of his confinement was his
reform and ultimate good. If he is made to believe that he is still
of some use and value, he will soon endeavor to act up to the
character which is set upon him." This kind of discipline, the managers argued, "will be willing, cheerful and lasting." The remarkably gentle—and from the lights of modern psychology, appropriate
—methods espoused by the Managers of the New York House of
Refuge came from a nineteenth-century theory about children
and the development of their personalities. As the Managers explained, men of the early nineteenth century believed that "the
minds of children, naturally pliant, can, by early instruction, be
formed and moulded to our wishes. An inclination can there be
given to them, as readily to virtuous as to vicious pursuits." Not
only can the plastic minds of children be turned to vice or virtue,
but earlier inclinations can be altered if the child is not too old:
"The seeds of vice, which bad advisers may have planted, if skill
is exercised, can yet be extracted . . . and on the mind which
appeared barren and unfruitful may yet be engrafted those principles of virtue which shall do much to retrieve the errors of the
past, and afford a promise of goodness and usefulness for the
future."

The Managers also reminded their readers that "these little vagrants, whose depredations provoke and call down upon them
our indignation are yet but children, who have gone astray for
want of that very care and vigilance we exercise towards our
own." They were nonetheless, misbehaving children, whose actions had to be condemned. Furthermore, "a regard for our property and the good of society, requires that they should be stopped,
reproved and punished. . . . But," the Managers continued, "they
are not to be destroyed. The public must in some measure take
the place of those who ought to have been their natural guardians
and protectors." Here the Managers of the New York House of
Refuge anticipated one of the key concepts of the Illinois Juvenile

Court Act of 1899—the idea that the public (in the Illinois law it was the state) has a collective responsibility to and for society's misbehaving children. Ironically, this provision of the Illinois law was hailed as a great innovation in the legal treatment of delinquent children.[22]

In order to carry out their theories, the officials at the New York House of Refuge adopted rules which prescribed continuous activity for the inmates during their waking hours. They were to be employed "every day in the year, except Sundays, at such labor, business, or employment as from time to time [would] be designated by the Acting Committee." Other rules indicated that all the children wore "coarse but comfortable apparel of the cheapest and most durable kind," which was made on the premises. Inmates who refused to work or who used profane or indecent language, or who fought with their fellow delinquents, would be punished. Punishments included deprivation of play periods, being sent to bed without supper, and bread and water. In more serious cases, the officials might force the recalcitrant boy or girl to drink a bitter herb tea which caused them to sweat profusely, or they might put the offender in solitary confinement. In extreme cases, corporal punishment or iron fetters might be used. The rules provided that corporal punishment could only be inflicted in the presence of the superintendent (or the matron in the case of misbehaving girls). The rules also indicated that "the females shall eat their meals and lodge in a separate building from the males, with whom they shall have no intercourse or communication, except at family or public worship." [23]

Scarcely a week passed without some sort of incident. On September 5, 1826, one of the worst troublemakers in the girls' department returned of her own accord after having escaped. She and the school teacher got into an argument, and he began whipping her. According to Superintendent Hart,

> She commenced swearing most bitterly, tore his shirt considerable & made battle with her fists—having a pen knife secreted about her, she succeeded in opening it with her mouth, & made several

attempts to stab him in his breast—to no purpose, but finally got it in the flesh of his arm and ripped a gash at least 1½ inches long and very deep.

The superintendent put the girl in irons. In December, 1826, two boys escaped through the attic of the male cell house, and an officer went to town to look for them. He found one of the boys "in a small rum hole in Anthony St. with girls and other company of ill fame." The boy drew out a knife, while one of the patrons of the establishment shouted "Stick him [!] Stick him [!]." The boy cut the officer severely on the arm and on the neck "near the jugular vein." When the police had returned this boy to the House of Refuge, the superintendent punished him "with a cowskin up on his bare back" and then put him in solitary confinement "without a book to divert his mind" on a bread and water diet. The boy remained in solitary for three days, after which the superintendent put him in a cell in the upper tier. The boy then attempted another escape:

> [He] tied three sheets & a cord together—broke through the plastered wall into the garret—again fastened the cord to the same place where he had been successful in making his escape but a few evenings since—but alas! no sooner than he had . . . [placed] his weight upon the cord thus fastened, it broke & he fell about 30 feet upon frozen ground & stones—broke his foot badly—pitched upon his face cut a hole over his eye to the skull bone & fractured it, broke his nose & drove the bones so deep as to endanger his life—cut his lip through nearly up to his nose. Thus he rolls in agony.

To prevent similar escape attempts the officers moved the older boys to the first tier and put the younger boys in their place.[24]

The House of Refuge, following the penal theories of men like Thomas Eddy, also instituted a rudimentary classification system. When they entered, the officials placed the inmates in one of four grades, ranging from "those who are vicious, bad and wicked" in class four to "the best behaved and most orderly boys and girls; those that do not swear, lie, or use profane, obscene or indecent language or conversation," in class one. Every Sunday, the superintendent, his assistant, and the teacher reclassified the children according to their behavior. The upper classes enjoyed extra recreation, and the lower classes found themselves on a reduced diet and suffered from the loss of other privileges. The system of treatment at the New York House of Refuge, rudimentary as it was, is another example of an improvement in penal practice made in a juvenile institution which would later be hailed as an "innovation" in adult reformatories.

A typical day in the Refuge illustrates this system. A bell would ring at sunrise to arouse the sleeping children. They had fifteen minutes to dress, make their beds, and straighten up their cells; then they assembled in the corridors and marched off to the washrooms. After washing, the inmates lined up for a personal inspection. They were at best a motley group. Their clothing had been cut from "a coarse, cheap material" to six standard sizes. In 1848 Elijah Devoe, formerly an assistant superintendent, recalled that they had "collectively a slovenly and untidy appearance." From inspection the children went to morning prayers, after which they went to school for an hour and a half. Then they sat down to a breakfast which usually consisted of bread, molasses, and rye coffee. After breakfast, the inmates trooped off to their various workshops, where they worked until noon. Washing up again and the noon meal occupied the next hour, after which the children returned to work. During this afternoon work period the children could gain extra recreation time if they finished their assigned tasks early. The work period ended at five o'clock; then there was a half-hour for supper and another hour and a half of school. Following the evening school session, there were evening prayers; the inmates then marched back to their cells, turned in, and followed a rule of silence for the night.[25]

The labor of the children in the House of Refuge was let out to contractors, who then paid the institution for the value of the work done by the children. While the contractors taught the children the skills necessary to perform their tasks, the officials of the House of Refuge maintained discipline. The girls worked mostly at sewing; and the boys made cane bottoms for chairs, various kinds of brushes, shoes, and boxes for soap and candles. The contractors represented an outside presence in the House of Refuge and an unending source of difficulty. On July 22, 1826, for example, two girls claimed that the shoemaker took them "into his dwelling & there perpetrated that heinous crime of seduction." An investigation quickly followed and on August 6, Superintendent Hart wrote that the shoemaker had "closed his business with us." On October 16, 1827, Hart noted in the daily journal that the parents of some of the boys in the House of Refuge had complained that their sons were not learning a trade since the shoemaker had set up an assembly line, assigning a separate task to each boy. "The remarks are in considerable degree true," Hart wrote, "& how the difficulty is to be obviated I cannot tell." It would take nearly half a century to eliminate the contract system.[26]

When the officials at the New York House of Refuge concluded that a boy or girl had sufficiently reformed to be trusted outside the institution itself, they often bound them out as apprentices. Some of the boys signed on as sailors in whaling ships, a practice which the managers endorsed heartily in the *Fifth Annual Report* because such a boy would find himself under "wholesome restraint and discipline" and would have the examples of "moral, industrious, and religious companions." Most of the boys, however, were apprenticed to farmers, including some in the West—a practice which anticipated the placing out system of Charles Loring Brace and the Children's Aid Society. Generally, the girls became servants in families not too distant from the House of Refuge. Boys were indentured until they were twenty-one, girls until they reached eighteen. To explain the purposes and methods of the New York House of Refuge, the superintendent sent a form letter to the masters of the apprentices, which warned against the overuse of corporal punishment and reminded the masters that "it has not been concealed from you, that this child has been a delinquent." The superintendent also addressed a form letter to the apprentice. "We should not have consented to part with you at this time," it began, "had not your conduct given us reason to hope, that the religious and moral instruction you have received since you have been under our care, have disposed you to lead an honest, industrious, and sober life." The letter to the apprentice also cautioned him against bad company, especially his former associates.[27]

IV

In 1820 a committee of the Massachusetts legislature began investigating the causes of poverty. In 1821 the committee recommended that the system of alms-giving then practiced throughout Massachusetts be abandoned and that cities and towns build work houses or houses of industry. As a result of this report, the town fathers of Boston launched an investigation of poverty in their city. They found the Boston Almshouse to be in deplorable condition. Crowded together were the poor who could not work, the able-bodied who were given make-work such as picking oakum, and those convicted of minor offenses such as drunkenness. The Boston investigators recommended the erection of a work house or industry for the able-bodied poor and a house of correction for minor offenders. By the summer of 1823 these new institutions were in use, but the south wing of the House of Correction remained empty. As in New York, hundreds of undisciplined and apparently homeless children roamed the streets of Boston. Their disturbing presence—the prosperous people of Boston also saw these waifs as a threat to society—and the creation of the New York House of Refuge stimulated the town fathers of Boston to do something about juvenile delinquency. Early in 1826 a committee of the City Council recommended that the unused wing of the House of Correction be converted to "a house of reformation for juvenile offenders." [28]

In March of 1826 the legislature passed an act authorizing the Boston City Council to use the House of Correction or any other building as an institution for juvenile offenders. This statute also gave the Commonwealth of Massachusetts a definition of juvenile delinquency. Like the act passed two years before in New

York, the Massachusetts law defined juvenile delinquents as "all
such children who shall be convicted of criminal offenses, or taken
up and committed under and by virtue of an act of this Commonwealth, 'for suppressing and punishing of rogues, vagabonds,
common beggars, and other idle, disorderly and lewd persons.'"
In addition, the Massachusetts General Court also provided that
the house of reformation could receive "all children who live an
idle or dissolute life, whose parents are dead, or if living, from
drunkenness, or other vices, neglect to provide any suitable employment, or exercise any salutary control over said children."
The Massachusetts law was the first legislative recognition of the
idea of preventing juvenile delinquency.[29]

The early years of the Boston House of Reformation were difficult. Ordinary citizens and members of the Boston City Council
disagreed about its design, and, as Mayor Josiah Quincy indicated
in his *Municipal History of Boston*, "the expenditures were immediate and considerable; the advantages distant and problemati-
cal." Many Bostonians felt that the institution should have been
supported by the state instead of the city. Mayor Quincy also
complained about parents who tried to have their sons removed
from the institution and about "tender-hearted philanthropists, who
regarded the length and nature of the restraint as severe, not-
withstanding [the fact that] the boys were committed by a court
of justice for serious offenses." The new institution was very fortunate, however, in the selection of its second superintendent, the
Reverend E. M. P. Wells. According to Mayor Quincy, "Strictness
without severity, love without indulgence, were the elements of
his system of management." Quincy was not alone in his praise of
Wells. In 1832 two French noblemen, Alexis de Tocqueville and
Gustave Beaumont, came to the United States on an official mission for the French government to study American prison systems.
They inspected several American prisons and the houses of refuge
at New York and Philadelphia, and naturally they came to Boston
and visited the House of Reformation. They were particularly impressed by Superintendent Wells and his administration of the
Boston institution. "It is possible to find superintendents who are

fit for the Philadelphia system," they wrote, "but we cannot hope to meet often with such men as Mr. Wells." [30]

What distinguished the House of Reformation in Boston from the New York House of Refuge and the House of Refuge established in Philadelphia in 1828 was its system of discipline. As Tocqueville and Beaumont noted, "the Boston discipline belongs to a species of ideas much more elevated than that established in New York and Philadelphia"; but it was difficult to practice because it was "entirely of a moral character." The Boston House of Reformation used a classification system based on the conduct of the inmates, but unlike the New York House of Refuge it required each child to evaluate his own conduct, and a jury composed of children in the institution tried cases of serious misconduct. In the House of Reformation there were six grades of conduct—three good ones and three bad ones. Each of the good grades carried with it certain privileges; boys in the highest grade could go outside the bounds of the House of Reformation by themselves. Conversely, each of the bad grades carried a degree of privation; boys in the two lowest grades were not allowed to speak unless it was absolutely necessary. Before the boys could participate in this system of discipline, they went through a period of probation. A new arrival met with the superintendent who interviewed him to determine his moral condition. Then, if the new inmate had been found guilty of a serious offense, he was placed in solitary confinement for two weeks so that he could reflect on his vices. Superintendent Wells then told him why he was in the Boston House of Reformation and explained the system of discipline. If the boy rebelled against the officials during his probationary period, they whipped him. Only at this first stage did the superintendent permit corporal punishment. At the end of the probationary period, the superintendent assigned the child one of the bad grades and encouraged him to move up.[31]

While the Society for the Prevention of Pauperism in the City of New York began concentrating on the problem of youthful offenders in its city, the Society for Alleviating the Miseries of Public Prisons met in Philadelphia and appointed a committee to investigate the conditions of vagrant children in the prisons of the city. At that time, juvenile vagrants and young offenders in Philadelphia were placed in the Walnut Street jail along with adult criminals. In May, 1824, the committee recommended that the Guardians of the Poor provide a suitable place for the reception of juvenile vagrants. In the meantime the Society had appointed another committee to consider what should be done about juvenile offenders. This committee recommended the creation of a House of Refuge for discharged prisoners, but soon after they filed their report "an association of females" petitioned the Society to create a House of Refuge for Juvenile Offenders. So the committee investigated again and decided that such an institution was desirable but beyond the means of the Society for Alleviating the Miseries of Public Prisons. The Society then called a public meeting in February, 1826, to find additional support for the proposed House of Refuge. The assembly adopted a resolution calling for the creation of such an institution for juvenile offenders and appointed a committee to draw up "articles of association" for that purpose and to ask the legislature for "such powers in law, as may be necessary to carry the designs of the association into full effect when it may be organized." The legislature readily acceded to the request and passed an act of incorporation for the Philadelphia House of Refuge in March, 1826. This act, like those statutes creating the New York House of Refuge and the Boston House of Reformation, provided that the Managers of the Philadelphia House of Refuge could receive "such children who shall be taken up as vagrants, or duly convicted of criminal offenses," but it also gave the managers the authority to receive children "who shall be taken up . . . upon any criminal charge." Thus, by law, children suspected of crime could be placed in the Philadephia institution.[32]

To accomplish their goals the Managers of the Philadelphia House of Refuge expected to rely on a combination of strict discipline, a classification similar to that used at the House of Reformation in Boston, work at a useful occupation, education, and moral instruction. The first step in such a program was "to raise

the delinquent in his own estimation . . . to change his whole
course of thought: to awake his latent pride and sensibility: to
direct his ambition to useful and honorable pursuits: and thus to
conduct him unconsciously as it were to the practical charms and
advantages of a virtuous life." The managers expected to retain
control over delinquents who entered the House of Refuge until
they reached a majority, but the managers hoped to place the
children out as apprentices well before they reached the upper
age limit.[33]

V

The public image of an institution, derived in part from the reports of well-publicized visitors and investigations and also from
the institution's own annual reports, is rarely a complete picture
of its daily life. In a book that amounted to a polemic against the
New York House of Refuge, Elijah Devoe, a discharged assistant
superintendent, contended that the New York institution had
deliberately falsified its public face. He charged that officials had
altered the records to give a higher rate of reformation and that
the day-by-day practices in the institution were far more cruel
than any outsider realized. The routine was "a stern, brutal, co-
ercive government and discipline, entirely the opposite of that
paternal establishment so amiable and ingeniously pictured in the
'annual reports.'" Devoe also indicated that the rule prohibiting
corporal punishment unless in the presence of the superintendent
was a dead letter: "Corporal punishments are usually inflicted
with the cat or a ratan. The latter instrument is applied in a great
variety of places, such as the palm and back of the hands, top and
bottom of the feet, and lastly, but not rarely or sparingly, to the
posteriors over the clothes, and also on the naked skin." Ratans
were readily available and "liable to be used everywhere and at
all times of the day." In addition, Devoe deplored the mixing of
"hardened culprits over fifteen years" of age with "small, younger,
and less corrupt children." The older boys were just as likely to
corrupt the younger ones as hardened adult criminals were to

corrupt juveniles in prison; it was therefore an injustice that "boys under a certain age, who become subject to the notice of our police, either as vagrants or houseless, should be thrust into the society of confirmed thieves, burglars, and robbers, and subjected to the same discipline and punishments." [34]

Devoe's account, which was the work of an unhappy former employee, nonetheless provides an "inside view" of an early nineteenth-century juvenile institution. It seems probable that the annual reports of these institutions, which were made in response to state law and which represented to some extent arguments for state appropriations, presented only the most favorable aspects of houses of refuge and ignored the day-to-day activities which deviated from the high ideals set by the managers. In some respects, however, the view of juvenile institutions presented in their annual reports is more valuable than the "inside story," because the annual reports gave the public its only look at juvenile institutions. Thus, they are a rudimentary index to what nineteenth-century Americans knew about institutions for juvenile delinquents.

The creation of special institutions for juvenile offenders in the second decade of the nineteenth century indicated a growing awareness on the part of American city-dwellers of the problem of juvenile delinquency, and the new institutions also represented a modification in the application of criminal laws to young people. Under the common law as Blackstone explained it, children under seven were presumed to be unable to distinguish between right and wrong. Between the ages of seven and fourteen, "though an infant shall be *prima facie* adjudged to be *doli incapax* [not mentally competent]; yet if it appear to the court and jury that he was *doli capax*, and could discern between good and evil, he may be convicted and suffer death." That this understanding of the common law was generally adopted in the United States may be illustrated by a case involving a twelve-year-old Negro boy in New Jersey in 1828. The boy had been found guilty of the murder of a sixty-year-old woman by a lower court, and the case had been appealed to the New Jersey Supreme Court on the grounds that the boy was too young to be found guilty of such an offense. The

Supreme Court upheld the verdict of the lower court, finding that the judge had correctly charged the jury with the relevant points of law in the case. The lower court judge had told the jury that "with respect to the ability of persons of his age, to commit crimes of this nature, the law is, that under the age of seven, they are deemed incapable of it. Between seven and fourteen, if there be no proof of capacity, arising out of this case, or by testimony of witnesses, the presumption is in their favor; a presumption however, growing weaker and more easily overcome, the nearer they approach to fourteen." The judge went on to explain that a twelve-year-old boy in New Jersey at that time probably possessed "sufficient capacity" to commit murder. Finally he told the jury: "you will call to mind the evidence on this subject; and if you are satisfied that he was able, in a good degree, to distinguish between right and wrong; to know the nature of the crime with which he is charged; and that it was *deserving* of *severe* punishment, his infancy will furnish no obstacle, on the score of incapacity, to his conviction." [35]

None of the statutes which established the houses of refuge in New York, Boston, and Philadelphia changed the basic premises of the common law, but in effect they raised the age below which a child could expect to receive some kind of preferential treatment from the law. The sentiment behind the creation of the new institutions for juvenile delinquents recognized that children—even children over fourteen—required different treatment from adults. The new laws, although they did not mention any ages except those for the end of minority, created institutions which would provide that treatment. The laws also provided a legal definition of juvenile delinquency. A juvenile delinquent was a child who broke the law, or who was in danger of breaking the law, and the community hoped to keep him from becoming an adult criminal by providing reformatory treatment in a house of refuge.

The creation of the House of Refuge, a unique institution in the United States, posed some new legal problems, which soon led to court action. In the case of *Commonwealth* v *M'Keagy*, heard before the Court of Common Pleas in Philadelphia in 1831, the

issue was a plea for a writ of habeas corpus on behalf of one
Lewis L. Joseph, who had been convicted on evidence supplied
by his father of being "an idle and disorderly person" and sent
to the Philadelphia House of Refuge. After reciting the relevant
sections of the statute establishing the Philadelphia House of
Refuge, the court noted that "great power is given to the managers of this institution, a power which could only be justified
under the most pressing public exigencies, and whose continuance
should depend only on the most prudent and guarded exercise of
it." Particularly unusual, according to the court, was the power
given to any magistrate or justice of the peace, "on a charge of
vagrancy or crime . . . to take a child from its parent and con-
sign it to the control of any human being, no matter how elevated
or pure." The overseers of the poor generally had the power to
provide for orphans and dependent children and even to bind
them out as apprentices until they reached their majority. "Why
is it that in some shape, and if necessary, in a more decided
shape," the court asked, "the public cannot assume similar guardianship of children whose poverty had degenerated into vagrancy?" The court agreed that the House of Refuge indeed did
have the power to receive and control children whose vagrancy
fell within the categories the court had outlined. However, the
court continued, "it is when the law is attempted to be applied to
subjects who are not vagrants in the just and legal acceptation of
the term"; when "preservation becomes mixed' with a punitory
character, that doubts are started and difficulties arise, which
often and necessarily involve the most solemn questions of individual and constitutional rights."

Having thus stated its position, the court proceeded to find
that Lewis Joseph was not a vagrant. His father, who had committed him, was not a pauper, and the boy, while he had misbehaved, was not a fit subject for the House of Refuge. The
Superintendent of the House of Refuge had told the judge that
the boy had been very well behaved there and had been very
receptive to discipline. As the court said, "it is manifest, that
gentle but firm discipline was all that was necessary to root out

from his mind the luxuriant weeds produced by weak indulgence, bestowed by an erring parent of a sportive and volatile disposition." In opposing the petition for a writ of habeas corpus the lawyer for the House of Refuge had argued that the boy's father had transferred his parental authority to the managers of that institution, which now acted *in loco parentis*. But the court rejected this view, saying that the House of Refuge could only receive vagrant and criminal children; it was not "a place to correct refractory children." Accordingly, the court ordered Lewis L. Joseph released from the Philadelphia House of Refuge.[36]

In a later case, *Ex parte Crouse*, which the Pennsylvania Supreme Court heard in 1839, a similar petition for a writ of habeas corpus challenged the constitutionality of the statute which created the Philadelphia House of Refuge. The petition had been filed on behalf of Mary Ann Crouse by her father. "The House of Refuge is not a prison, but a school," the court said in opening its argument. The use of the House of Refuge "as a prison for juvenile convicts who would also be committed to a common gaol" is clearly constitutional, but in the case of juveniles admitted as vagrants or potential criminals, the constitutionality was open to some question. The main purpose of the House of Refuge was clearly reformation and not punishment; education was one of its principal activities. If a child's parents did not, for one reason or another, provide it with adequate education, the state by virtue of its power of *parens patriae* could provide the child with the necessary education. Such was Mary Ann Crouse's case: "The infant has been snatched from a course which must have ended in confirmed depravity; and not only is the restraint of her person lawful, but it would be an act of extreme cruelty to release her from it." [37]

These two cases illustrate that the House of Refuge was a legal institution with certain well-defined powers. Primarily, it was an institution designed to reform youthful criminals, but it also functioned to prevent crime by accepting young vagrants who were potential juvenile criminals. Once a house of refuge received a child, the managers had a wide latitude of authority over him. In effect, they had the same powers over their charges that a natural parent had over his own children. Thus the state, by chartering a private or municipal association to take the place of inadequate or missing parents, had taken a bold step in the direction of providing for the welfare of its children. In addition, such a step appeared almost too attractive to resist. When houses of refuge first appeared, they seemed to have a good chance of preventing or drastically reducing the rate of adult crime. They not only gave the community something to do with juvenile offenders and vagrant children, they promised to cut future welfare and prison costs. When they insisted that the inmates of houses of refuge be taught a useful trade, the managers shrewdly responded to a community prejudice which not only condemned idleness as a sin but also linked it with serious crime. By teaching juvenile offenders how to work then, houses of refuge were exorcising sin and providing for the future security of life and property. The creation of the New York House of Refuge and similar institutions in Boston and Philadelphia marked the beginning of nineteenth-century America's concern for wayward children. It also marked the beginning of the process of separating juvenile delinquents from adult criminals—a process that would not be complete until the creation of the juvenile court in 1899. But the house of refuge had one essential weakness as an institution—it was a charity, which, although chartered by the state, private citizens operated. The involvement of private citizens had been necessary to launch the first institutions for juvenile delinquents, but once their worth had been proved, many philanthropists felt that the reformation of juvenile offenders was a duty for which the state should take full responsibility.

4

Mary Carpenter and Charles Dickens: English Contributions to the Study and Treatment of Juvenile Delinquency

In Dickens's novel *Oliver Twist*, published in 1838, young Oliver had just run away from his "place" as an apprentice to the undertaker, Mr. Sowerberry, when he met a boy about his age named Jack Dawkins. Dawkins promised to take Oliver to London and introduce him to "a 'spectable old genelman as lives there, wot'll give you lodgings for nothink . . ." Dawkins, who told Oliver that his friends called him "the artful Dodger," took the young runaway to a strange room in the slums of London:

> The walls and ceiling of the room were perfectly black with age and dirt. There was a deal table before the fire upon which were a candle, stuck in a ginger beer bottle, two or three pewter pots, a loaf and butter, and a plate. In a frying pan, which was on the fire, and which was secured to the mantelshelf by a string, some sausages were cooking; and standing over them, with a toasting fork in his hand, was a very old shrivelled Jew, whose villainous-looking and repulsive face was obscured by a quantity of red hair. He was dressed in a greasy flannel gown, with his throat bare; and seemed to be dividing his attention between the frying pan and a clothes-horse, over which a great number of silk handkerchiefs were hanging. Several rough beds made of old sacks, were huddled side by

side on the floor. Seated round the table were four or five boys, none older than the Dodger, smoking long clay pipes, and drinking spirits with the air of middle-aged men.

Jack Dawkins introduced Oliver to the group, who crowded around to make the new boy welcome. The next day, the old man, Fagin, began teaching Oliver to pick pockets, but "for many days" the new boy remained in the dark room. Oliver wanted to go outside and be "actively employed," because

> of the stern morality of the old gentleman's character. Whenever the Dodger or Charley Bates came home at night emptyhanded, he would expiate with great vehemence on the misery of idle and lazy habits, and would enforce upon them the necessity of an active life by sending them supperless to bed.

At length Oliver went out with the Dodger and Charley Bates, still unaware of what Fagin's boys did. The three boys approached an old man reading a book at a street stall:

> What was Oliver's alarm as he stood a few paces off, looking on with his eyelids as wide open as they would possibly go, to see the Dodger plunge his hand into the old gentleman's pocket and draw from thence a handkerchief! To see him hand the same to Charley Bates, and finally to behold them both, running away round the corner at full speed!
>
> In an instant the whole mystery of the handkerchiefs, and the watches, and the jewels and the Jew, rushed upon the boy's mind.

Here was juvenile crime organized and deliberate; Dickens's portrayals of the artful Dodger and Charley Bates are probably the most graphic literary descriptions of juvenile delinquents in literature. In *Oliver Twist* one of his purposes was to show just how miserable life among the lower and criminal classes was. "It appeared to me," he wrote in 1841 in the preface to the third edition,

> that to draw a knot of such associates in crime as really do exist; to paint them in all their deformity, in all their wretchedness, in all the squalid poverty of their lives; to show them as they really are, forever skulking uneasily through the dirtiest

paths of life, with the great, black, ghastly gallows closing up
their prospects, turn them where they may—it appeared to me
that to do this would be to attempt something which was
greatly needed and which would be a service to society.

Exactly. Charles Dickens, for all of his immense (and continuing)
popularity was essentially a social critic who used the novel as
propaganda. He depicted the lives of the "dangerous classes"
vividly, and his work, which appealed to mass audiences, did
much more than government reports to arouse concern about the
social ills of nineteenth-century England. His images also influenced Americans to see their own social problems more clearly.

More prosaic than the writings of Dickens, but equally important, both for Americans and Englishmen, was the work of an
obscure Englishwoman, Mary Carpenter. Dickens, in novels like
Oliver Twist and *Hard Times* and in articles in his magazines, *All
the Year Round* and *Household Words,* made the public aware of
the conditions of life for the swarms of juveniles, vagrants, criminals, and laborers who infested the low quarters of England's great
cities. Quietly and efficiently Mary Carpenter devoted her life to
social reform. She worked in city missions, ragged schools (make-
shift institutions for the street urchins whose tattered clothing
kept them out of regular schools), reformatory schools, and industrial schools; wrote three significant books about the duty of
the state toward its less fortunate young citizens; testified before
parliamentary committees; and helped to organize two national
conferences on reformatory schools for juvenile delinquents.[1]

II

To the average law-abiding Englishmen in the middle of the
nineteenth century, life must have been increasingly unsettling.
With foreign security reasonably assured, Englishmen turned from
Continent-watching to the contemplation of the evils of their own
society. Yet they learned about the reality of life in the closed
courts and blind alleys of the slums of the large cities in a sporadic
and haphazard way. First they read the novels of Dickens, which

moved them to sympathize with the likes of Oliver Twist, Charley
Bates, and Jack Dawkins, the artful Dodger. They could have dismissed what Dickens wrote since it was only fiction, had it not
been for the deluge of supporting documentation. Select committees of parliament published the results of their investigations
of child labor, vagrant children, and juvenile offenders; and people
like Mary Carpenter, Matthew Davenport Hill, and Edmund
Edward Antrobus wrote books that confirmed with examples and
statistics Dickens's vivid pictures of the life of homeless children
in the cities. Thus the writings of Charles Dickens and the efforts
of Mary Carpenter molded the public sentiment which made
possible nineteenth-century British legislation for improved treatment of juvenile delinquents. Working alone they might not have
succeeded. Dickens aroused the sympathy of the public; he appealed to their emotions and he followed the dramatic career of
Oliver Twist. Mary Carpenter appealed primarily to men's minds.
She argued about the injustice of the government's neglect of the
country's vagrant and criminal children and outlined a comprehensive program for the prevention of juvenile offenders. She
supported her arguments with specific examples and impressive
statistics.[2]

The link between the two approaches could be found in the
addresses on behalf of child labor legislation and ragged schools
given by Lord Shaftesbury. On one occasion Shaftesbury (then
Lord Ashley) told the House of Commons:

> Of the existence of . . . evil no one can doubt who peram-
> bulates the streets and thoroughfares of this vast city, and
> observes the groups of filthy, idle, tattered children either
> squatting at the entrances of the courts and alleys, or engaged
> in occupations neither useful to themselves nor creditable to
> the locality. If he proceed to estimate their moral by their
> physical condition (and it will be a just estimate)—if he ex-
> amine the statements before the police offices, or the records of
> various tribunals—or above all, if, by personal inspection, he
> seek to understand the whole mischief, he will come to the
> conclusion that these pressing and immediate evils must be met
> by the application of an immediate remedy.[3]

Shaftesbury had Dickens's gift for vivid, emotional description, but he also marshalled his facts in the same way that Mary Carpenter did in her books.

In July, 1833, the Reverend Joseph Tuckerman, a minister to Boston's poor, left for a year long visit to Europe. In December he stopped at the home of a colleague, Dr. Lant Carpenter, in Bristol. While there he was particularly impressed with one of the Englishman's daughters, Mary, who only a year before had resolved to devote herself to helping the less fortunate members of society. One day, while the Reverend Mr. Tuckerman and Miss Carpenter were walking through the streets of Bristol, a ragged urchin darted across their path and disappeared down an alley. "That child," Tuckerman said, "should be followed to his home and seen after." Mary Carpenter would remember the incident well, for Joseph Tuckerman inspired her to spend the rest of her life working with poor children and juvenile delinquents.[4]

In 1846, Mary Carpenter decided to establish a "ragged school" for the children of the poor of Bristol. The idea of special schools for very poor children was not a new one. In 1783, Robert Raikes, while visiting the Bridewell in Gloucester, decided to do something about the human wreckage he saw. It seemed to Raikes that there was little difference between the children in the Bridewell and "the multitudes of wretches" who filled the Gloucester streets with their "noise and riot, playing at chuck, and cursing and swearing in a manner so horrid, as to convey in any serious mind an idea of hell rather than any other place." Raikes founded a Sunday School whose purpose was to teach moral principles and deportment to undisciplined urchins. His idea soon caught on, and philanthropists founded Sunday Schools in most of England's major cities. The extension of the ideas underlying the Sunday Schools to week-day and evening schools led to the creation of so-called "ragged" schools.[5]

The basic idea of a ragged school was simple: one needed a place big enough for a classroom, a teacher, and to advertise the existence of the school. Mary Carpenter began teaching in her

own school in August, 1846. "It is literally a 'Ragged School,'"
her mother wrote soon after it opened, "none have shoes or stock-
ings, some have no shirt, and no home, sleeping in casks on the
quay, or on steps and living, I suppose by petty depredations."
The supporters of this impromptu educational idea formed the
Ragged School Union in 1848. They hoped to extend the number
of such schools and ultimately to persuade the British government
to provide for universal public education. England finally provided for public (government-supported) schools in the Forster
Education Act of 1870.[6]

A ragged school was a place where "a number of wild and
generally vicious children assemble together, for an object which
many of them cannot understand, without any effective curb on
their wildness, without any authority . . . to subdue them." As
Mary Carpenter wrote: "to attempt such a work, zeal and qualifications of no common order are required. . . . It is not enough
ardently to desire to do this work, . . . it is needful also to know
how to teach, and how to adapt one's language and manner to
these children so as to make oneself really intelligible to them."
The ragged school had a twofold purpose. Like the Sunday
School it sought to impart a certain amount of moral education,
but it also attempted to teach basic skills such as reading and
computation.

In 1850 a reader of the *Morning Chronicle* in London complained about the schools for the children of the streets. He
argued that in the years from 1844 to 1848—in the period when
ragged schools grew rapidly—juvenile arrests had also increased
and that these schools were in part responsible for the increase.
Partly to refute this argument and partly to outline a coherent and
rational program of treatment for juvenile delinquents, Mary
Carpenter wrote *Reformatory Schools for the Children of the
Perishing and Dangerous Classes, and for Juvenile Offenders*, published in 1851. She argued that ragged schools did not cause
juvenile crime, but that they were one of the most important
agencies for preventing it. She admitted that poorly run schools
probably did more harm than good because "large numbers of

children, of . . . wild and lawless habits, are collected together without sufficient moral force to control them." Despite the fact that some of the schools probably did nothing to prevent the increase of juvenile crime, Miss Carpenter denied that there was any direct relationship between ragged schools and children's law-breaking. In addition to their primary purpose of preventing juvenile and adult crime and pauperism, the schools also brought England's upper and lower classes together. "The rich and titled," Miss Carpenter wrote, "have felt their human sympathies awakened by coming into actual contact with the wanderers of the highways. . . . There may have been much that was unnecessary; much that was unwise in what has been done, and in the manner of doing it; but it has tended to establish the practical conviction that we are all of one human race."

Mary Carpenter proposed three new types of schools: free day schools for children of the working classes, who could not otherwise afford to go to school; industrial (vocational) schools for children who had come to the attention of the police, but who had not yet committed a serious offense; and reformatory schools for juvenile offenders. In defending her proposals she aimed pointed criticism at the methods then being used in England to deal with juvenile delinquents. She particularly objected to the practice of imprisoning youthful offenders. "The only school provided in Great Britain by the state for her children," she thundered with righteous indignation, "is the gaol!" [7]

Despite the distinctions of the common law, which held that children under seven were not responsible for their actions and that children between seven and fourteen were presumed to be incapable of telling right from wrong unless there was evidence to show that they did, English judges regularly sentenced children to jails. Not long before Mary Carpenter wrote her book a judge in Liverpool was confronted with a tiny seven-year-old girl. She had been arrested for begging on the streets; her mother had sent her out and had threatened her with punishment if she did not return with a stated sum. Rather than send her home to face a whipping or worse, the judge sentenced her to jail.[8] This case was all too typical; England's large cities teemed with "thousands of neglected children . . . prowling about the streets begging and stealing for their daily bread." Often such children had been sent out by their parents and told to bring home a certain sum; the child who failed would be punished severely. Many of the street children appeared to have no parents at all and lived either in cheap lodging houses (when they could afford it) or found shelter in doorways, old packing crates, under stairways, and anyplace else that offered a modicum of shelter. Some lived by begging, others were petty thieves and pickpockets, and a good many of the girls were prostitutes.[9]

When such children were arrested, as they so often were, the judge could either dismiss them or sentence them to a short term in jail. Some English prisons attempted to separate their young prisoners from the adults, but in many cases the facilities did not permit such a separation. For most of the juveniles thus imprisoned, confinement did not necessarily mean punishment. For the term of their sentence at least they had both food and shelter, both of which were often better than what could be obtained outside.

By the middle of the nineteenth century several other critics had joined Mary Carpenter in condemning England's treatment of her juvenile offenders. A justice of the peace for Middlesex, Edmund Edward Antrobus, agreed with Miss Carpenter's indignation as he wrote: "Send a child to prison for taking an apple, an orange, a few walnuts, . . . even for snatching some trifling article, imprudently or culpably exposed in the streets, or for having a vagrant parent, the act is monstrous, and can only tend to increase the immoral pestilence which reigns, and which all deplore." Once a child had been sent to prison, Antrobus explained, he had lost his good name and society made it difficult if not impossible for him to find honest employment. Thus, convict a child and you set him on the road to adult crime. Another critic complained about the effect of the ceremony on the minds of street children: "The pomp and panoply of justice only gives to these lads a feeling of self-importance," but which, the critic adds, "might, if properly acted upon, be turned to the advancement of industry and honest emulation." To other observers, the trouble with prisons was that they removed the child's healthy fear of punishment and thereby encouraged rather than deterred crime. While the body of criticism of the treatment of juvenile offenders mounted, the government responded slowly and cautiously.[10]

III.

The earliest organized efforts to do something about the problems of juvenile crime in England seem to have been in the eighteenth century. In 1756 the Marine Society started a school for the children of convicts; the Philanthropic Society, organized in 1788, continued that work and began the practice of placing such children as apprentices. In 1804 the Society broadened its scope to include juvenile offenders and opened a small vocational school at Hoxton. But only a very few juvenile offenders found themselves in the custody of the Philanthropic Society; most of them went to prison.[11]

In 1837 the government did provide a special institution for juveniles, Parkhurst Prison on the Isle of Wight. Parkhurst Prison was accurately named. For all practical purposes it was simply an adult prison with younger inmates. It had been established primarily for youthful offenders who had been sentenced to transportation, and the officials there used a rigid, military-like discipline to soften their charges before allowing them to go to Western Australia or Van Diemen's Land. The discipline at Parkhurst was itself controversial among the critics of the official treatment of juvenile offenders. An article in the *Law Times* referred to "the difficult and all but hopeless task of controlling and correcting the inmates, who, although young in years are old in crime, and who, bearing about them the brand of convicted felons, are insensible to those incentives of industry and good conduct." Mary Carpenter complained that the discipline attempted to turn the boys there into "machines instead of self acting beings." She claimed that the system would eventually fail, because "it is utterly vain to look for any real reformation where the heart is not touched, and where the inner springs of action are not called into healthful exercise." For the first four months a new boy at Parkhurst was kept in a solitary cell to break his spirit. Then for the next two or three years he learned a trade. Finally, he would be sent to one of the colonies where a "Guardian of Juvenile Emigrants" would try to place him with a settler's family.[12]

Not long after the opening of Parkhurst Prison one of the recorders of Birmingham, Matthew Davenport Hill, developed a new system for youthful offenders. He told the Select Committee on Criminal and Destitute Juveniles that many of his fellow magistrates had often released juveniles convicted of a first offense to the custody of their parents or masters if they were respectable. In 1841 Hill himself began the practice and also kept track of the young people he thus discharged and the persons who had agreed to take charge of the young people. From time to time Hill had a policeman check up unexpectedly on both parties. Thus, in an informal way Matthew Hill anticipated what would later be one of the main components in the treatment of first offenders both juvenile and adult—the probation system.[13]

In the same year that Hill began his probation system Sheriff Watson of Aberdeen established a voluntary industrial school where children could receive vocational training and a free meal. But many of Aberdeen's problem children did not come in spite of the meal, and so in 1849 the police of the city rounded up all of the vagrant children and forced them to attend the school. The purpose of the school was to prevent both juvenile and adult crime by teaching Aberdeen's vagrant children a trade. Although the Philanthropic Society began in a limited way to try to prevent juvenile crime by working among the children of convicts, the efforts of Recorder Hill of Birmingham and Sheriff Watson of Aberdeen represent the earliest official efforts to prevent juvenile delinquency in Great Britain.[14]

Meanwhile the agitation against juvenile imprisonment had begun to have an effect. In November of 1836 Lord John Russell had written to the members of the Royal Commission on the Criminal Law recommending separate trials for juveniles. The Commissioners did not favor separate trials, but they did recommend summary jurisdiction—non-jury proceedings in which a magistrate might assess certain limited punishments—for children under fifteen who committed minor offenses. Eventually, in 1847 Parliament passed the Larceny Act or Juvenile Offenders Act, which provided that juveniles under fourteen who committed certain minor offenses could be "privately whipped" instead of being imprisoned. The two magistrates who heard cases in summary jurisdiction could also sentence youthful offenders to prison for up to three months. The purpose of this act was to protect youthful first offenders from the scandal of a public trial, but the fact that most young offenders were sent to prison indicated that in 1847 England retained the concept of retribution in all aspects of its penal system. Magistrates who ordered whippings soon discovered that they, too, did not provide much of a deterrent to juveniles, although they did find that the boy who would willingly submit to a flogging from a cat o'nine tails, hated to have his whipping from a birch rod. The "cat" was a man's punishment; the cane the punishment of a child.

In the conclusion to *Reformatory Schools for the Children of the Perishing and Dangerous Classes,* Mary Carpenter outlined four basic assumptions which she believed England needed to make in order to begin a proper program for the elimination of juvenile delinquency. She believed that all children, "however vicious and degraded" were capable of becoming useful members of society, but the present system did not deter or reform them. To accomplish the goal of a useful, honest life for these young lawbreakers, she advocated penal reformatory schools, conducted on Christian principles with "a wise union of kindness and restraint." She believed that parents were probably more guilty than the children and proposed that they should pay the cost of food, clothing, and shelter for their children in reformatory schools. To win support for these ideas and for both the ragged schools and the industrial schools, in the summer of 1851 Mary Carpenter helped to organize a nation-wide conference on juvenile delinquency and reformatory education.[15]

The congress convened in Birmingham on December 9, 1851. Mary Carpenter advocated to the conference the principles she had expounded in her book, and the recorder of Birmingham, Matthew Davenport Hill, spoke about the children who came before him, standing "on tiptoe raising their eyes over the bar and meeting the gaze of the pitying spectator with an indifference revolting at any age, but doubly painful to witness at this early period." Although judges and magistrates knew that they often ruined the future life of a child brought before them for a minor offense, they had no choice. "We feel that we are compelled to carry into operation an ignorant and vengeful system," Hill told the conference, "which augments to a fearful extent the very evil it was framed to correct." Before the congress adjourned, the delegates passed resolutions calling on the Government to establish three new schools for the "perishing and dangerous classes": free day schools for children who, because of their poverty, could not attend the regular schools; industrial feeding schools for children guilty of minor infractions of the law such as vagrancy; and finally, reformatory schools for those guilty of more serious offenses.[16]

The government responded by appointing a "Select Committee on Criminal and Destitute Juveniles," which made a preliminary report in June, 1852, and a final report with recommendations in June of the following year. The Committee painstakingly heard evidence from prison officials, magistrates, and others who dealt with juvenile criminals. It also listened to concerned private citizens like Mary Carpenter and an American, Joseph Reed Ingersoll. "In the English law, as far as I understand it," Miss Carpenter said, "children are considered incapable of guiding themselves, they are therefore entirely submitted to the guidance of their parents." Children could not bind themselves out as apprentices in order to learn a trade; nor could they will property. "But," she continued, "the moment the child shows he is really incapable of guiding himself by committing a crime, from that moment he is treated as a man." [17]

In its report the committee concluded that "a great amount of juvenile destitution, ignorance, vagrancy, and crime has long existed in this country, for which no adequate remedy has yet been provided." They noted that other countries such as Germany, France, Switzerland, and the United States had faced the problem of juvenile delinquency and had done something about it. They recommended that Great Britain adopt similar measures in order to reduce the adult crime rate and transform its youthful criminals into "honest, virtuous citizens." They specifically endorsed tax-supported industrial (vocational) and reformatory schools. Shortly after the committee made its report, a member of Parliament from Staffordshire, C. B. Adderly, introduced a "juvenile offenders' bill" which embodied the Select Committee's recommendations. Adderly had not introduced his bill in the hope that it would pass, but only to succeed in getting a bill on juvenile delinquency printed and to win a promise from the administration that it would sponsor such a bill.[18]

Pondering her testimony before the Select Committee, Mary Carpenter decided that she had not said enough in her first book, and so early in 1853 she published *Juvenile Delinquents: Their Condition and Treatment*. As before she advocated free day schools, industrial feeding schools, and reform schools, and she claimed that her principles had been, for all practical purposes, already carried out in the United States. She noted the existence of free public schools in states like Massachusetts and applauded such reformatory institutions as the New York House of Refuge and the Boston Asylum and Farm School. She also discussed the efforts of some of the continental countries to deal with the problem of juvenile delinquency and wrote with appreciation of the French Agricultural Colony for juvenile delinquents at Mettray and a similar institution, the *Rauhe Haus* near Hamburg in Germany.

Between the sessions of Parliament, the philanthropists working for reform of the treatment of juvenile offenders held another con-

ference in Birmingham and debated again the relative merits of
Mary Carpenter's recommendations. A thorny question at this
second conference was whether or not the doctrines of the Church
of England ought to be introduced into the recommended reformatory and industrial schools. For years the religious question
had stymied efforts of educational reformers to create a universal
system of free public schools in England, and so this was a serious
question. Finally, the delegates at the conference agreed not to
press the issue of religious doctrine in the schools they proposed.

On August 10, 1854, Parliament passed the Youthful Offenders
Act. It provided for the establishment of private "reformatory
schools" which the government would inspect from time to time
and which would receive government funds for their operations.
Juvenile offenders under sixteen could be sent to these new reform
schools only after they had served at least fourteen days in prison.
The law also provided that the parents of any youthful offender
sent to a reformatory school should have to pay as much as they
could afford toward the cost of maintaining their child in the
school. This act established the first official, specialized treatment
of juvenile delinquents in England. The Juvenile Offenders Act
of 1847 had only provided for separate treatment of young offenders; in all other respects they were treated as adults. To many
philanthropists, such action was long overdue. As early as 1806,
when the Philanthropic Institution first received juvenile offenders,
they had recognized that juvenile delinquents required special
care if they were not to grow into adult criminals, but it took the
government half a century to accept that proposition. Although
the Youthful Offenders Act did promise state support for privately
founded reform schools, it did not provide for industrial schools,
and it required that children who went to the state-supported reformatories should first serve a prison sentence. To many this
added an element of pathetic irony. The main purpose of the
reform schools was to prevent children from becoming adult criminals and costing the state money to keep them in prison. Now,
before they could benefit from these new institutions, they had to
repay society for their crimes by serving a prison term. This pro-

vision came from a peculiarly English point of view. Anyone who broke the law had to pay the penalty. Since the reformatory schools were basically educational rather than penal institutions, a sentence to one of them did not represent punishment.[19]

In September of 1853, Mary Carpenter began working at Kingswood, a reformatory for boys and girls in Bristol. She found girls much more difficult to reform and decided to begin a reformatory school for girls only. With the aid of her friend and patron, Lady Byron, she established Red Lodge, a girls' reformatory school also in Bristol, in October, 1854.[20]

Although the Youthful Offenders Act of 1854 had made it possible for approved reformatory schools to receive state aid, the government had done nothing about either industrial schools or free day schools. In 1856 Sir Stafford Northcote introduced a bill which would have provided for state aid to industrial schools. A bill in a different form from that proposed by Northcote passed. The bill was permissive—and allowed but did not require magistrates to send vagrant children to industrial schools, and the children could not be compelled to remain in them. In a letter to Lady Byron written in April, 1859, Mary Carpenter explained why she opposed the Industrial Schools Act of 1857: "We have been striving to do by law what Sheriff Watson did without law some 18 years ago—to have a right to take hold of these children and give them the needed training." [21]

Mary Carpenter founded her own industrial school on the model of those in Aberdeen which she had written about eight years before. By this time she was working in all three types of institutions which she had long advocated. She continued to work with Bristol's ragged schools, she managed Red Lodge, and she founded and managed a new industrial school. Even as she began work with this new activity, she found herself writing another book to make her principles clear. The publication of *The Claims of the Ragged Schools to Pecuniary Educational Aid* explained why the government ought to provide funds for the ragged schools. In June of 1856 the state had begun to provide small sums for the ragged schools and for meals to be served to the children. The government's definition of a ragged school had been too vague, and all sorts of operations eager to claim what amounted to free money soon caused expenses to soar. The Government cancelled the program and then reinstated it on such a reduced scale that Mary Carpenter protested. The Government at first claimed it was trying to eliminate the ragged school class and raise educational standards. Mary Carpenter exploded: "Does the Government of our country remain passive and allow of the existence of dreadful evils, because these things ought not to exist?" For the next two years she continued to champion the cause of ragged schools and advocate a comprehensive compulsory law on industrial schools.[22]

The passage of the Industrial Schools Act of 1866 and the Forster Education Act of 1870 marked the acceptance of Mary Carpenter's basic principles for the treatment of juvenile delinquents in Great Britain. In 1863 she turned her attention to adult convicts and in her book, *Our Convicts,* published in 1863, she argued that England ought to imitate the Irish system of prison discipline. Except for a four-year stay in India, she spent the remainder of her life working on the question of the reformation of criminals. She visited the United States in 1873 and inspected a number of American prisons and institutions for juvenile delinquents. She was appalled at the conditions in both types of institutions, especially the houses of refuge, because they had become little more than juvenile prisons.

Meanwhile Parliament enacted new legislation which gradually approached the ideal of the industrial school that Mary Carpenter had outlined. The Industrial Schools Act of 1866 provided for government support of schools which received only children who had been found guilty of minor offenses. These schools provided food and lodging for their inmates in addition to industrial training. The statute also provided that where the parents were able, they could be compelled to pay for the maintenance of their children who were sentenced to industrial schools. It was not until 1876, however, in the Elementary Education Act that Great Britain provided state aid for industrial day schools which gave their pupils one or more meals, and not until 1908 did Great Britain completely eliminate the imprisonment of children.[23]

IV

The English began working with juvenile delinquents well before Americans did, but during most of the nineteenth century the official treatment of juvenile delinquents in Great Britain was considerably harsher and less enlightened than the treatment given youthful offenders in the more advanced American states. Nonetheless, there was a considerable exchange of ideas about juvenile delinquency across the Atlantic. The founders of the New York House of Refuge consciously imitated the institution which the Philanthropic Society had established at Hoxton, and many American reformers read the works of Mary Carpenter. Mary Carpenter praised American institutions for juvenile delinquents before a Select Committee of Parliament, and Oliver Twist was probably the best-known boy in the English-speaking world.

Mary Carpenter worked for the establishment of state-supported institutions for juvenile delinquents in England. In the United States, the man who had inspired her, the Reverend Joseph Tuckerman worked with the vagrant boys of Boston, and his efforts there led indirectly to the creation of the first state-supported institution for juvenile delinquents in the United States, the Massachusetts State Reform School for Boys. Similar direct links between English and American ideas and practices continued through the nineteenth century. Moreover, England also served as a channel through which some of the continental ideas about juvenile delinquency passed to America.

5

Johann Wichern and Theodore Lyman: The Family System and State-Supported Institutions for Juvenile Delinquents

In September, 1833, a young theology student, Johann Henry Wichern, and his mother moved into an old farm cottage at Horn, near the free city of Hamburg in the German Confederation. The cottage had a rustic name, *Rauhe Haus* or "rough house" which was meant to be descriptive of its simple accommodations rather than to apply to the character of the young people who came there. Depressed by the failure of society to care for the vagrant and criminal youth of Hamburg, one of Europe's larger commercial cities, Wichern resolved to do what he could for them in this simple cottage. What these unfortunate young people lacked most, Wichern thought, were the blessings of family life. Shortly after they moved to the *Rauhe Haus*, Wichern and his mother had twelve boys living with them. They hoped that the home-like atmosphere would encourage the boys—of whom four had criminal parents and the rest were illegitimate—to form good habits of industry and hard work and develop a sound moral character. Wichern's efforts with this original group were so successful that he soon expanded his operation, although he retained its fundamental principles. As more troubled young people came to his institution, now known simply as *Rauhe Haus*, he trained additional staff members and established new "families." Each of Wichern's families contained only twelve children. The family lived as a unit, working cooperatively under the direction of an "elder brother." The program of the institution combined agricultural labor with religious devotion and more formal instruction. Attached to the reform school was a society known as the brethren of the *Rauhe Haus*. The brethren were young men who had come to Wichern's institution to become teachers or "social workers" with the young people there. After a two-year stay, during which they lived with and helped one of the families, they became members of another society, the Inner Mission, which sponsored similar efforts throughout Europe.[1]

By the early 1840's the *Rauhe Haus* had gained an international reputation as one of the most successful reformatories for juvenile delinquents in the world. Wichern's basic principle was the family system. By attempting to re-create the atmosphere in a normal middle-class family, he had found a means of controlling and teaching some of the most recalcitrant boys and girls in Hamburg. Visiting philanthropists hailed his system as a novel approach, but it was in effect an application of the principles first set forth by Pestalozzi and embodied in the poor boys' school taught by Joseph Vehrly at Hofwyl.

In 1837 the judge of a Paris court, M. Frederic Auguste Demetz, who had become concerned about the problems of juvenile delinquency—possibly from his judicial experience—traveled to the United States to study American juvenile institutions. The New York House of Refuge particularly impressed him. Shortly afterward he went to Hamburg and visited the *Rauhe Haus*. When he returned to Paris, Demetz began working for the creation of an institution especially for juvenile delinquents which would combine the best features of the New York House of Refuge and Wichern's system. The result was the *Colonie Agricole* at Mettray which opened in 1840 and which, like the *Rauhe Haus,* had "families." In addition, it had borrowed the features of larger units from American institutions. Here the families numbered forty inmates instead of twelve. Despite this major difference, the *Rauhe Haus* and

Mettray were remarkably similar. Both depended on specially trained personnel to administer their "family" system. Both stressed the importance of agricultural labor and the need to breathe fresh clean country air. Both relied on sentiment and religious feeling to motivate their charges, and finally, both of them served as the chief models for new reformatory institutions for juvenile delinquents—particularly in the United States.[2]

II

In 1826 the Unitarian Association of Massachusetts appointed the Reverend Joseph Tuckerman as minister to the poor of the City of Boston. To Tuckerman the main difficulty with the lower classes there was not poverty but pauperism, the chronic ailment of people who seemed unable or unwilling to help themselves. The best way to eliminate this social disease, he thought, was to make sure that children did not grow up to be paupers or criminals. Consequently, Tuckerman devoted most of his efforts to the children of the poorer classes. They often had no formal education at all, and, lacking that, no regular employment. This idleness presented young people with all kinds of temptations and Tuckerman thought that as a result they lacked moral fiber. Tuckerman spent the remainder of his life trying to rescue the children of Boston's streets from their unfortunate environment. He fought to place them in the city schools, to find jobs for them, and he helped to found a new reformatory institution.[3]

Not long after he had accepted his new position, Tuckerman complained about the hordes of young boys who thronged in the streets and at times disrupted the operations of the city market. "An authority should exist somewhere," he wrote, "and he to whom it is entrusted should use it, to dispose of lads who own no master, who regard no law, and who, if not in a legal sense *vagrants*, because there is a place in the city which they call their *home*, are yet known to be profane, intemperate, dishonest and as far as they may be at their age, abandoned to crime." Tuckerman also complained about the Boston House of Reformation.

Only boys who had been convicted and committed could be sent there. Boys who were in need of reformatory discipline, but who were not offenders simply roamed the streets, and a good many who should have been in the House of Reformation were still free because witnesses often failed to show up for criminal proceedings against them. It seemed clear to Tuckerman and many of Boston's most prominent citizens—men like the scholar and educator, George Ticknor, John Tappan, a leading merchant, and the Reverend E. M. P. Wells, the former superintendent of the Boston House of Reformation—that Boston needed a new institution for young people, one which would fill the gap between the regular schools and the House of Reformation. In January, 1832, on a Friday afternoon, they met at the Tremont Bank and agreed to create a "farm school" for "the morally exposed children of the city." They collected money from private citizens and bought Thompson's Island in Boston Harbor. By 1832 they had established the Boston Asylum and Farm School for Indigent Boys, which, with the Reverend Mr. Wells as superintendent, stressed agricultural training and an academic education.

In the early 1840's among the directors of this school was Theodore Lyman, who had served as Mayor of Boston from 1834 to 1836 and who was a well-known shipping magnate. Lyman took his duties very seriously and worried about the possibility that vicious boys might corrupt young and impressionable boys at the Farm School. While Lyman was mulling over this problem, a movement to create a new state institution for juvenile delinquents began.[4]

III

Outside the City of Boston, the Commonwealth of Massachusetts had made no provision for the specialized treatment of youthful offenders. In the winter of 1846 three separate petitions urged the legislature to create a state institution for the reformation of juvenile delinquents. The committee to which the petitions found their way took up the question and wrote letters to many of Massachusetts's public officials, including the Sheriff of Essex County, Judge Markham of the Court of Common Pleas, and a member of the staff of the State Lunatic Hospital. The committee then presented the legislature with a resolution calling for the establishment of a State "Manual Labor" School. In 1847 the legislature appropriated ten thousand dollars and authorized the governor to appoint a commission to study possible sites for such an institution.

When Theodore Lyman learned of the possibility of a state-supported institution for juvenile delinquents, he wrote a letter to the head of the commission, Alfred D. Foster of Worcester. Lyman indicated that he had been associated with the Farm School for five or six years and that he thus wrote from first-hand experience. "I am rejoiced that the state have entered on this business," he said, "because I am sure that a vast deal of good can be done in a simple and easy way, and without a great expense in proportion to what shall be obtained." Lyman asked Foster to keep his letter private and indicated that he would donate some money to the proposed school. In a later letter to Foster, Lyman offered to donate $10,000, an amount equal to the state appropriation, which Lyman had felt was too small. "I do not think that sum is sufficient to have an experiment of the results of such an institution fairly tried," he wrote, "and as I consider it exceedingly important that a school of the kind should be founded in this commonwealth, I am willing to give to it a similar sum, namely ten thousand dollars." Again he asked Foster to keep their correspondence secret.

The committee completed its investigation and recommended a site near Westborough because of its central location. On April 9, 1847, the law creating the Massachusetts State Reform School for Boys passed the Massachusetts General Court. This new school was the first fully state-supported institution for juvenile delinquents in the United States. It was not, however, the sort of school that Lyman had hoped it would be. In his exchange of letters with Foster, Lyman had recommended that the school take in only boys under fourteen: "Boys of that age are difficult to manage," he explained, "if they have been for some time in a vicious course, they become by 14 or 15 hardened, bad themselves, and very fit to make others bad." Lyman wanted the state school to be much like the Farm School on Thompson's Island. It would take in young boys who had committed minor offenses and prevent them from becoming more serious offenders and criminals. Older boys had little chance of reformation in his view, and he favored sending them to houses of correction. In spite of his concern for young offenders Lyman did not favor an especially soft approach:

> The institution should be considered a place of punishment as well as a place for reform, and as under the authority of the State. . . . I should give no character of disgraceful punishment to the institution, but the character of a state school, with an established system of rules of government and discipline, where boys are received because they are not fit to be at large, and where they are kept and trained till they are considered fit to be restored to society.[5]

However, the law fixed the upper age limit at sixteen, and the new institution soon took on the character of a house of refuge. Most of the inmates were the older, tougher boys that Lyman had wanted to keep out. Nonetheless, Lyman continued his support of the institution. Before the school had opened he gave another $10,000 to the commissioners. The following year he gave another $2,500, and in that year he added two codicils to his wills providing for another payment of $50,000 to the school.[6]

The Massachusetts State Reform School for Boys was the first fully state-supported institution for juvenile delinquents in the United States to open its doors, but New York can claim to have been the first state to authorize such an institution. In 1838 the New York legislature had begun to receive petitions from residents in the western parts of the state urging it to create a new institution for juvenile delinquents in their region. Two factors accounted for this growing demand. The laws of New York had provided that juvenile delinquents outside the City of New York could be sent to the New York House of Refuge, but the county from which this commitment was made had to pay the cost of the youth's transportation. Consequently, it was common in the western counties to overlook a great many juvenile offenses. A situation developed, however, which made this course all but impossible. A number of young boys (a New York legislative committee estimated their number at 5,000) worked at various jobs along the Erie Canal. During the winter or when business was slow, they were laid off. Many of these boys were orphans, and they began living by their wits in the canal towns. Thus, as a result of business fluctuations and seasonal variations in the work force, juvenile delinquency increased rapidly in the western part of the state. The New York legislature in May of 1846 passed an act which created the Western House of Refuge at Rochester. Patterned after the New York House of Refuge, it opened its doors a year after the Massachusetts State Reform School for Boys.[7]

IV

The first American institution for juvenile delinquents, based on the family system, was the Massachusetts State Reform School for Girls at Lancaster established in 1855. A state institution for girls to complement the State Reform School for Boys had been contemplated since at least 1850, when one of the commissioners appointed to study the creation of such an institution wrote to the well-known Boston reformer, Samuel Gridley Howe, and asked for his advice. In reply, Howe, who had been a director at the Boston House of Reformation and who was familiar with most of the juvenile institutions in Europe, advocated a placing-out system for delinquent girls in which the state would pay private families to take them in. He argued that girls were less likely to benefit from a stay in a house of refuge than boys and more likely to benefit from "the virtuous influences of a private family." Howe also argued that such a system would be cheaper than a reform school with its initial heavy capital outlays and subsequent depreciation. But this approach was too radical for Massachusetts at that time; in fact it took four years to provide for the creation of a state institution for delinquent girls. In 1854 the legislature resolved to create "a State Reform School for girls, similar in purpose to the State Reform School for boys at Westborough," and appropriated $20,000 for the purpose. These funds would not be available, however, unless an equal amount could be raised by private donation.[8]

Once again the commissioners wrote to Howe, who replied: "I am glad to see that the sacred social duty of attempting to reform vicious or viciously disposed girls is at last to be undertaken by the State. But I am sorry to see, as I do, in the spirit of the Resolutions of the Legislature, . . . that this delicate and difficult task is to be attempted by the machinery of an establishment similar to the great Reform School for boys at Westborough." Again, Howe recommended a placing out system and included a copy of his earlier letter in his second reply to the commissioners for a state reform school.[9] The law creating the State Reform School for Girls at Lancaster passed the Massachusetts legislature in 1855. This act did not follow Howe's recommendations, but the Massachusetts State Reform School for Girls became the first American institution to use a family system like that employed at the *Rauhe Haus* and Mettray.[10]

The year after the establishment of the Massachusetts State Reform School for Girls, the Ohio legislature passed a measure authorizing the Governor of Ohio to appoint three commissioners to find a site and make recommendations for a state reform school for boys. In 1857 Ohio passed a series of acts designed to provide a comprehensive system for the treatment of juvenile offenders, including an institution labeled the Ohio State Reform Farm. The act providing for the creation of the institution indicated that it would be conducted on the "family system"—with forty boys to each family. This was the first institution on the family system for *boys* established in the United States. The size of its "families" indicates that the model for the Ohio State Reform Farm was Mettray rather than Hamburg.[11]

The creation of the Ohio State Reform Farm marks the close of a phase in the development of institutions for the treatment of juvenile delinquents in the United States. Before 1824, except in isolated and individual cases, there had been no specialized handling of young offenders. Between 1824 and 1857 philanthropists working either within local reform societies or through their state legislatures created first houses of refuge, then state-supported and state-managed reform schools. Finally, they began to adopt the more promising family system. By 1860 there were twenty institutions for juvenile delinquents in the United States. Seven of them were municipal houses of refuge; three, the New York House of Refuge, the Boston Asylum and Farm School, and the New York Juvenile Asylum, functioned as state-regulated private corporations; and the remaining ten were state reform schools. Only two of the institutions, the House of Refuge in New Orleans, which had opened in 1847, and the House of Refuge in Baltimore, opened in 1855, were located in the South. In general, houses of refuge were municipal institutions located in and intended for the troubled youth of a particular metropolis. "Reform schools" received young delinquents from all parts of the state. Two states, New York and Pennsylvania, called their state reform schools "houses of refuge," but by the 1850's the distinction between "reform school" and "house of refuge" was fairly well understood. By then "houses of refuge" had acquired a reputation for being strict, and so only the harder cases were sent to them. New institutions like the Boston Asylum and Farm School and the New York Juvenile Asylum, which opened in 1850, appeared to accommodate juveniles guilty of only petty offenses, and who were not yet hardened in crime.[12] By the early 1850's the evolution of juvenile custodial institutions—whether they were houses of refuge or reform schools on the family plan—had reached a point of stagnation. The next important change in the treatment of juvenile delinquents would abandon the custodial path already well trod and take a new direction. The pleas of Samuel Gridley Howe for the creation of a placing-out system for delinquent girls in Massachusetts were answered in part, but not in Massachusetts and not quite in the way Howe had envisioned.

6

Charles Loring Brace and the Children's Aid Society of New York

One Sunday in October, 1849, Charles Loring Brace, a young theological student at Union Seminary, preached in the New York County Almshouse on Blackwell's Island. Afterwards he visited the prisoners and hospital patients confined there. "I never had my nature so stirred up within me," he later wrote. "You felt you were standing among the wrecks of the Soul; creatures cast out from everything but God's mercy." This experience helped to begin the erosion of the young man's determination to become a clergyman, and in a letter to his father he criticized "the inefficiency of religion"—particularly in New England. "There is so much of the dogma," he complained, "and so little of what makes men better men." [1]

Brace now began to look at the City of New York in a new way, probably seeing for the first time the effect of an urban environment on the children of the poorer classes of society. He wrote to his sister, Emma, about the "immense vat of misery and crime and filth" in New York and challenged her to "think of *ten thousand children* growing up almost sure to be prostitutes and rogues." [2]

Of the Americans who worked with juvenile delinquents in the nineteenth century, Charles Loring Brace was the most important. He reflected in his work and writing the efforts of the entire century to solve the problems of youthful crime and misbehavior. In his support of certain types of institutions such as the industrial schools he reflected the attitudes of the first half of the century, but in his stress on the family as "God's reformatory" he moved away from the almost total reliance on formal education as a means of reforming wayward young people. Brace differentiated among various types of "problem" children and thereby extended Mary Carpenter's crude system of typology among the children of the "perishing and dangerous classes" of England's great cities. He also tried to harmonize the work of the Children's Aid Society with the latest scientific and evolutionary thought and so reflected the intellectual outlook of late nineteenth-century America.

At first glance Brace would appear to be significant only because of the many new programs he introduced while serving as secretary of the Children's Aid Society, a philanthropic organization which sought to help the juvenile vagrants of New York. The key to Brace's importance, however, lies not in his innovations so much as in his systematic approach. He was not the first to use placing-out in the United States, but he developed the practice into a specialized system. Brace argued that the family was the natural place for a child and that a child without a home or with an inadequate home was a threat to society. Furthermore, the city was an evil place; it was full of temptations and unsavory associates and compared most unfavorably with the healthy and wholesome life possible on a farm. Consequently, the Children's Aid Society devoted most of its resources to placing the street children of New York on western farms. Brace and the Children's Aid Society also developed educational programs designed to meet the needs of some children. For the boys who sold papers and shined shoes during the day they provided evening classes at the Newsboys' Lodging House. This establishment stressed the dominant values of mid-nineteenth-century America by requiring boys who stayed there to pay for beds and meals; boys without funds could borrow money which they were expected to repay.

For children who lacked the skills to work and who were too poor to attend the regular schools of the city, the Children's Aid Society established neighborhood Industrial Schools where volunteers from the New York's upper classes taught the children vocational skills and the common branches of learning. Besides their educational functions these agencies also served as funnels to the placing-out system. In many respects these schools were remarkably similar to the ragged and industrial schools of England. What made them different, however, was their relationship with the placing-out system.[3]

Another index of Brace's significance was his continued ability to attract support from the public and the State of New York during his term as General Secretary for the Children's Aid Society. Because of the nature of Brace's public appeals, the Society received generous financial support from the public and some substantial subsidies from the State. Brace described the Children's Aid Society as one of the most useful of charities since its programs sought to eliminate the roots of pauperism and crime. Because it dealt with children on an individual basis and because its programs conformed to natural laws, Brace regarded the Society as a "scientific" charity. Unlike "sentimental" and "softhearted" welfare agencies, the Children's Aid Society did not engage in "indiscriminate alms-giving," a practice which Brace condemned as perpetuating pauperism.[4]

II

Charles Loring Brace was born June 19, 1826, in Litchfield, Connecticut. His father, John Brace, had gone to Williams College, planning to be a minister; instead he taught in a school for girls maintained by his aunts. He married Lucy Porter of Maine in 1820, and in 1833 he moved his family to Hartford, where he became the principal of the Female Seminary. Mrs. Brace, who suffered from poor health, died in 1840, leaving four children: Mary, Charles, James, and Emma. In Hartford the Brace family joined the congregation of Dr. Horace Bushnell, one of New England's best-known preachers, and there John Brace began guiding Charles's formal education. By the time he was fourteen Charles was ready to enter college, but he delayed his entry for two years to study French and German and to read history.[5]

Brace entered Yale in the fall of 1842, and after receiving his degree, taught school for a year. In 1847 he returned to New Haven to attend theological school, but left there a year later to go to Union Theological Seminary in New York. Although Brace's path to the ministry seemed clearly marked, he was beginning to have some doubts about his career.[6]

In the summer of 1847 a life-long friend, Frederick Law Olmsted, encouraged those doubts when he wrote Brace: "There's a great *work* wants doing in this our generation, Charley, let us off jacket and go about it." Six months later, Olmsted wrote Brace again. "I think, Charley," he said, "I never knew the man that had graduated at a Theol[ogical] Seminary that showed ordinary charity in his heart." [7]

In the summer of 1850 Brace and Olmsted departed for a "grand tour" of Europe, but Brace, his mind probably on questions of charity and his future career, spent a great deal of time at philanthropic and correctional institutions such as the *Rauhe Haus* near Hamburg. That fall, when Olmsted returned, Brace remained in Europe. In November he wrote to another old friend, Fred Kingsbury, that "I have a kind of feeling growing on me that my only and great business in the world is men-helping." Before returning home, Brace toured central Europe, and from Vienna in April, 1851, he wrote John Olmsted that his "hopes of steadily working for men" were "much more cheery" and that he was ready to work in "any or all movements for the poor or the miserable." [8]

Brace returned to New York hoping to "raise up the outcast and homeless." He began working at the Five Points Mission, with the Reverend Lewis M. Pease, a Methodist city missionary, who had been active in the area for over a year. The Five Points district, deep in the older section of New York, was one of the most depressed neighborhoods in the city. Narrow, crooked alleys wandered between dilapidated and decaying buildings, and the people living there seemed incapable of mustering the effort needed to leave the district. When Charles Dickens visited the Five Points in 1842, it reminded him of some of the scenes in his own writings. "This is the place," he said, "these narrow ways diverging to the right and left, and reeking everywhere with dirt and filth. Such lives as are led here, bear the same fruits here as elsewhere." Dickens noted that "nearly every house is a low tavern," and concluded that "all that is loathsome, drooping, and decayed is here." [9]

The Reverend Mr. Pease had bought an old brewery in the area and converted it into a mission. As Brace worked with the missionary he quickly became disillusioned with the lack of success in his endeavors. "What soon struck us all engaged in those labors," he recalled, "was the immense number of boys and girls floating and drifting about our streets with hardly any assignable home or occupation, who continually swelled the multitude of criminals, prostitutes, and vagrants." In October, 1849, in a report to the Mayor, the Chief of Police for the City, George W. Matsell, had called attention to "the constantly increasing numbers of vagrant, idle and vicious children" who swarmed in the public places of the city. "Their numbers are almost incredible," the Chief continued, and he warned that "each year makes fearful additions to the ranks of these prospective recruits of infamy and sin, and from this corrupt and festering fountain flows a ceaseless stream to our lowest brothels—to the Penitentiary and to the State Prison!" Chief Matsell estimated that there were about three thousand such children and recommended that they either be compelled to attend school regularly, or be apprenticed to some suitable occupation. Some of the city's clergymen responded to this challenge with special Sunday services for the vagrant boys of the city, and the Reverend Thomas L. Harris recommended the creation of a home for children which would provide "reformation, education, and remunerative employment." Another minister, Dr. George Cheever, argued that the vagrant youth of the

city needed "a pastor to look after them during the week," to see
that they went to school and to church on Sunday and to "get
places of steady industry for them." [10]

Even before the Chief's report, the Reverend A. D. F. Randolf,
pastor of the Carmine Street Presbyterian Church, had been ex-
perimenting with special services for vagrant boys. After the report a number of other men including William C. Russell, Benjamin Howland, John L. Mason, and Brace established similar
"Boys' Meetings." They hoped to influence the "wild and un-
tutored young Arabs" where "ordinary agencies were of no avail."
For many of these men the boys proved to be almost too much.
At the early meetings they fought over benches, threw rocks at
the speaker, and in general made any kind of service impossible.
Brace recalled the occasion when "a pious and somewhat sentimental Sunday-school brother" had been droning on with a "vague
and declamatory religious exhortation." Soon the boys began
whispering and the words "Gas! Gas!" in high sibilant tones
coursed through the room. Some of the speakers knew how to appeal to the boys, however. Dramatic oratory on bold or heroic
themes usually held the boys' attention, but the meetings seemed
to have little effect on the behavior of the "Arabs" for whom they
were intended. In January, 1852, Chief Matsell underscored the
failure of the Boys' Meetings when he complained that the conditions described in his report of 1849 were "in no degree diminished." Since these early efforts had failed, the Chief recommended new laws and new agencies to deal with the problem of
the street children.[11]

The men who had supported the boys' services discussed other
steps they could take to reduce the number of idle and vagrant
children on the streets. They must have talked about the Reverend
Mr. Harris's plan for a children's home and Dr. Cheever's idea of
a special minister to the children. At any rate, these men, early in
1853, organized what became the Children's Aid Society and selected Charles Loring Brace as their chief officer. Brace was surprised by the offer, but his life as a city missionary while working
at the Five Points Mission led him to reject for the time the idea

of becoming a regular minister. "I have hesitated a good deal," Brace wrote to his father, "as it interrupts my study and training, but this is a new and important enterprise." The other men, Russell, Mason, and Howland, became trustees of the new organization, and in March it issued its first *Circular*.[12]

The Children's Aid Society, the *Circular* announced, had been created "to meet the increasing crime and poverty among the destitute children of . . . New York." The almshouses which society had provided to deal with the vagrant classes could not contain this growing "evil," and the immigration of poor foreigners who abandoned their children added to the growing numbers of vagrant and homeless young people on the city streets. These children lived deplorably; they slept in cellars, in old barns, or in "low lodging-houses." Nevertheless, they were "shrewd and old in vice" while other children remained in "leading strings." It was true that benevolent people had responded to the begging entreaties of this class by dropping "a trifle into the extended hand," but as they did so they feared that they were encouraging idleness and vagrancy. The new association, however, would provide a means through which these benevolent people could contribute to "the poor children of the city" and be sure that idleness and vagrancy were not encouraged.[13]

The Children's Aid Society proposed to continue the Boys' Meetings and in connection with them to start "industrial schools" where the boys could learn a trade. In addition the Society had made arrangements to provide "five hundred jobs" for idle boys and would endeavor to find "homes in the country with farmers" for the homeless. On its editorial page the *New York Times* assured its readers that the trustees of the Society were "businessmen of active benevolence," which guaranteed that the Society would be "managed in the best way, and its funds sacredly devoted to the best purposes." [14]

III

The Children's Aid Society opened an office at 638 Broadway, and Brace soon found himself working a full day. He spent the mornings at the office keeping books and writing letters, and in the afternoons he ranged about the city. In his wanderings in the older part of the city Brace had come to know "certain centers of crime and misery." Along Pitt and Willard Streets was the "rag-pickers' den" where "the wild life of the children soon made them outcasts and thieves." In Cherry and Water Streets little girls who "flitted about with baskets, and wrapped in old shawls, became familiar with vice before they were out of childhood." In the "thieves' lodging houses" of the lower wards of the city older pickpockets and burglars, reminiscent of Fagin, trained street boys to follow their "nefarious callings"; and in "Poverty Lane" along Sixteenth and Seventeenth Streets there was "a dreadful population of youthful ruffians and degraded men and women." And there were other "fever-nests": "Dutch Hill" near Forty-second Street on the East side, the area around Corlear's Hook where copper pickers and wood-thieves congregated, and the Italian quarter in the Sixth Ward, which was full of organ-grinders and little street-sweepers.

The Children's Aid Society hoped to concentrate its efforts on these areas and first tried workshops where boys could earn money and learn a trade. These workshops failed, however, because the boys for whom they were intended would not come regularly, and because the shops could not compete with other factories using machinery. Nevertheless, the Society continued to stress the idea of self-help which had been implicit in the creation of the workshops.

The Society opened its first "industrial" or vocational school in the Fourth Ward on Roosevelt Street in December, 1853. In the neighborhood, which was one of Brace's "fever-nests," a number of ragged little girls were "fast training . . . for the most abandoned life." Brace recalled, that "it seemed to me if I could only get the refinement, education and Christian enthusiasm of the better classes fairly to work here among these children, these terrible evils might be corrected at least for the next generation." Brace persuaded some of the city's leading women to try to teach vocational skills to vagrant little girls of the district. When the

school opened, "a flock of the most ill-clad and wildest little
street girls" greeted the ladies. The girls fought and swore and
for a time the women wondered if the school would ever begin.
Most of the girls had no shoes, and they were dirty, ragged, and
unkempt. Neither the ladies nor the girls knew quite what to do
with each other, but the ladies persisted in their efforts to establish order and finally had the school operating. The school concentrated on sewing, knitting, and crocheting; and the ladies "began to show the fruits of a high civilization to these poor little
barbarians." Brace later claimed that industrial schools for girls
helped to reduce the number of arrests for female vagrancy in
New York and argued that the moral influences of the upper-
class women who worked in such schools kept many young girls
from becoming prostitutes.[15]

The Fourth Ward Industrial School, despite Brace's claims, had
little effect on the army of vagrant children that thronged in the
streets of New York. These children supported themselves in a
variety of ways, legal and otherwise. They picked rags, sold goods
on the streets, blacked boots, begged money from affluent citizens,
picked pockets, stole, and some of the girls turned to prostitution.
The children who endeavored to make an honest living seemed to
be heroes struggling against the forces of evil. Newsboys and
bootblacks in particular appeared to be juvenile personifications
of the American self-help cult—the philosophy that an honest,
industrious, frugal, and virtuous young man could not fail to rise
in society. The newsboys became a favored group with Brace and
the founders of the Children's Aid Society because they seemed to
embody the virtues which the Society was trying to inculcate
among the street children of the City. Many who observed the
newsboys regarded them as heroes in the Great American Adventure; and a novel, *The Newsboy*, by Elizabeth Oakes Smith
romanticized this view. Mrs. Smith saw the newsboy as "a great-
soul'd boy whose nobleness I dared not fathom." She explained
that there was "no appearance of vice among newsboys." There
was "no idleness of the eyes, no bloated face, no pallid debauchery." The newsboy was "self-reliant, self-maintained, [and] hon-

est." Another writer who romanticized the newsboy was Horatio
Alger. Since *The Newsboy* was published in 1854, it seems reasonable to assume that Alger read it. Much of Alger's material, however, came from his firsthand experiences with the newsboys
themselves. Like Mrs. Smith's book, many of Alger's works, such
as *Ragged Dick* and *Luke Walton,* include as a central character
a stereotype, the heroic newsboy. Charles Loring Brace saw the
newsboys in this light, but he also saw their vices. In his writings
Brace commended the newsboy's lightheartedness but explained
that the newsboy's morals were "not of a high order" because he
lived in "a fighting, swearing, stealing and gambling set." But the
boys had a code: they did not drink; they paid their debts, and
they helped each other in hard times.[16]

As he studied the newsboys, Brace concluded that what they
needed most was a place to sleep, and so he began an effort to
provide such a place. To obtain money for this project he went
to some of the city's leading citizens, wrote newspaper articles,
and appeared before church congregations. The Children's Aid
Society secured the loft in the old *Sun* Building, where in March,
1854, it opened the Newsboys' Lodging House. Boys who came
there did not find charity, but a good bargain. In keeping with
the self-help tradition Brace proposed to "treat the lads as independent little dealers, [and] gave them nothing without payment."
A night's lodgings cost six cents and supper four cents. At first
these low prices made the boys suspicious, and when the superintendent explained that every boy had to take a bath before he
could have a bed, they were sure that they had walked into a
trap. They thought that the superintendent, C. C. Tracey, was a
street preacher and that the lodging house was a scheme to catch
them and send them to the New York House of Refuge. But they
could not resist such a good bargain, and so they stayed.[17]

At first the lodging house offered only food, shelter, and baths;
but when it had won the loyalty of the boys, the superintendent
then began to make some effort to exert a moral influence over
them. The first such project was a night school, in which they
learned "the common branches." Later Tracey added a Sunday

religious meeting and a savings bank. The savings bank consisted of a drawer in a table with slots cut in the top. The slots led into compartments in the drawer so that each boy could drop his money into his own slot. The drawer remained locked until the boys voted to open it. To encourage savings, the Society paid a modest rate of interest on the money. The savings bank helped to make the depositors regular patrons of the Newsboys' Lodging House, and it gave them "a sense of property" and "the desire of accumulation." At the end of the first year of its operation of the Newsboys' Lodging House, the Children's Aid Society confessed that the lodgers were not "model boys," but the Society did contend that they were now "more saving, and industrious and cleanly." [18]

Brace believed that the benevolent societies in New York had overlooked the needs of young working girls, and so the Children's Aid Society, in order to protect these girls from temptation and prevent them from becoming prostitutes, created a Girls' Lodging House in 1862. It was supposed to be a haven for virtuous but homeless girls and not "a reformatory for Magdalens." Brace wrote: "To keep a house for reforming young women of bad character would only pervert those of good and shut out the decent and honest poor." Keeping virtuous girls from temptation proved to be an easier task than keeping those already fallen from corrupting the girls in the House. "Sweet young maidens, whom we guilelessly admitted," Brace complained, "turned out perhaps the most skillful and thorough-going deceivers, plying their bad trade in the day, and filling the minds of their comrades with all sorts of wickedness in the evening." Like the Newsboys' Lodging House the Girls' Lodging House was not a home, but an agency whose main purpose was self-help. As Brace explained, it was supposed to teach the girls "to work, to be clean and to understand the virtues of order and punctuality; to lay the foundations of a housekeeper or servant; to bring the influences of discipline, of kindness, and religion to bear on these wild and ungoverned creatures." [19]

The industrial school and the lodging house became the main

institutions of the Children's Aid Society in the City of New York, and they soon multiplied. In 1863 the Society had eight industrial schools, and by 1892 the number had grown to twenty-one day industrial schools and twelve evening schools. In 1892 there were five lodging houses for the boys of the street, and of course, the Girls' Lodging House. Clearly, the Children's Aid Society did not abandon or repudiate the use of institutional and educational means to control juvenile delinquency. Where Americans earlier in the nineteenth century had sought primarily to reform juvenile delinquents, Charles Loring Brace and the Children's Aid Society attempted to prevent juvenile delinquency by using educational methods similar to those used in houses of refuge. The industrial schools taught the girls of the city streets skills they could use to make an honest and virtuous living, and the Newsboys' Lodging House encouraged the street boys to become calculating young capitalists who followed the tenets of the self-help tradition—to work hard, live moral lives, and save their money.[20] These institutions, however, took second place among the operations of Brace and the Children's Aid Society to prevent juvenile delinquency, adult crime, and pauperism.

IV

The placing-out system of the Children's Aid Society was the most important of its efforts, because it represented a change in thinking about the process of cultural transmission. Implicit in the use of houses of refuge to reform juvenile delinquents was the assumption that formal education could repair the cultural defects in deviant young people. A great faith in the power of education to remedy social evils and to mold American culture characterized the first half of the nineteenth century, but educational reformers in their zeal to convince the public of the need for tax-supported schools open to all children overstated the case for the possible achievements of education. They and the public-spirited citizens who established institutions for juvenile delinquents overlooked the significance of the family in transmitting the norms and values of a society. In Germany in 1833 Johann Henry Wichern had perceived the family's importance in passing on the basic aspects of a culture to the children. Wichern sought, as he developed the *Rauhe Haus*, to create an artificial family in order to remedy the cultural defects in juvenile delinquents.[21]

When Charles Loring Brace visited the *Rauhe Haus* on his European trip, Wichern's institution impressed him, and he later wrote that "the friend of man, searching anxiously for what man has done for his suffering fellows, may look far in both continents before he finds an institution so benevolent, so practical and so truly Christian." Later as Brace walked the streets of New York and learned of the tragic lives of the homeless children who thronged in the alleys and byways of the city, he must have recalled the *Rauhe Haus* and its emphasis on the need for family life.[22]

Brace also must have remembered the sermons of Horace Bushnell and probably had read his *Views of Christian Nurture*. The brief book which had been so controversial when it was first published in serial form in 1846. In it Bushnell complained that "the tendency of all our modern speculations is to an extreme individualism," and that Americans were overlooking the organic nature of society and its components. "All society is organic," Bushnell wrote, "the church, the state, the school, the family." Bushnell concentrated most of his work on the family's unique place in society and in the teaching of religion. "In maintaining the organic unity of the family," he explained, "I mean to assert that a power is exerted by parents over children, not only when they teach, encourage, persuade and govern, but without any proposed control whatever." The family did this because of its nature: "They do it unconsciously and undesignedly—they must do it. Their character, feelings, spirit and principles must propagate themselves." Clearly, Bushnell had stressed the importance of the family in the process of continuing and nurturing religion, but by implication, he also showed the significance of the family in the entire process of the transfer of culture from one generation to another.[23]

Besides the theoretical foundations for the placing-out system there were practical prototypes as well. Brace knew of the indenturing system of the New York House of Refuge and the newly created New York Juvenile Asylum. This institution, like the Children's Aid Society, had appeared in response to Chief Matsell's 1849 report on juvenile vagrancy and crime. It began operation in 1851, and attempted to concentrate on younger juvenile vagrants and petty offenders. The founders hoped to round up such children, train them briefly, and then, following the practice of the House of Refuge, bind them as apprentices to farmers in the country. While the system Brace advocated seemed to be the same as the practice of these two New York institutions, there was a significant difference. When western farmers accepted apprentices from the New York House of Refuge or the New York Juvenile Asylum, Brace argued, they took them as cheap labor, not as members of the family. Such a system not only prevented the children from being received into families, he continued, it often resulted in exploitation.[24]

Thus, from three sources Brace drew the ideas and practical details for the placing-out system. Superficially his system seemed to be the same as that used by the New York House of Refuge and the New York Juvenile Asylum. However, when the Children's Aid Society placed children with western families, the children were not bound as apprentices, and either party was legally free to end the arrangement. In its first circular the Society had stated that it hoped "to be the means of draining the City of vagrant children by communicating with farmers, manufacturers, or families in the country, who may have need of such." [25]

In 1854 the Society sent out its first party, a group of forty-six children, most of whom were orphans. They were a "bright, sharp, bold, racy" crowd between the ages of seven and fifteen who were bound for Michigan under the care of the Reverend E. P. Smith, an agent for the Society. Even before they reached Albany two of the children had been selected by the passengers on the *Isaac Newton* as the ship made its way up the Hudson. From Albany the group traveled by railroad and lake boat to Dowagiac, Michigan. There the Reverend Mr. Smith took the entire band to church where they caused quite a stir among the townspeople, and after the service the agent explained the purpose of the Children's Aid Society and how families might receive the children. On Monday morning Smith began receiving applications for the children, and by Saturday all of them had been placed.[26]

The Society gradually developed a much more regularized system of sending children to the West. It divided the City into districts and assigned a "visitor" to each one. The visitor would go from house to house, trying to persuade the families to send their children to the public schools or to the industrial schools of the Children's Aid Society. When a visitor found a homeless or neglected child, he took him to the central office of the Society, where, after securing the parents' consent—if they could be found —it prepared to send him to a farmer's home in the West. Before it sent children to the West, the Society used a rudimentary screening process. The Society generally excluded older children, particularly girls over fourteen, and those who had been found guilty of serious offenses. Instead of sending groups into towns without warning, the Society had resident agents in the West, who, well before the arrival of the children, selected a town, visited it, and arranged for the creation of a committee of prominent citizens to screen the prospective families. When the children arrived, they appeared as a group before the local residents, who then made their choices. After the children had been placed, the western agent of the Children's Aid Society was supposed to visit them and help to adjust any difficulties.[27]

The children were not indentured to the families and could leave—as some of them did—if they were not satisfied. The Society wrote to the families and asked about the children and their progress. It also encouraged the children to write directly to the New York office and regularly printed some of these letters in its *Annual Reports.* In 1855, for example, a boy wrote that he was well and had been to school. "I am five foot high," he went on, "and fat as a bear. I have got a good home. A farmer I should like

to be, when I grow up to be a man." These letters, in almost
every case, tell remarkable success stories, although the Society
admitted that some of its placements had been unwise. Throughout the nineteenth century, however, the *Annual Reports* of the
Children's Aid Society stressed the overwhelming success of the
placing-out system.[28]

The fact that after the Civil War the Society came to enjoy
strong financial support from the people of New York indicated
that the Society's approach appealed to the monied classes of the
City. One of the most important aspects of the appeals of the
Children's Aid Society for public support was that it could claim
concrete results from its operations. The *Annual Reports* contained impressive statistics which the Society used to argue that
its operations had reduced crime in the City of New York. In
1855, for example, the Society placed out 800 children and claimed
that "our operations are saving to the State, the expense and
punishment of crime hereafter by its prevention now." By 1884
the Children's Aid Society had placed out over 60,000 children.
Brace admitted that not all of the children sent to families did
well, but estimated the failure rate at less than 10 per cent. In
1900 the Society analyzed the placing-out system and concluded
that 87 per cent of the children had been successful. As further
proof of the effectiveness of the programs of the Children's Aid
Society, Brace cited the decline of arrests for female vagrancy in
New York City. Over 5,000 women had been committed for that
offense in 1860, but by 1871 the number had fallen to 548. In
1860 the ratio of arrests for female vagrancy to the number of in-
habitants in the city was 1 to 138.5; by 1881 that ratio was 1 to
647. In 1884 Brace also claimed that there had been a 25 per cent
decline in the number of crimes against property since 1877.[29]

Another reason for the strong public support of the Children's
Aid Society was the fact that it enjoyed a very favorable image
in the city's most influential newspapers. In an editorial in March,
1865, the *New York Times* praised the "quiet labors" of the Society, which it said were "drying up the very sources and springs
of childish misery and criminality" and the New York *Sun* called

the Society's placing-out system "one of the most remarkable discoveries of the age." The *New York Tribune*, however, worked closely with the Society in some of its efforts to place children in the West. In March, 1879, a man from New England who asked to remain anonymous, sent $1,000 to Whitelaw Reid, the editor of the *Tribune*, and instructed him to use his judgment and apply the money to the relief of the destitute. Reid selected the Children's Aid Society as the charity most deserving of such assistance; shortly afterward the *Tribune* carried a front-page story describing Reid's part in sending a party of thirty-two homeless boys to the West.[30]

In addition to strong public support, the Children's Aid Society also had critics. What Brace called the "asylum interest"— institutions such as the New York House of Refuge and the New York Juvenile Asylum—argued that the Children's Aid Society was threatening the peace and security of life in western America by sending out vagrant and criminal city children. Brace's reply contended that the children which the Society placed out were not criminals and that the cost of the placing-out system was far less than that of asylum care. Brace also disagreed with the view of those in favor of asylum care that their approach—of two or three years' institutionalization to "reform" the children—was necessary before such children could be sent to the country. Such an approach was artificial, and the behavior taught in such institutions stressed "the external virtues" and had an "alms-house flavor," which made a child "very weak under temptation, somewhat given to hypocrisy, and something of a sneak." [31]

Many Catholics—particularly those associated with the Protectory, incorporated in 1863, which was a reformatory for Catholic juvenile delinquents modeled after the New York House of Refuge—echoed the arguments of the "asylum-interest." They also charged the Children's Aid Society with proselytism, because they believed that the Society often deliberately took Catholic children and placed them in Protestant homes. Brace rejected this criticism and accused the priests of New York of being envious of the success of the Children's Aid Society. Whether such charges were true probably cannot be known, but Brace's attitude toward Catholics was far from tolerant. In an article entitled "Pauperism" which appeared in *The North American Review* he implied that Catholicism encouraged poverty. "The influence both of general suffrage and of the Protestant faith," he wrote, "is to cultivate individual self-respect and independence; and wherever these are, there can be little of the spirit of pauperism." [32]

Westerners also criticized the placing-out system. At the National Prison Reform Congress in 1874 a delegate charged that the children sent out by the New York Children's Aid Society were filling western reform schools. The following year at the National Conference of Charities, Hiram Giles of Wisconsin repeated the accusation. In 1876 Brace answered the charges in a paper he sent to the National Conference of Charities. The Society's western agent, Charles R. Fry, Brace said, had investigated the charges and had found only five children, who had been placed out by the Society, in western reform schools. In the three states which Fry investigated the Society had placed approximately 15,000 children, and the rate of delinquency among those children was much lower than the rate among the native children.[33]

However, the charge did not die. Instead it became a focal point for arguments between supporters of the institutional approach to the reformation of juvenile delinquents and advocates of some kind of placing-out system. In 1879 Brace gave a paper at the annual meeting of the American Social Science Association on "The Care of Poor and Vicious Children" in which he vigorously defended the placing-out system of the Children's Aid Society. He argued that juvenile reformatories failed to accomplish their purpose and that such institutions should be used only for "the vicious and those who had committed criminal offenses." A lively discussion followed Brace's paper. One of the founders of the Industrial School for Girls at Middletown, Connecticut, objected to Brace's negative view of the value of institutional life, and a delegate from Michigan read a letter from J. P. Alden, principal of the Michigan State Public School for Poor Children. Alden argued that many of the children who had been in his institution had "repeatedly been placed in homes, where they failed," but who, after receiving training, "are now doing well in homes." Other delegates lined up on either side of the now familiar debate.[34]

At the National Conference of Charities and Corrections in 1882 J. H. Mills, the superintendent of an orphan asylum in North Carolina, charged the Children's Aid Society with inadequate supervision of the boys it had placed in that state. Mills said that some of the ex-slave owners in his state had been treating the boys from New York "as the children of slaves were treated." A delegate from St. Paul, Minnesota, added that boys often wandered away from their new families and came to the city. An Ohio delegate complained that some of the children from New York were "born constitutional thieves." Next the defenders of the placing-out system began to state their side of the continuing debate. Philip Gillett, the superintendent of the Institution for the Deaf and Dumb at Jacksonville, Illinois, wondered "why these children from the East should be judged differently from our own. Some turn out badly and some well. We magnify the evil and overlook the good." Another delegate charged that agencies such as the Children's Aid Society did not screen the children properly before sending them to the West. In an effort to calm the delegates, Frederick H. Wines, the Secretary of the Illinois State Board of Charities, reminded them that "the great practical difficulty in the administration of public and private charity is to descend from generalities and to exercise a wise discrimination." Now Hiram Giles, who had earlier accused the Children's Aid Society of polluting western society with criminal youths from New York, repeated his charge: "These boys are gathered up from the streets; they are wild as Mexican mustangs, and they should be treated as such." But Franklin B. Sanborn, the best-known man in American charity work and one of the founders of the National Conference of Charities, had the last word in this debate. He suggested that Brace might have been out of touch with his agents and therefore unaware of the quality of their supervision.[35]

Once again Brace sent Charles Fry and other agents to investigate the accusations leveled at the Society. When the Society announced that this investigation showed no unusual number of juvenile delinquents among its western placements, this did not settle the dispute. Andrew Ellmore, a member of the Wisconsin Board of State Charities, replied: "I have seen street-Arabs from New York, and I have seen a score of them in the Industrial School at Waukesha. I have never seen one that made a good boy." In a letter published in the *New York Tribune* Fry asserted that "for fifteen years, with the exception of the past two years, my entire time has been devoted to the important work of visiting these children in their Western homes. I have advised, protected and procured new homes for thousands during that time." Brace himself responded to the critics in a paper given before the American Social Science Association in September, 1883. He pointed out that some of the undesirable children in the West might have been sent under the auspices of other agencies such as the New York Juvenile Asylum. He defended the supervisory system of the Children's Aid Society and stressed the fact that it had placed over 60,000 children in the country, most of whom had prospered. Thus, he concluded that the Children's Aid Society had not been increasing crime in the West. While reducing crime in New York City, it had also been enhancing western prosperity.[36]

Meanwhile, the Secretary of the Minnesota State Board of Corrections and Charities, Hastings H. Hart, had conducted an investigation of his own into the children sent by the New York Children's Aid Society to Minnesota. Hart reported his investigation to the 1884 National Conference of Charities and Corrections and explained that of 340 children placed in Minnesota in the three years just passed only six had broken the law and nine had been returned to the Society as incorrigible. There had been five or six cases of abuse, but there were also some false stories circulating. In spite of this favorable evidence Hart concluded that the Society had been negligent in its placement system. The selection of families to receive children had been inadequate because the applications screening committee rarely rejected a local resident. Furthermore, the Society's method of supervising the children once they had been placed provided no way for them to redress their grievances. Hart thought that the Society ought to be more careful in the selection and supervision processes and limit its placement operations to children under twelve.[37]

In spite of the criticism and controversy surrounding it, the Children's Aid Society of New York had a number of imitators. Children's Aid Societies appeared in Baltimore in 1860, Boston in 1864, and Brooklyn in 1866. Philanthropists organized similar state-wide agencies in New York in 1872, in Pennsylvania in 1882, and in Connecticut in 1892. In addition, the system organized by Dr. Thomas J. Barnardo in England closely paralleled the operations of the New York Children's Aid Society.[38]

Dr. Barnardo's life was remarkably similar to Brace's. Both had begun other careers—Barnardo had studied medicine—and both came to devote their lives to disadvantaged children. Like Brace, Barnardo began his first charity work in the slums of a large city. He volunteered to help in a ragged school and soon became its superintendent. Barnardo was struck by the number of homeless children, however, and soon after his association with the ragged schools began, he founded the first of a series of children's homes, which were very much like the lodging houses of the Children's Aid Society. In a haphazard way he began placing these children in foster homes, and in 1882 he began sending them west—to Canada. Like Brace, Barnardo justified his work as being essentially preventive, but his operations were much more systematic than those of the New York Society. Children sent to Canada came only from Barnardo's homes and schools. Only those children with good conduct records, good physical health, and no blemishes on their past histories were permitted to go to Canada. Barnardo employed a resident agent in Toronto, who received applications and checked on the children after they had been placed. Despite Barnardo's care the placement of children in Canada became controversial, and Canadians, just as Americans had done, passed laws regulating the activity.[39]

Michigan passed the first law regulating the interstate placement of children in the United States in 1887. In 1895 Michigan also passed a law requiring out-of-state child-placing agencies to post bond for children they brought into the state. Four years later Indiana, Illinois, and Minnesota passed similar but stricter laws which in effect prohibited the placement of incorrigible, diseased, insane, or criminal children within their boundaries. These laws served as models for other western states, and within five years Kansas, Missouri, Kentucky, Iowa, North Dakota, South Dakota, and Ohio had passed similar laws.[40]

V

In many respects Charles Loring Brace was one of the most important figures in the history of American thought. Although he did not contribute many distinctive ideas, Brace reflected the mainstream of American intellectual development in the nineteenth century.

In defending his approach to the problems presented by dependent and delinquent children Brace used the ideas of a number of his contemporaries. He must have borrowed from Horace Bushnell, for example. In his later years Brace recalled that "among the especial blessings of his life [was] that his boyhood and youth were passed under the pastorate of Dr. Bushnell." While he was away at Yale he wrote his father that "if there is one thing I miss especially here which I had at home, it is Mr. Bushnell's sermons." Both *Christian Nurture* and Brace's placing-out system stressed the importance of the family in the life of the child, but where Bushnell sought to lessen the importance of the clergy and increase that of the Christian family in the process of transmitting the essential elements of the Christian faith, Brace saw the family in the larger context of transmitting most of the values of society to the child. Bushnell wanted families to understand their role in the process of making a Christian. Brace saw the family as "God's reformatory," and as a substitute for the usual prison-like institutions for juvenile delinquents. When he published *Christian Nurture*, Bushnell found himself a controversial figure because, by implication, his work indicated that ministers and schools were less efficient and less important in transmitting values than society had thought. Consequently many leading clergymen and educators attacked him, and the Sunday-school union which had been serializing *Christian Nurture* stopped its publication and tried to suppress it. In a way Bushnell served as a lightning rod for Brace's more comprehensive and practical explication of the same idea—that the family was the basic means of transmitting the values of a society.

From Theodore Parker and writers like Mary Carpenter, Brace borrowed the idea that the "perishing and dangerous classes"—the lower orders of society made up of criminals and paupers—represented one of the greatest threats to modern society. He had written to Parker in 1853 that "I am reading your sermons with intense interest and am happy and surprised to find that difference of view on historic questions has not in the least produced a different moral view." With Parker, Brace felt that the perishing and dangerous classes were in part the result of social development rather than individual wickedness. Brace divided the causes of crime and poverty into preventable and non-preventable categories; and among the preventable he listed ignorance, intemperance, over-crowding, and bad legislation. Parker referred to the perishing and dangerous classes as the "victims of society." Where Parker proposed no specific remedies to the problem, Brace argued that the work of the Children's Aid Society was "the best method" of dealing with this increasing threat to society. Brace believed that by concentrating on children, society could ultimately eliminate the problems of pauperism and crime.[41]

Brace's justifications of the operations of the Children's Aid Society and his appeals to the public for funds provide valuable insights into American thinking about social problems in the decades immediately following the Civil War. His argument that the Children's Aid Society approached social problems scientifically dovetailed with the ideas of other social reformers and philanthropists—such as Franklin B. Sanborn and Josephine Shaw Lowell—who contended that charity ought to be both organized and individualistic in its approach. The Children's Aid Society assured its benefactors that their money was not wasted. The

Society considered each case on its merits and placed children in the West on an individual basis. Furthermore, the Society did not perpetuate pauperism because it stressed the principle of self-help in all of its institutions and in the placing-out system. Unlike old-fashioned and unscientific charities the Children's Aid Society did not give alms indiscriminately and therefore did not encourage a dependence on charity.[42]

Brace also cited other reasons for his contention that the Society was scientific. By taking children from the crowded slums of the city where the supply of labor exceeded the demand and transporting them to the West where labor was scarce, the Children's Aid Society acted in conformity with the natural law of supply and demand. In addition by placing the homeless children of the city with families, the Society obeyed the natural laws of human development and began the process of remedying the cultural deficiencies of New York's street children.

This approach also harmonized with the Darwinian theory of evolution—particularly the principle of natural selection. Implicit in Darwin's theory was the importance of environment—not in determining the patterns of evolution but in providing the challenge against which the natural variations struggled. Thus to improve a given variation's chances of survival one might give it a more favorable environment. That is exactly what Brace sought to do. He believed that cities were evil and full of temptation. The country by contrast was free from temptation, and in the clean country air the children could learn the virtue and dignity of labor by working in the life-giving earth. In the developing West the culturally deprived children of the city could learn to help themselves in a society free from the stifling and degrading competition among the lower classes of the cities. Thus Brace argued that his approach to the problems of dependent and delinquent children was clearly scientific, and by citing impressive statistics he claimed remarkable success for his programs.[43]

In spite of his strong advocacy of the placing-out system Brace conceded that juvenile reformatories had a place in society's response to the challenge of juvenile delinquency. Brace felt that the family or cottage plan was the best way to administer such institutions, but he admitted that the older, hardened juvenile offenders might be better off in congregate institutions such as the New York House of Refuge. For young delinquents guilty only of vagrancy or of one minor offense Brace rejected an institutional approach and argued that these children needed the love and affection of a natural family. They did not need the artificial rules and discipline of a juvenile reformatory. Such places —as their names indicated—sought to "reform" or make over young criminals. But Brace believed that juvenile vagrants and minor offenders were not really criminals, only children, who through no fault of their own had found themselves outside the limits of acceptable behavior. For the most part such children were homeless, and if not homeless they came from very unsatisfactory homes. They needed not so much "reforming" as initial "forming." They had not learned the standards and norms of behavior which society expected of them because their families had failed to transmit those norms and values. Only the natural and scientific approaches of the Children's Aid Society, Brace contended, could remedy these deficiencies.[44]

Brace's philosophy rested on the idea that children deserved a full and free opportunity to develop themselves, and he stressed the need for self-help. Brace and the Children's Aid Society represented a significant departure from the earlier, group-oriented efforts of institutions such as the New York House of Refuge. Before nineteenth-century Americans could create an institution as flexible and sophisticated as the juvenile court, they had to learn a great deal more about human behavior and the nature of crime, but without Charles Loring Brace and his work it might have taken them much longer.

7

Ragged Dick and Huck Finn: Juvenile Delinquency and Children's Literature

In April, 1875, James T. Fields, the well-known member of the firm of Ticknor and Fields, publishers, visited Jesse Pomeroy in his cell. Fields asked Pomeroy if he liked to read. Fields later recalled that the boy claimed he read everything he could—including dime novels. A memoir published after Fields's death records the following conversation:

FIELDS: "What were the books about?"

POMEROY: "Killing and scalping injuns and so forth and running away with women; a good many scenes were out of the plains."

FIELDS: "Were there any pictures in the books?"

POMEROY: "Yes, Sir, plenty of them, blood and thunder pictures, tomahawking and scalping."

FIELDS: "Do you think these books were an injury to you, and excited you, and excited you to commit the acts you have done?"

POMEROY: "Yes, Sir, I have thought it all over, and it seems to me now they did. I can't say certainly, of course, and perhaps if I should think it over again, I should say it was something else."

FIELDS: "What else?"

POMEROY: "Well, Sir, I really can't say."

FIELDS: "Would you earnestly advise the other boys not to read these books you have read?"

POMEROY: "Indeed, Sir, I should." [1]

This conversation, even if it cannot be substantiated, reveals a basic attitude about juvenile delinquency in the late nineteenth century. In more recent times in the continuing debate about the causes of juvenile misbehavior, self-styled authorities have accused comic books, motion pictures, and television of causing or encouraging juvenile delinquency. In the late nineteenth century similar authorities attacked dime novels and newspapers on the same grounds.

Before mid-century, writers of juvenile literature in the United States and England operated on the Wordsworthian notion of children as "beings from God," and they produced vapid, moralistic books with stilted and unbelievably "good" children. The material intended for children consisted almost entirely of "tracts thinly disguised as stories," but after the Civil War some children's books eliminated the overly obvious preaching and included more realistic characters. Unlike the earlier books these new works were written by men who knew and understood children and not by men whose detachment made their child characters seem to be miniature, and very stuffy, adults. [2]

After the War, parents began to permit their children to read for recreation, and as a result there was a tremendous expansion in various types of children's literature. Special magazines for children such as *Our Young Folks, Riverside Magazine,* and *St. Nicholas* appeared along with the Horatio Alger books and the infamous dime novels. Not only was there more for children to read, but there were also books about real children. This growing bulk of children's literature suggests that in the last half of the nineteenth century there was an increasing awareness of children and child life in all parts of American society. [3]

One of the reasons for this new awareness of and interest in children came from the growing influence of Charles Darwin's

theory of evolution. Darwin's *Origin of the Species* had appeared
in 1859, but caught up in the Civil War, Americans did not appreciate the implications of Darwinism until after the end of the
War. Evolution suggested a development from lower to higher
orders, and the romantic inference that "the child is the father of
the man" seemed correct and natural. John Fiske, an early popu-
larizer of evolutionary theory and a disciple of Herbert Spencer,
advanced the view in *The Meaning of Infancy*, published in 1883,
that the long childhood of humans accounted for man's moral
feelings. To understand human nature and human behavior, according to Fiske, one must first study childhood. One of the
consequences of Darwinism, then, was a new concern about
children. This concern, like that of Wordsworth and the romantics,
focused on children, but the new attitude saw children not as
"beings from God" but as primitive savages. G. Stanley Hall, one
of America's leading psychologists, in his "general psychonomic
law" contended that the development of the individual organism
recapitulated the evolution of the race. According to this view, as
the person matured, his mind would evolve through the various
stages of social development, with adulthood and civilization
coinciding at the end. G. Stanley Hall agreed with John Fiske that
to learn the processes of society and to understand human nature
fully, one must first study the child. Thus because of the emphasis
on evolution, there emerged a new interest in the child. One of
the consequences of that interest was a notable increase in books
for and about children.[4]

In England, more natural children had appeared earlier in
books for children, and believable children has also appeared in
English fiction for adults well before they did in similar American
books. What may well be the best-known book about children of
all time was the first novel in English to focus on the life of a
child, Dickens's *Oliver Twist*. It was not until *Our Young Folks*
began serializing Thomas Bailey Aldrich's *The Story of a Bad Boy*
in 1869 that the United States had a book which focused on the
life of a real child.[5]

Why had British fiction depicted children more realistically earlier? Perhaps the same forces were at work in England as in the United States. By the 1830's most of England's cities were crowded and unhealthy; and miserable, grueling working conditions had become the lot of the English labor force, which included a good many women and children. In the 1830's Parliament at last roused itself to investigate the effect of the industrial revolution on the people of England. It discovered that, if anything, Dickens's vivid portrayals of life among the lower classes were too rosy. This public awareness of the conditions of life, the miserable state of many of her children, the romantic tradition of the noble child as father of the man, and the technical advances in printing all combined in England to launch a new children's literature nearly three decades before the same thing occurred in the United States. The impact of the industrial revolution on American life and the growth of American cities in the decades after the Civil War paralleled similar occurrences in British cities thirty or forty years before. Thus, one reason for the new American interest in children was the influence of the industrial revolution.[6]

II

By the time the final excerpt of Aldrich's *The Story of a Bad Boy* had appeared, American boys had found new reading passions— dime novels and the books of Horatio Alger. Alger was the best-known nineteenth-century author of books for boys. During his lifetime he wrote well over one hundred books and became one of the leading interpreters of the values of American society as applied to children. Alger had at first intended to be a clergyman like his father but had given that up some time before the War. He began writing books and decided to become an author. Not any of his first books were much of a success, but shortly after the Civil War, Alger met Charles O'Connor, the superintendent of the Newsboy's Lodging House, which had been established by the New York Children's Aid Society in the loft of the old *Sun* building. O'Connor invited Alger to live in the Lodging House and gather material for books about boys. From that first-hand experience and from Elizabeth Oakes Smith's *The Newsboy,* Alger drew the material which he used in his first successful book, *Ragged Dick,* published in 1868.[7]

Ragged Dick was the story of one of New York's vagabonds who supported himself as a bootblack. According to Alger, Dick "wasn't a model boy in all respects. . . . He swore sometimes, and now and then he played tricks upon unsophisticated boys from the country." However, like Bob in Elizabeth Oakes Smith's *The Newsboy,* his "nature was a noble one." The book consisted of a loosely connected series of incidents whose only unity was that they involved Dick. Dick saw himself as "a pretty rough customer" but not "as bad as some." He hoped to "grow up 'spectable.'" Although Alger modeled his character after the boys who lived at the Lodging House, and the boys delighted in the familiar haunts and scenes found in his books, he also used his books as sermons. An inventor told Dick that "all labor is respectable [:] . . . you have no cause to be ashamed of any honest business." Such an indirect approach might not have been convincing, and so Alger made his moral message perfectly clear. Dick decided to become a success, and Alger explained the process:

> He knew that, in order to grow up respectable, he must be well advanced, and he was willing to work. . . . His street education had sharpened his faculties, and taught him to rely on himself. He knew that it would take him a long time to reach the goal which he had set before him, and he had patience to keep on trying. He knew that he had only himself to depend upon, and he determined to make the most of himself,—a resolution which is the secret of success in nine cases out of ten.

Clearly, Alger accepted and preached the self-help gospel, and became one of America's most prolific and accepted authors of books for boys. Society approved of him because he expressed its values and its approach to social problems so clearly and so consistently. The rags-to-riches story was a part of the self-help gospel. Horatio Alger was the high priest of that gospel.[8]

Ironically, none of Alger's heroes achieved fame and fortune by adhering to the self-help gospel that he preached. All began as

poor and disadvantaged children—as members of Charles Loring
Brace's "dangerous classes," but they did not reach the high pinna-
cle of success through hard work and penny-pinching economy.
Ragged Dick, after he had resolved to become a success, achieved
his goal when a grateful father gave him a job for saving a child
who had fallen from a ferry. Success always came fortuitously to
Alger heroes, and although Alger modeled his characters after real
boys, the characters always changed from reasonable likenesses of
real street boys into noble, self-sacrificing types—for no apparent
reason. Thus Alger pleased two sets of readers—the newsboys
who enjoyed the stories about themselves, and the respectable
members of society who liked the nobility of the characters, their
virtuous actions, and their invariable success. Indeed, to the
arbiters of American taste, Alger's books seemed to voice that era's
universal prescription for the prevention of juvenile misbehavior:
the inculcation of a sober morality and the encouragement of hard
work. When stories for children lacked this moral overview,
society often condemned them.[9]

Among the reading materials for children that the self-appointed
consciences of American society roundly condemned were dime
novels. Inexpensive paperbound dime novels with their vivid
illustrations had first become popular with the soldiers in the
Civil War. The earlier examples were mostly historical fiction and
almost as moral as the Alger books. The best-known publisher of
dime novels, Erastus F. Beadle, insisted that his books should
have a certain amount of verisimilitude and that they should not
contain "subjects that carry an immoral taint." Their themes of
heroic greatness focused on the frontier, and although they moved
at a fast pace, they never showed evil triumphant. To give his
western books authenticity Beadle employed experts like Buffalo
Bill and Sam Hull as technical advisers, and he even made a trip
to the West himself to be sure that the books were true to the
real frontier. Like the Alger books, the Beadle dime novels lauded
rugged individualism, but they were less concerned with the rags-
to-riches story. To parents and ministers, however, they seemed
sensational and too bloody.[10]

The earlier dime novels did not deserve the criticism leveled at them nearly as much as did the later ones. The house of Beadle and Adams, which began the publication of dime novels, soon attracted competitors who were more concerned about sales than about the propriety of their books. Crude desperadoes, city sharpers, and all kinds of reprehensible underworld characters replaced the pioneer heroes of the Beadle books, and the criticism against dime novels mounted. When these later books began appearing in the 1880's, such criticism was justified, but some of the earlier charges that the Beadle dime novels encouraged immorality probably came from established publishers who feared the new competition.[11]

The dime novels did not, as did the Alger books, focus on young people. Instead, they were books with adult characters, read by both children and adults. However, dime novels and the Alger books do illuminate popular thinking about juvenile delinquency in the late nineteenth century. Many civic and social leaders, ministers, editors, and administrators of agencies like the Young Men's Christian Association regarded Alger's books as the kind of reading material which might prevent juvenile delinquency. At the same time, they regarded dime novels as one of the chief causes of juvenile delinquency. After all, Jesse Pomeroy had read dime novels. But the Alger books were not the only ones to have children as the central characters, and some of the books which focused on children sought to depict real, believable young people. The first important book of this type was Aldrich's *The Story of a Bad Boy*, which appeared in 1869. Aldrich was the first to discard the Wordsworthian romanticism which had become typical of fictional juvenile characters. The boy was "bad" in the sense that he often got into mischief and did things that "real" boys did, but he was no vagrant. He had a home and family, did not steal, and although he sometimes disturbed the peace, society never considered him to be a problem. Aldrich's boy was no juvenile delinquent.[12]

Better known and more significant than *The Story of a Bad Boy* were Mark Twain's *Adventures of Tom Sawyer* and the *Ad-*

ventures of Huckleberry Finn. Taken together these two books are probably the best American fiction ever written about boys, and some critics regard *Huckleberry Finn* as the greatest American novel. Their appearance and continued popularity show that Americans then as now appreciated real boys. The popularity of the books makes them excellent material for a consideration of public attitudes about boys—including juvenile delinquents—in the years between the Civil War and the turn of the century. Huck Finn in the *Adventures of Tom Sawyer* is a classic juvenile delinquent. As Twain wrote,

> Huckleberry was cordially hated and dreaded by the mothers of the town, because he was idle and lawless and vulgar and bad—and because all their children admired him so, and delighted in his forbidden society, and wished they dared to be like him. . . . Huckleberry was always dressed in the cast-off clothes of full-grown men, and they were in perennial bloom and fluttering with rags. His hat was a vast ruin with a wide crescent lopped out of its brim; his coat, when he wore one, hung nearly to his heels and had the rearward buttons far down the back; but one suspender supported his trousers; the seat of the trousers bagged low and contained nothing; the fringed legs dragged in the dirt when not rolled up.
> Huckleberry came and went, at his own free will. He slept on doorsteps in fine weather and in empty hogsheads in wet; he did not have to go to school or to church, or call any being master or obey anybody; he could go fishing or swimming when and where he chose, and stay as long as it suited him; nobody forbade him to fight; he could sit up as late as he pleased; he was always the first boy that went barefoot in the spring and the last to resume leather in the fall; he never had to wash, nor put on clean clothes; he could swear wonderfully.

Huck Finn was a juvenile delinquent not so much for what he did but because everybody in town thought he was. The very mention of his name caused a reaction. Once when Tom Sawyer was late for school the master demanded to know why. "I stopped to talk with Huckleberry Finn," Tom replied. "The master's pulse stood still, and he stared helplessly. The buzz of study ceased." Such an admission was clearly incredible. "You—you did what?"

the master said. Again Tom admitted that he had talked to the notorious Huckleberry Finn. "Thomas Sawyer," the master said, "this is the most astounding confession I have ever listened to. No mere ferule will answer for this offence. Take off your jacket." The master whipped Tom until he was tired "and the stock of switches notably diminished." [13]

The character of Huckleberry Finn in *Tom Sawyer* shows that the same stereotype of the juvenile delinquent which inspired the creation of the New York House of Refuge still held the popular mind late in the nineteenth century. Delinquents were still vagabonds, homeless, rootless children who neither worked nor went to school. Idle children ignored "the necessity and dignity of labor," and thus they were delinquents. But Huck Finn was no mere personification of a stereotype. In the first place, although the community regarded Huck as a delinquent, technically he was not one, for he was never caught doing anything illegal. Secondly, Mark Twain made it clear that it was the community which judged Huck; Mark Twain and the boys rather liked him. Of Huck, the author said, "everything that goes to make life precious that boy had. So thought every harassed, hampered, respectable boy in St. Petersburg." Finally, near the end of the *Adventures of Tom Sawyer*, the attitude of the community toward Huck changed. Huck and Tom had found a cache of money which they could not return and which made them rich. "Huck Finn's wealth and the fact that he was now under the Widow Douglas' protection," Mark Twain wrote, "introduced him into society. . . ." When he could stand no more of "civilization," Huck "turned up missing." According to the author, "the public were profoundly concerned; they searched high and low, they dragged the river for his body." Tom Sawyer found Huck in one of his "hogsheads" and persuaded him to return to the Widow Douglas. At that point the *Adventures of Tom Sawyer* ended.

The Adventures of Huckleberry Finn opened with Huck somewhat reluctantly civilized. He was even going to school. "At first I hated the school," Huck said, "but by and by I got so I could stand it. Whenever I got uncommon tired, I played hookey, and

the hiding I got next day done me good and cheered me up."
Huck's character changed in the second book, and in the course
of his adventures he acquired a conscience. He and Miss Watson's
Jim, who was running away toward freedom, were floating down
the Mississippi on a raft, and Huck began to wonder if he should
turn Jim in. Jim had been talking about buying his children out of
slavery or stealing them if necessary:

> Here was this nigger which I had as good as helped to run
> away, coming right out flat-footed and saying he would steal his
> children—children that belonged to a man I didn't even know;
> a man that hadn't ever done me no harm.
>
> I was sorry to hear Jim say that, it was such a lowering of
> him. My conscience got to stirring me up hotter than ever, until
> at last I says to it, "Let up on me—it ain't too late, yet—I'll
> paddle ashore at the first light and tell."

But Huck did not tell. Even when two men asked him about Jim,
Huck said that Jim was white. Nevertheless, Huck continued to
worry about breaking the law and helping a slave to run away.
At another point in the story, he wrote a note to Miss Watson to
tell her where Jim was, but it bothered him:

> It was a close place. I took it up and held it in my hand. I
> was a-trembling, because I'd got to decide, forever, betwixt
> two things, and I knowed it. I studied a minute, sort of holding
> my breath, and then says to myself:
>
> "All right, then, I'll *go* to hell"—and tore it up.
>
> It was awful thoughts, and awful words, but they was said.
> And I let them stay said; and never thought no more about re-
> forming. I shoved the whole thing out of my head; and said I
> would take up wickedness again, which was my line, being
> brung up to it, and the other warn't.

Later Jim was captured and Tom Sawyer turned up. Tom agreed
to help steal Jim and this puzzled Huck:

> Here was a boy that was respectable, and well brung up, and
> had a character to lose; and folks at home that had characters;
> and he was bright and not leather-headed; and knowing and
> not ignorant; and not mean, but kind; and yet here he was,
> without any more pride or rightness, or feeling than to stoop to

this business, and make himself a shame, and his family a shame, before everybody.

In the end Huck and Tom learned that Jim had been free all along and Huck decided to "light out for the Territory" before Aunt Sally civilized him.[15]

In *Tom Sawyer* Huck Finn was a juvenile delinquent in the town's eye and a hero in the eyes of the boys. Yet the townspeople's acceptance of him late in the book and the fact that Tom persuaded him to return to the Widow Douglas suggest that he was a delinquent in the process of reforming. At the beginning of *Huckleberry Finn* he seemed to have reformed. Although Huck's father dragged him back to vagabond life, Huck did reform. He gained a conscience and made a difficult moral choice. Mark Twain overtly suggested that Huck's decision to aid Jim was consistent with his earlier anti-social character, but there is a tension here. The reader, particularly the nineteenth-century American, thought that this decision to help a runaway slave was moral. Thus, Huck, despite society's disapproval of him in *Tom Sawyer*, became a hero for Mark Twain. He even took on a certain nobility, but unlike the heroes of the Horatio Alger books, Huck came by his nobility clearly and honestly—it came from his growing friendship with and respect for Jim. At the end of the book the author almost overplayed this theme. Huck's decision to "light out for the Territory" meant that he would go west, just as many other Americans (including Mark Twain himself) had done, in response to the myth of manifest destiny. By the end of *The Adventures of Huckleberry Finn,* Huck had gone from being a juvenile delinquent to becoming a typical young American.

In *Tom Sawyer* in sketching the character of Huck Finn, Mark Twain delineated a "typical" juvenile delinquent as society viewed him. In the earlier book Huck was something of a foil, and his personality was not fully developed. In *Huckleberry Finn* Huck came into focus, and he was not a simple stereotype. Indeed, he was a very complex young man, who manfully faced (and solved to the reader's satisfaction) a difficult moral choice. As Mark Twain depicted Huck Finn, so society came to regard its problem

children. Until after the Civil War Americans did not see their
children as children. It was as if the metaphysical systems which
sought to unify science and all other knowledge had dropped a
shade over Americans' eyes, who then saw their children only in
silhouette. But the new children's literature helped to remove that
shade, as Mark Twain's handling of Huck clearly shows.

III

Like their twentieth-century descendants who worried about the
possible connection between motion pictures, comic books, television and juvenile misbehavior, nineteenth-century Americans
worried about threats to juvenile morality. In 1878 William
Graham Sumner, a Yale professor of political economy and a
leading Darwinist, wrote "What Our Boys Are Reading" for *Scribner's Monthly*. Sumner discussed the recent changes in literature
for boys and commented on the new subjects of the stories—
"hunting, Indian Warfare, California desperado life, pirates, wild
sea adventure, highway men, crimes and horrible accidents, . . .
the life of vagabond boys, and the wild behavior of dissipated boys
in great cities." What disturbed Sumner about the new literature
was not that it was profane or obscene but that it was vulgar. To
Sumner "vulgar" meant dangerous or worse. He complained that
the heroes were either "swaggering vulgar swells of the rowdy
style" or "in the vagabond mass" below such swells. The heroes
and principal characters seemed always to be in the company of
"criminals, gamblers, and low people who live[d] by their wits."
Sumner also contended that such books taught boys to rely on
physical strength, to cheat their father, to hang around theaters
and saloons, and to learn to drink. In addition the books implied
that a quiet home life was unmanly, that the police were stupid,
and that a young man could escape his troubles by assuming a
light manner. "These papers," Sumner wrote, "poison boys' minds
with views of life which are so base and false as to destroy all
manliness and all chances of true success." The fact that Sumner

found the new books for boys dangerous when they failed to show a normal home life indicates the degree to which late nineteenth-century Americans had come to understand the importance of the family in transmitting and preserving the values and norms of society. Sumner also complained that the new literature did not mention "industry and economy in some regular pursuit." Thus the new books, because they poisoned boys' minds and failed to depict a normal home life and because they mocked the gospel of self-help, represented a serious threat to American society, and in Sumner's mind they probably had a great deal to do with the increasing rates of juvenile delinquency.[16]

A more vigorous and vitriolic critic than Sumner was Anthony Comstock, the chief self-appointed conscience of late nineteenth-century America. In 1871 Comstock joined with the New York Y.M.C.A. in a campaign to suppress obscene literature and thereby to rescue young men from its nefarious influences. In 1873 he lobbied successfully for the passage of a federal anti-obscenity law which prohibited the use of the mails for the transmission of such material. Comstock became a special agent for the Post Office and vigorously joined the effort to track down and prosecute the publishers of obscenity. In 1883 he paused from his zealous labors long enough to write *Traps for the Young*, a book designed to "awaken thought upon the subject of Evil Reading, and to expose to the minds of parents, teachers, guardians, and pastors, some of the mighty forces for evil that are to-day exerting a controlling influence over the young."

As he contemplated America in the late nineteenth century, Comstock saw Satan's snares all around young people, even in the home. There was light literature, for example, which was "a devil trap to captivate the child by perverting taste and fancy." It led to an enslavement of the imagination, and it lacked both a moral and an elevating tone. A second trap found in the home was the newspaper, which was particularly reprehensible because it gave the lurid details of crime. "The youth who reads such loathsome details," said Comstock, "might almost as well pass his time in the society of criminals."

The following passage illustrates Comstock's style of moral invective at its best:

> And it came to pass that as Satan went to and fro upon the earth, watching his traps and rejoicing over his numerous victims, he found more room for improvement in some of his schemes. The daily press did not meet all his requirements. The *weekly* illustrated papers of crime would do for young men and sports, for brothels, gin mills, and thieves resorts, but were found to be so gross, so libidinous, so monstrous, that every decent person spurned them. They were excluded from the home on sight. They were too high priced for children, and too cumbersome to be conveniently hid from the parent's eye or carried in the boy's pocket. So he resolved to make another trap for boys and girls especially. . . . These sure ruin traps comprise a large variety of half-dime novels, five and ten cent story papers, and low-priced pamphlets for boys and girls.

With such an approach, beginning with Satan and linking him directly to dime novels, it is not surprising that Comstock failed to note the relatively harmless character of the early dime novels. But Comstock had more to say about dime novels. They bred "vulgarity, profanity, loose ideas of life, [and] impurity of thought and deed." They also encouraged a host of other evils and disparaged "honest toil" and made "real life a drudge and a burden." "What young man," Comstock asked, "will serve an apprenticeship, working early and late, if his mind is filled with the idea that sudden wealth may be acquired by following the hero of the story?" [17]

Comstock went on to list other traps: advertising—especially of theaters, which he called "the recruiting stations of hell"; gambling—"death traps by mail"; quack or false medical traps; free love traps; artistic and classical traps in which "art" and the classics throw their protective shields over "the most obscene representations" and "foulest matters in literature"; and various "liberal traps" which would keep the government from regulating such nefarious traffic. Nonetheless, when he condemned dime novels, Comstock, like Sumner, struck the chord of the self-help gospel. What made the new children's literature which had appeared after the Civil

War so dangerous, both men agreed, was that it failed to stress the importance of hard work and it encouraged idleness. In effect, the new literature had created a fantasy world which had little relation to the ideal world envisioned by the leaders and movers of society.[18] This fantasy world threatened the continuity of society because it envisioned new and different values. Thus, dime novels caused juvenile delinquency, not because they depicted dangerous criminals but because their heroes did not seem to do any work and did not have a regular home life. When they read such books, boys would therefore be encouraged to leave home and abandon their jobs. By leaving their families the boys would separate themselves from the source of their values and standards of behavior. By becoming idle, boys would sink into the "perishing and dangerous classes" and quickly become juvenile delinquents. Such were the dangers of these "traps for the young."

IV

The dime novels and Horatio Alger books that American children read in the last half of the nineteenth century perpetuated the romantic view of children which had been prevalent in American fiction before the Civil War. The publication of Thomas Bailey Aldrich's *The Story of a Bad Boy* in 1869, the appearance of other similar works, and the popularity of Mark Twain's books show that some Americans were beginning to abandon these generalizations about children.

The emphasis on real children in literature paralleled a greater concern for the children of American society. The crusade against child labor, the child study movement, and the modification of institutions and agencies for children, including those for juvenile delinquents, are all evidence of this concern. "Child study" is a vague term, but its vagueness accurately reflects its nineteenth century nature, when it might have meant a mother's observation of a single child, or an elaborate "scientific" investigation of a large group of children. G. Stanley Hall was an early exponent of child study in the 1880's, but a significant national movement in the field did not begin until the twentieth century. Hall's interest in children and the beginning of child study, however limited, show that scientists and educators believed that children were worth studying.[19]

America's children began to come into focus as individuals. Not only did American fiction discard some of the literary stereotypes of children, but Americans themselves seemed to be more aware of children. Because of the growing industrialization of American society, the already sad plight of many of America's children became worse in the years after the Civil War. The crowded cities, the exploitation of children in factories and sweatshops, the armies of "Arabs" on the streets of large cities had by the end of the century attracted society's attention and aroused its sense of outrage. When society began to see children as they really were, it recognized that their ideas about problem children did not fit real children. They were, in fact, assumptions about adults which had been indiscriminately and uncritically applied to children. Society abandoned these generalizations in two separate ways: through the development of individualized treatment in institutions for children, and through the application of new empirical methods to the study of individual juvenile delinquents.

8

Elbridge Gerry and William Pryor Letchworth: The Delinquent in the City

The narrow, crooked streets in lower Manhattan south of Fourteenth Street had always formed a maze. Before the Civil War tenements and cheap lodging houses had already appeared in this part of the city, and portions of the district had become slums. In 1845 John Griscom, one of the founders of the New York House of Refuge, wrote a treatise "The Sanitary Conditions of the Labouring Population of New York" in which he discussed the effects of slum living on "the dewllers in the courts and ill-ventilated garrets" of the city. They were "depressed and prostrated by the want of stimulus given by nature" and were therefore "unable to enjoy the feelings guaranteed by an unfailing abundance of oxygen." In 1857 a committee of the New York legislature investigated tenements in New York and Brooklyn and concluded that the tenement house was "the parent of constant disorders, and the nursery of increasing vices." [1]

These early slums would seem almost like a paradise compared with the later ghettos that appeared when increasing numbers of immigrants poured into New York. The immigrants mingled with equally impressive numbers of young people who had migrated from the country to make their fortunes. The quickening of the industrial revolution, the revival of American trade after the Civil War, the growth of the railroads—the entire spectrum of the gigantic expansion of the American economy in the late nineteenth century stimulated and fed upon an equivalent expansion in the population of American cities. The newcomers crowded into existing slums and the slums themselves expanded. Noisy, teeming streets filled to overflowing with people, among whom were thousands of children. The children played in dirty, refuse-laden alleys, in garbage piles, and in the cellars and basements of the "human hives" in which they lived. The odors of the slum district almost defied description. A reporter for the *New York Times* who ventured into the Thirteenth Ward complained about the "pestiferous atmosphere," one exposure to which was "enough to poison those who live in a purer neighborhood." On his tour the reporter found a pool of "refuse slops" and "unwholesome effluvia" in which several small children were "paddling with their hands, which disturbing motion" made the "surrounding atmosphere anything but agreeable." The children were extremely dirty, and one of them "looked as if he had raked the mud from the bottom of the pool and rubbed it over his cheeks." [2]

The late nineteenth century saw the creation of a series of organizations such as the Young Men's Christian Association and the Society for the Prevention of Cruelty to Children which were designed to cope with the growing social ills of American cities. Existing agencies such as the New York Association for Improving the Condition of the Poor and the Children's Aid Society found their responsibilities increasing. In part this was because of the great crowding of American cities in the period after the Civil War, but it was also due to a growing awareness of the complexity of social problems. Many of these agencies, both old and new, by accident or design, found themselves concerned with juvenile delinquents. As they dealt with poverty, crime, and disease, these agencies built up a body of ideas about such problems. For the most part these ideas were those of the observant layman, and as such they provide an index to popular thinking. Thus, a study of the social agencies of one American city, New York, furnishes a guide to late nineteenth-century popular ideas about the nature and causes of juvenile delinquency.

II

In an editorial entitled "Where Crime Is Bred," which appeared in 1875, the *New York Times* explained that the conditions in the slums caused youthful lawbreaking:

> Now, the tenement house gives no sense of home. Anything like home life is almost an impossibility there. Enter one of those human hives on a summer's evening. There is no sign of privacy. The most anxious mother cannot preserve . . . [her children] from the contaminating influence of the most vicious adults. At an age when children should be innocent as lambs, they are too often steeped in the knowledge of every sort of vice and crime.

The *Times* went on to say that in small houses mothers could keep their children from such influences. Accordingly, the editorial argued, it was "the duty of the wealthy and philanthropic to take the urgent need of suitable accommodations for the working classes into consideration." The *Times* even went so far as to comment that there were "many millionaires who ought not to think of a possible loss of one or two per cent when a scheme of such moment to the City where they make their money is at stake." [3]

The juvenile crime that the *Times* had editorialized about seemed almost constant. "Nearly every day," the paper reported, "small boys commit highway robbery—usually by snatching the purses of ladies—in the streets of New York and Brooklyn." In the summer of 1890 two "knee-high youngsters" found themselves charged with horse-stealing. The two young culprits were Michael Givigia, age seven, and William Naegee, age ten. Naegee was already familiar with the craft of horse-stealing. Earlier he had stolen a wagon and its team, a goat-cart, and a horse. Naegee and Givigia found a horse and wagon untended at Pier 29 and took off on a joy ride. The police arrested the boys, however, and locked them in jail. Later they were released to their parents. [4]

More disturbing than cases such as these, however, were the activities of juvenile gangs. In 1873 the *New York Times* complained about "half-drunken, lazy, worthless vagabonds," who prowled the streets after dark and sometimes fired pistols to frighten passers-by. Sometimes the gangs even terrorized people in their own homes. There were a great many organized gangs in New York such as the "Nineteenth Street Gang," the "Dean Rabbits," and the "Short Boys." These gangs often had close connections with a local saloon-keeper, who in return for the gang's muscle in political campaigns provided them with protection from the police. Usually the leaders of such gangs were not juveniles, but young men. When they were not active, the gangs met together and read dime novels, played cards, and generally amused one another.[5]

Gangs, juvenile theft, and the idle, dirty, and potentially criminal children of the streets were symptoms of the growing cities' deeper social problem. City administration and government had not kept pace with the tremendous growth in population in American urban areas. As they had before the war, governmental authorities relied heavily on private agencies to alleviate poverty and suffering among the lower classes. The magnitude of this task was more than existing agencies could handle, and so new charities appeared. Some of these agencies dealt primarily with children and juvenile delinquents, but nearly all of the charitable and philanthropic organizations in the city had some contact with or concern about juvenile delinquency. As these organizations, both old and new, moved to try to cure the growing ills of American society, they said a great deal about the nature and causes of juvenile delinquency.[6]

One of the most important charities in New York was the Association for Improving the Condition of the Poor, organized in 1843. The primary purpose of this agency was to assist poor families, but it also conducted investigations to discover the "causes" of the poverty and misery of the people it tried to help. Shortly after it had been founded, the Association came to the conclusion that the housing of the poor was morally debasing.

The agency's basic attitude toward the poor, however, was that they were individually responsible for their poverty. Like Brace and others, the Association urged the poor to leave the slums, where they congregated like "driftwood," and migrate to the West.

The Association operated with volunteer visitors who dispensed advice and investigated potential clients. In 1853 these visitors began a campaign to eliminate juvenile street-begging and vagrancy. The visitors tried to persuade parents to send their children to school, and the Association supported a bill to provide for compulsory education for "idle and truant children," which passed in April, 1853. Because of the crowded conditions in the public schools, the new law could not be enforced. Nevertheless, the Association continued to stress education as a means of preventing poverty and social misery. "Why is it that the neglected children of our city have so long furnished the class which endangers life and property among us, and tenants our prisons and penitentiaries?" the secretary of the agency asked. "It is because mere moral influence, opposed by parental authority, has been incompetent to effect their recovery." In short, the secretary reminded his fellow New Yorkers that it would take more than sermons to prevent juvenile delinquency. The Association for Improving the Condition of the Poor continued to function throughout the nineteenth century and continued to stress the idea that individuals ought to remedy their own difficulties. As a result of the investigations of the Association, New Yorkers could better understand the connection between the squalid conditions in the slums and the increase of juvenile delinquency.[7]

In 1850 the Association resolved to take a more direct interest in juvenile delinquency. In January of that year a committee of the AICP resolved to create "a suitable House of Detention" for the "morally exposed children and youth" of the city. They expected the house to remove the children from "dangerous and corrupting associations and place them in such circumstances as will be favorable to reform, and tend to make them industrious, virtuous, and useful members of society." The result of that resolution was the creation of the New York Juvenile Asylum, which the

State of New York chartered in 1851 and which opened in 1853. This institution received the same sort of children that the Children's Aid Society sought to help: truants, disobedient children brought by their parents, and first offenders. It also received neglected and destitute children.[8]

Like the Children's Aid Society the Juvenile Asylum placed children in the West. Usually it sent only those children whose parents could not be found. The Asylum kept the children in custody until they had "shown sufficient improvement," and unlike the Children's Aid Society, indentured the children to the families with which they had been placed. In 1872 in the case of *People* ex rel. *Splain* v *New York Juvenile Asylum,* a mother challenged the constitutionality of such an apprenticeship. The New York Supreme Court found the practice of apprenticeship to be both constitutional and beneficial. The legislation empowering the Asylum to indenture its inmates, said the court was "essential to the good order and protection of the community." It was based on the general police power of the state, and the court concluded that "that power cannot be more humanely and usefully exercised than it is by making salutary and wise provisions for the education, improvement, comfort and security of the destitute, homeless and needy children found in the large cities of the state." [9]

When a delinquent came before a magistrate, the magistrate usually sent younger, first offenders who had committed trivial crimes to the New York Juvenile Asylum. The magistrate sent older delinquents who had committed more serious offenses to the New York House of Refuge. He did this because the public generally regarded the Asylum as the milder of the two places. In 1876 a member of the New York State Board of Charities, William Pryor Letchworth, visited the Asylum and talked with the superintendent, E. M. Carpenter. At the time Letchworth was compiling a report on all of the child-caring agencies in the State. Letchworth appeared unannounced, but he found Carpenter eager to explain his institution. "I aim at good family discipline," Carpenter told him. "I educate my officers and teachers to the same ideas. The result is the establishment of a public sentiment

among the children, that is for the good. Such is the basis of good
family government, and we make it the basis of our discipline
here." Carpenter also claimed that the Asylum refused to accept
boys that were "hardened and better fitted for the refuge." In
1896, however, the Asylum received a boy that the House of
Refuge had rejected—with nearly disastrous results.[10]

The New York House of Refuge had been a comprehensive
institution which accepted all kinds of delinquents. With the creation of the Juvenile Asylum and the Children's Aid Society, however, it began to receive only the older and more hardened juvenile delinquents. The founding of the Catholic Protectory in 1863
further reduced the number of delinquents going to the House of
Refuge, but it continued to receive a substantial number of inmates. The House of Refuge was the largest and oldest reformatory in the United States. Located on Randall's Island in the East
River, it presented a handsome façade to a viewer from Manhattan. With high, narrow windows along a six hundred-foot front
and with taller central and end buildings, it was an imposing,
dignified structure.

Inside, the routine was little changed from the early days. The
children got up early, worked what amounted to a full day, and
also attended school. As had always been the case, the girl's department was entirely separate. During the late nineteenth century two great controversies involved the House of Refuge. In a
sense both were old issues. Catholics had long objected to the
Refuge's practice of requiring all of the inmates to attend a "non-
sectarian" but decidedly Protestant Sunday religious service. This
objection flared up into a controversy after the Civil War. The
second controversy concerned the contract labor system. This
method of hiring outside contractors to furnish employment for
the inmates had been a standard procedure at the House of Refuge
since its founding in 1825. In the late nineteenth century however,
two groups—trade unionists who feared the competition of the
inmates' labor and reformers who were concerned about the welfare of the children—objected to the system.[11]

In May, 1872, the boys working in one of the contractor's shoe shops at the House of Refuge revolted. The leader, a boy named Thomas McDonald, who had been "very insubordinate," stabbed the foreman and his assistant. The officials at the House of Refuge called in two companies of police to put down the riot. As a result of the disturbance, a committee of the New York State Board of Charities launched a full-scale investigation of the House of Refuge. The New York newspapers took up the controversy and published a list of "charges" against the management. The committee members considered these accusations first. They rejected the charges that the Managers of the House of Refuge had withheld wages from the boys, that the food at the institution was inadequate, and that the superintendent was incompetent. They also found no evidence that the Managers subordinated the interests of the inmates to those of the contractor. Finally, they rejected the charge that the officials at the Refuge used cruel and unusual punishments. Only one charge—that the Managers of the House of Refuge had not provided adequate religious services for Catholic inmates—impressed the committee as having any substance, but they left this charge for the consideration of the full Board of State Charities. In effect the investigation had given the New York House of Refuge a vote of confidence.[12]

More significant than any immediate results from this investigation were the activities of a new member of the State Board, William Pryor Letchworth. At the age of fifty Letchworth had retired from active business to devote his life to public service and charity work. He was appointed in August of 1872 and focused his attention on institutions for children in New York State. In 1874 he submitted a special report describing conditions in county poorhouses and almshouses and strongly advocated that children not be kept in such institutions. As a result of his report, the New York legislature passed a law in 1876 which required the removal of all children from almshouses and poorhouses.

In 1879 Letchworth began investigating the New York House of Refuge and other similar institutions and decided that he needed more information on the reformation of juvenile delinquents. Therefore he went to Europe to study institutions and

returned full of admiration for the *Rauhe Haus* near Hamburg
and the cottage or family system of managing juvenile reformatories. What disturbed Letchworth most about the New York
House of Refuge was its failure to make adequate provision for
those it discharged. The Managers indentured only a small percentage of the inmates they discharged; the rest were "discharged
to friends," which meant that they would return to their old
neighborhoods and associations. The main reason for this failure,
Letchworth thought, was the contract system. He did not agree
with the earlier charge made in the New York newspapers that
the Managers of the House of Refuge deliberately subordinated
the interests of the children in their care to those of the contractor
and to the profit motive, but he thought the system had that effect anyway. "Under the contract system in reformatory institutions," Letchworth explained, "there is a strong temptation to
retain as long as possible, boys who are most valuable to the
contractor. Those children generally belong to the most dutiful
class, and are really entitled to [the] earliest discharge." The
scheme, Letchworth argued, had been designed for adult prisons
and was not appropriate for an institution for children which
should have a "home atmosphere." [13]

Letchworth's efforts led to the introduction and passage of a
bill to eliminate the contract system in institutions for juvenile
delinquents in New York State. This effort, however, produced a
vigorous debate on the best methods of reforming juvenile delinquents. This debate provides some significant insights into popular ideas about juvenile delinquency. In July, 1879, the *New York
Tribune* carried a detailed "feature" story on the New York House
of Refuge, which described the daily schedule and explained the
purposes of the institution. A *Tribune* reporter found the Refuge
"very picturesque and quiet" from the outside and witnessed "a
busy scene" within. He came away impressed with the efficiency
of the institution and wrote a very favorable story, which praised
the contract system. The reporter explained that when children
were released from the House of Refuge, they usually went to

farms and that "in the majority of cases their experience in the House of Refuge seems to awaken in them a new view of life."

The president of the Society for the Prevention of Cruelty to Children, Elbridge Gerry, joined Letchworth in his efforts to eliminate the contract system. Gerry thought that the Managers ought to spend more time training the children in skills that would be of use to them once they left the institution, and on its editorial page, the *New York Tribune* now agreed. "If the chief end of a reformatory is to reform," the *Tribune* argued, "then its chief end cannot be to farm out the labor of the children who are to be reformed."

The Managers of the House of Refuge defended the system and claimed that it had been misrepresented and misunderstood. A *Tribune* reporter interviewed one of the Managers, Richard M. Hoe, who explained that the elimination of the contract system would mean "a large additional expense to the State," but claimed that most of the children remained at the House of Refuge such a short time that "it would prevent their learning more than the rudiments of a trade. I consider it not of so much importance to try to teach the boys a trade . . ." Hoe argued, "as to impart to them habits of industry, punctuality and order, to train their hands to work and to inure them to just discipline." In conclusion Hoe reminded the *Tribune* that the House of Refuge was the oldest institution of its kind in the United States. "It has always been conducted on philanthropic as well as economical methods," he said. "I wish Mr. Gerry and Mr. Letchworth, instead of constantly pulling such institutions to pieces, would come and join us and find a better way of conducting the management."

This last remark prompted Gerry to reply. "The House of Refuge," he began, "is one of the best reformatories, in my judgment, in this state." But, Gerry added, it had two glaring defects: the use of cells and the contract system. "The object of the contractor is to get all the work he can out of the children," Gerry continued. Although his Society would not interfere in the management of reformatory institutions, Gerry concluded that "it certainly will, so long as I have the honor of presiding over it, raise its voice against the infliction of unnecessary physical pain and suffering upon their inmates." [14]

III

In 1874 Elbridge Gerry was the counsel for Henry Bergh's Society for the Prevention of Cruelty to Animals. Late that year a city missionary, a Mrs. Wheeler, had gone to visit a woman dying of tuberculosis. The woman refused to go to a hospital but asked the missionary to do something for the little girl next door. Her stepmother beat her, and the little girl's screams had alarmed the entire building. The missionary went to the police who told her that they could do nothing unless she had proof that an assault had taken place. She made the rounds of the charities in the city that aided children. The charities could help homeless children, or those sent to them by the courts, but no one was willing or able to interfere between a parent and a child. Finally, the missionary turned to Henry Bergh. Bergh and Gerry decided to make the situation a test case, and Gerry secured a warrant for the presence of the child in court. The judge ordered that the little girl be placed in the temporary care of the Society for the Prevention of Cruelty to Animals, and they arranged for her placement in a foster home. The need for an agency to handle similar cases was clear, so the Society for the Prevention of Cruelty to Children was organized in 1875, with Gerry as president.[15]

In 1874 the New York legislature had passed a law designed to eliminate child-begging. The Society for the Prevention of Cruelty to Children concentrated on this problem as one of its first major efforts. One of the sadder aspects of child-begging was the practice of having girls sell flowers. They used it as a cover-up for prostitution. In 1877 the SPCC reported the arrest of three girls, aged twelve, thirteen, and fourteen, for "peddling flowers, disorderly conduct and annoying passers-by." According to the SPCC, these girls were "some of the most notorious characters with which our city abounds, and have, no doubt, initiated more girls of

tender years into vice and immorality than many old offenders."
By 1879, however, the SPCC claimed to have all but eliminated
the child-beggars and flower-sellers from the city.

Frequently, the police justices of the city asked the SPCC to
investigate the home circumstances of children brought before
them. Thus, the Society was able to provide the court with social
information that helped it decide what to do with the children
before it, a practice which would become standard procedure in
the juvenile courts created a generation later. In 1892 the Society
supported a law which provided that children could be tried at
different times, "separate and apart from the trials of other criminal cases, of which session a separate docket and record shall be
kept." Although it did not require a separate court for juvenile
offenders, this law established the principle for such a court in
the State of New York.[16]

In 1877 the Society for the Prevention of Cruelty to Children
successfully supported a law against child-begging. This law also
prohibited children under fourteen from going into saloons or
dance-halls and in effect provided a modernized definition of juvenile delinquency. Children found begging or in saloons, dance-
halls, or houses of prostitution, or "found wandering and not having any home or settled place of abode, or proper guardianship or
visible means of subsistence," could be arrested and sent by the
court to various institutions such as the New York House of Refuge, the Juvenile Asylum, or the Catholic Protectory. The act also
provided that "no child under restraint or conviction, apparently
under the age of fourteen years shall be placed in any prison or
place of confinement, or in any courtroom or in any vehicle of
transportation to any place in company with adults charged with
or convicted of crime, except in the presence of the proper authorities." Although this act did not provide for the complete
separation of juvenile offenders from adult convicts, it did establish the principle of separating juveniles from adults—not just at
the end of the sequence of arrest, confinement, trial, and sentence,
but throughout the process. This, too, would be one of the basic
provisions of juvenile court laws in the next generation.[17]

One factor which made the tasks confronting the Society for the Prevention of Cruelty to Children more formidable was the fantastic population growth of the City of New York. Most of this increase came from immigration. By 1890, for example, New York and Brooklyn contained more foreign-born residents than any other city in the world. For the most part these newcomers crowded into ghettos and pressed on the available housing of the cities. They compounded the problems of the slum and tenement districts and added new tensions to the American urban environment.[18]

In 1911 the report of the famous Dillingham Commission on Immigration noted that

> of late years the general impression that owing to immigration the poorer districts of large cities are greatly overcrowded and even degrading has been so prevalent that it seemed desirable to make a thorough investigation on this question. . . . As was to be expected, many extremely pitiful cases of poverty and overcrowding were found, at times six or even more people sleeping in one room, sometimes without light or direct access to window or door to the open air. On the whole, however, the average conditions were found materially better than had been anticipated.

Nevertheless, most of the immigrants were unskilled or semi-skilled laborers, and most of them lived on the edge of poverty.[19]

Policemen, reformers, and philanthropists had long regarded immigrants as the chief source of crime and pauperism. In the decade before the Civil War, Chief Matsell, in his report on the vagrant children of New York, claimed that most of them were of Irish or German parentage, and Charles Loring Brace complained that immigrant families increased the "dangerous classes" of the city. It was easy to blame the immigrants for poverty and crime because they lived in the cheapest housing in the worst parts of the city. They crowded into ghettos which took on some of the characteristics of their residents' native countries. As they increased their wealth, however, these newcomers moved away from the poorer parts. Other groups, often of a different nationality, took their places. New York's Lower East Side clearly illustrated this pattern. In the years before the Civil War the area was predominantly Irish and German in population. After the War the Irish and Germans moved northward on Manhattan Island or over to Brooklyn. As the "new" immigration, which consisted of the peoples of southern and central Europe, began increasing, the Lower East Side changed from a German and Italian neighborhood to an Italian and Polish ghetto. The Italians formed the largest group in the "new" immigration, and like earlier immigrant groups they were accused of fostering more than their share of crime and poverty.[20]

Taken as a whole, immigrants, regardless of their native country, represented another challenge to American society and American culture. There is no statistical evidence to suggest that, as a group, the immigrants committed more crimes or had more illegitimate children, or became public charges more often than native-born Americans, but the children of immigrants were more likely to become juvenile delinquents or adult criminals than the children of native-born parents. This was true because the children of the foreign-born usually were in the lowest levels of society, where crime and misbehavior have always been more prevalent and because they had to adhere to two sets of values, those of the Old World culture of their parents and the mores and norms of American society. Thus, the influx of immigrants affected the increase of juvenile crime during the late nineteenth century in American cities; it also brought other problems—such as the "padrone" system.[21]

A *padrone* or entrepreneur would contract with the parents of a boy from one of the poorer provinces of Italy for a three-year indenture. The *padrone* then paid the parents a small sum and took the boy to the United States. In the larger cities of the United States hundreds of these little boys played musical instruments on the streets and begged money from passers-by. The *padrones* took all of the boys' earnings and often mistreated them. Relying on the child-begging law of 1874 the SPCC prosecuted a number of *padrones*, but this law proved ineffective. With the aid of the 1877 child-begging law and the cooperation of the Italian government, which passed regulatory legislation, the SPCC had, by the early 1880's, nearly succeeded in suppressing the *padrone* traffic. The campaign against the *padrones* illustrates the distinction society had drawn between self-employed children and those employed by others. In general, society romanticized the self-employed children—such as newsboys and bootblacks—as heroes in the great American dream of success. On the other hand, reformers were ready to move against employers who exploited children openly as the *padrones* did. Nevertheless, more than a generation would pass before society seriously considered the harmful effects of child labor on all children.[22]

The work of the Society for the Prevention of Cruelty to Children and that of older organizations like the Children's Aid Society and the Association for Improving the Condition of the Poor increased the city's awareness of its neglected and delinquent children, but these agencies sometimes seemed to be working without coordination or cooperation. The panic of 1873 and the depression which followed, when combined with the tremendous increase in population in the City of New York led to a burden on the city's charities that proved impossible to meet.

In 1869 the various charities of London had joined to form the London Society for Organizing Charitable Relief and Repressing Mendicancy. This organization provided the model for similar unifications of charities in American cities. Charities in New Haven and Philadelphia formed Charity Organization Societies in 1878. Boston followed in 1879 and New York in 1882.[23]

These societies sought to make giving more effective and to make sure that only the deserving received aid. The leaders of the societies thought that by combining their forces they might succeed in eliminating poverty and crime from American cities. In short, the main purpose of the Charity Organization Societies was to rid the city of the "dangerous classes." To mount an attack against the forces of evil and degradation, the leaders felt that they had to be businesslike. That is, they would grant relief only if an investigation showed that such relief was needed, and they would, like scientists, gather the information necessary to make such a judgment with great care. Thus, they were engaged in "scientific philanthropy." Two aspects of their activities made the Charity Organization Societies significant in the development of nineteenth-century America's response to juvenile delinquency: their stress on the individual case, and the premium they placed on cooperation and coordination among relief-giving agencies.[24]

IV

The period between the Civil War and the turn of the century witnessed considerable public debate about the continuing problem of juvenile delinquency, but with the exception of the Society for the Prevention of Cruelty to Children, it saw the creation of no new agencies for children. The debate about juvenile delinquency indicated that the public was beginning to realize that the traditional explanation of crime and pauperism was inadequate. The idea that people freely chose a life of crime or yielded to pauperism because of a lack of moral fibre began to give way to a growing awareness of the operation of social factors in causing such deviant behavior. Nevertheless, charity workers and philanthropists tried to check the growth of poverty and crime with individualized investigations and case study methods, which they called "scientific philanthropy."

Before the Civil War people, such as Theodore Parker and Charles Loring Brace, who appreciated the important contribution of social factors to deviant behavior were comparatively rare, and often they seemed to reject the full implications of such a view. Brace regarded the city as an evil place and urged the poor to escape its clutches, but when the poor remained, he returned to the moral exhortation which was the standard approach to the "dangerous classes" for philanthropists of the traditional school. After the war, the Association for Improving the Condition of the Poor, the Children's Aid Society, and other charities began to collect evidence that pointed to the magnitude of the problems among the lower classes of New York; and the public came to appreciate, although only in a vague, general way, that there was a link between the growing population, slums, tenements, and filth and such problems as crime, poverty, and disease.

This increasing awareness of the complexity of causes for deviant behavior included an erosion of the view that juvenile delinquents were young people who committed offenses as a result of a free choice. It led further to the view, best expressed by Brace, that the prevention of juvenile delinquency might be a better method of reducing crime and pauperism than the reformation of juvenile delinquents. This question, whether reformation or prevention was the best approach, was the central issue for people who worked with juvenile delinquents in the late nineteenth century. Philanthropists, reformers, and officials of reform schools and houses of refuge argued about the effectiveness of institutions for juvenile delinquents and whether or not "placing-out" the neglected and dependent children of the city really prevented juvenile crime. While these men were arguing, however, the American people had come to see that a wide variety of evils might lead to juvenile delinquency. They joined in crusades against dime novels and read Anthony Comstock's *Traps for the Young*. They worried about the gangs in New York and puzzled over the troubles of the New York House of Refuge. They applauded when Charles Loring Brace proclaimed that his Society was clearing the streets of juvenile vagabonds and when Elbridge Gerry pressed for the exclusion of juveniles from saloons, theaters, and houses of ill fame. Their ideas about the nature of children probably changed as well. They now found realistic, believable children in novels and stories, and there were even books like *Huck Finn* and *Peck's Bad Boy* about somewhat disreputable children. They could add the grim facts about life in the tenements and slums, which came from the *Annual Reports* of agencies like the AICP, from the columns of the daily newspapers, and from their own fleeting experiences with the children of the street—the bedraggled and begrimed newsboys and the pathetic flower girls—to the fictional characters in the realistic novels and begin to appreciate the miseries of life for children, particularly for homeless children, in a great city. Despite all of this, however, a flat, highly romanticized view of child life persisted. The independent, self-reliant hero of Elizabeth Oakes Smith's *The Newsboy* dominated the public mind and the *Annual Reports* of the Children's Aid Society. Even the Gerry Society did not move against self-employment when it sought to eliminate the exploitation of children by the *padrones*.[25]

Nevertheless the successful campaign by the Society for the Prevention of Cruelty to Children against the *padrones*, the creation of the Society itself, and the continued existence of a variety of institutions designed to aid, reform, or care for problem children prove that Americans in the late nineteenth century did not lack compassion for such children. But by later standards they did not understand children or the mainsprings of human motivation and behavior, and as a result their efforts were inadequate to meet the challenges of the period. They were beginning, however, to see the slums and the tenement as alien elements in the American environment. As mounting waves of immigrants poured into the United States, the agencies for assimilating these newcomers into American life, for transmitting American culture to them, became overloaded and then ceased to function. Consequently crime and pauperism, both anathema to American culture, increased. Before the War the cities had had slums, which showed that the process of cultural transmission was not perfect, but in that era the attractions of the vast American continent and the sparse population drew enough of the immigrants away from the coastal cities to keep the slums from growing too rapidly.

Juvenile delinquency was a symptom of this failure of cultural transmission among the lower classes in large cities, and in the late nineteenth century Americans tried a number of new remedies for this social defect, the most notable of which were the settlement house and the juvenile court.

9

Zebulon Brockway and William R. George:
The Older Delinquent

In 1870 at the annual meeting of the National Prison Association, the superintendent of the Detroit House of Correction, Zebulon R. Brockway, read a paper "The Ideal Prison System for a State" in which he recommended the use of an indeterminate sentence. The basic idea of such a sentence was that a convict's behavior, his "reformation," would determine the length of his stay in prison. Among the fifteen reasons Brockway gave for adopting such a plan was that "it utilizes for reformatory ends, what, though ever the strongest motive, is now the greatest hindrance to reformation, in the mind of prisoners, viz: the love of liberty, or the desire to be released." He also argued that the indeterminate sentence "removes the occasion and so mollifies the feeling of animosity usually felt towards the law and its officers." It put "the personal interest of the prisoner plainly in line with obedience to rules," and thereby made "safe and simple the disciplinary department." [1]

Brockway, who had been born in 1827 at Lyme, Connecticut, entered prison work as a guard at the Connecticut State Prison at Wethersfield in 1848. Writing about his childhood, Brockway recalled that as a boy he had gone to look at a "giant insane

Negro" who had been "chained to the center of a vacant room awaiting the dilatory unorganized action of the town authorities." The Negro seized the boy, but before he could do anything, passers-by rescued the young Brockway. "This insane man, the damage he had done and manifestly was liable to do," Brockway wrote, "showed the need of systematic, effective care and treatment of dangerous individuals."

Soon after he started work as a guard at the Wethersfield Prison, Brockway became the clerk; and his duties now included bringing in convicted and sentenced prisoners from the county jails to the State Prison. "It now seems almost incredible," he recalled, "that, stripling as I was, I should have been sent on those country road journeys, which often extended to late evening hours, unarmed, without an attendant guard, yet conveying at one time several prisoners to serve long, even life sentences." Brockway remained at Wethersfield until 1851, when he moved to the Albany County Penitentiary at the request of the warden there, Amos Pillsbury. In 1853–54 Brockway served a year as the superintendent of the Municipal and County Almshouse at Albany. In 1854 he became the superintendent at the Monroe County Penitentiary where he remained until 1861. Here for the first time Brockway questioned his determination to spend his life in prison work. As he explained, "belief was prevalent that every good must come mysteriously and directly from the supernatural source. More and more the chaplain preached and prayed and redoubled his persuasiveness; yet no miraculous changes were manifested." Not only were the prisoners unaffected by all of this clerical labor, but Brockway himself seemed unable to do anything constructive for the prisoners. "I seemed powerless," he recalled, "either to originate or support measures for reclamation or restraint from fresh crimes when soon again they must be released."

Because of this depression, Brockway gladly accepted the offer to manage a new institution in Detroit, which was supposed to concentrate on young offenders between the ages of sixteen and twenty-one. The 1861 law under which such prisoners were to be transferred from the State Prison to the Detroit House of Correction proved, however, to be unconstitutional, and Brockway did not work with young offenders in Detroit. While at the Detroit House of Correction, Brockway's most notable activity was his effort to win support for the principle of the indeterminate sentence. In 1869 he drafted the bill which became Michigan's "three-years law." This law required the sentencing to the Detroit House of Correction for a period of three years of every woman over the age of fifteen convicted as a common prostitute. According to Brockway, "immediately upon the enactment of the law and its publication in the newspapers there was an exodus of disorderly women from Detroit and the populous cities of the state." While such women could be sentenced to the House of Correction, the purpose of the law was to secure their reformation by making their early release conditional on evidence of that reformation.

In 1870 Brockway presented to the Michigan legislature the draft of a bill designed to extend the principle of the "three-years law" to all offenders, but this bill did not pass. In that same year Brockway read his paper before the National Prison Conference meeting in Cincinnati. In the following year a full-scale investigation of the finances of the House of Correction—instigated by an alderman seeking publicity—resulted in a complete exoneration of Brockway's management. This investigation in addition to the failure of the indeterminate sentence bill in the legislature convinced Brockway that there was little chance for his ideas to win support in Detroit, and so he resigned as superintendent of the House of Correction in 1872. Brockway spent nearly two years in private business before the effects of the Panic of 1873 forced him out.

II

In May, 1876, Zebulon Brockway received a telegram from Louis Pillsbury, the son of Amos Pillsbury, offering him the position as superintendent of the unfinished New York State Reformatory at Elmira. This institution, created in response to petitions signed by a number of prominent citizens of New York, took shape in legislation over an eight-year period. An 1869 law provided for the selection of a site; in 1870 the legislature authorized the creation of a building commission. In 1874 a building superintendent succeeded the building commission, and in 1876 the Board of Managers took over the administration of the unfinished reformatory. Louis Pillsbury became the president of the Board of Managers and persuaded the other members to employ Brockway. The first prisoners arrived in 1876, but the laws governing the reformatory proved inadequate, and the legislature passed Brockway's draft of an indeterminate sentence law in 1876.

After he had become superintendent at Elmira, Brockway established a system which sought "the modification of character by rational means and methods." What this meant in practice was that prisoners found that good, or cooperative behavior led to tangible benefits and a shorter stay in the reformatory. Such behavior, Brockway argued, was no accident. "This great reformatory with its large expenditures," he wrote, "either reclaims criminals or intensifies them; by it society is protected or crimes are multiplied with fearful progression." In order to avoid multiplying criminality Brockway contended that "the good must be actually accomplished and the most important difference of results depends very largely upon discipline." Brockway explained his ideas about discipline very carefully: "Neither coddling, nor undue severity should characterize the discipline, but since new habits must be formed, a high standard of behavior is essential, which can only be maintained by most minute regulations, very complete supervision, with wise and vigorous management." Such an approach was not retributive but was designed "to recover the criminals one by one from the turbulent, predatory class, to orderly, industrious citizens." [2]

Brockway's approach at Elmira recalls the practice of juvenile reformatories on the congregate plan. Like their officers, Brockway placed great emphasis on cooperative behavior as evidence of "reformation," but where they stressed moral regeneration as well as correct behavior, he argued that only the actions of a prisoner were significant. It was a new principle of penology, he explained, "that the state shall not judge the heart's intentions, and not judging or knowing, shall not designedly trespass on the mystical field of the soul's moral relations; but instead shall remain devoted to the regulation of the prisoner's conduct with sole regard to the public security." Brockway appreciated the possibility that the public might be uneasy about an approach that appeared to be lacking an emphasis on the true morality of the heart. He argued that his system, despite its behavioral stress, led to a genuine reformation. The indeterminate sentence, similar to those which confined juvenile delinquents to reform schools, was "irksome" to prisoners, but they soon learned that their conduct determined the length of their stay. The public naturally feared that this would lead to the kind of "institutional piety" which Charles Loring Brace had criticized as being characteristic of juvenile reformatories. But the focus on release, Brockway said, made good conduct "a motive equivalent to that of the fixed idea." The system worked a genuine reformation because "habitual careful attention with accompanying expectancy and appropriate execution and resultant clarified vision constitute a habitus not consistent with criminal tendencies." [3]

This emphasis on the external, observable behavior of the convicts was a fundamental change in American penology. Until the creation of the New York State Reformatory at Elmira, the dominant mode of thinking about crime and punishment had stressed the spiritual reformation of the offender through silence and penitence. The chief institution in this mode was the penitentiary, literally, a place for penitence. When the Pennsylvania system, which provided for solitary confinement, failed to have the desired effects, and indeed when it seemed to drive its inmates insane, American penologists compromised with the Auburn plan. This approach retained the basic idea of the traditional school—that the inmate should reflect on his crimes and sins and seek penitence and spiritual reformation. Under the Auburn plan inmates slept in solitary cells where the mind and spirit could work their reformation, but worked during the day in groups. According to Brockway, reformation was no longer a matter of mind and spirit; it depended on the inmate's behavior.[4]

In part Brockway's innovation had come from institutions for juvenile delinquents. Perhaps the best example of an early behavioral approach would be that devised by the Reverend E. M. P. Wells at the Boston House of Reformation. Under Wells's system good conduct led to rewards—more privileges and clear recognition from the group. Furthermore, at the House of Reformation Wells regarded a record of good conduct as evidence of reformation. In spite of this stress on behavior, early juvenile reformatories remained heavily influenced by the traditional school with its emphasis on the rational free will of man. While such institutions used a behavioral model to evaluate the characters of their inmates, their managers tried to judge the true moral character of their charges. Finally, in addition to their behavioral procedures—usually a combination of work and school—juvenile reformatories also stressed religious and moral exhortations as means of character building. No one thought to extend the behavioral model, even with its character-building moral and religious emphases, to adult criminals because most penologists believed that adults lacked the capacity for moral improvement possessed by children whose minds and characters remained plastic.[5]

Curiously, Brockway did not acknowledge his debt to American juvenile institutions for the indeterminate sentence and the behavioral approach. Instead he cited the practices of Recorder Matthew Davenport Hill as well as the work of Alexander Maconochie and Sir Walter Crofton in England. Crofton's Irish system anticipated in most respects the system used by Brockway at Elmira, but the practices of American juvenile reformatories preceded that of Crofton.[6]

According to Brockway, what made the extension of the practices of juvenile institutions to a reformatory for adults possible was the development of the sciences of human behavior. As he explained, during the last three decades of the nineteenth century "better biological and moral conceptions, largely due to the investigations and publications of Charles Darwin, enabled the enactment of more rational criminal laws." Throughout his tenure as superintendent of the New York State Reformatory at Elmira, Brockway stressed the "scientific" nature of his system. The purpose of the new penology, he contended, was the "education of the whole man, his capacity, his habits and tastes, by a rational procedure whose central motive and law of development is found in the industrial economies." [7]

Brockway and the Elmira Reformatory soon gained an international reputation, and in 1891 Havelock Ellis called the system there an "epoch-making movement" in "the practical treatment of criminals." Sometimes the public confused the Elmira Reformatory with juvenile reform schools, despite Brockway's efforts to remind them that such was not the case. "This reformatory," he wrote,

> should not be classed as one of the juvenile reformatories. Such a conception of it is erroneous. The prisoners here are not children, nor are they, properly speaking, "boys," a term so often inappropriately applied to them. The reformatory is a prison, a reformatory prison, certainly, but nevertheless a prison for adult offenders. The prisoners are males, having been convicted and sentenced for offenses punishable by imprisonment, and are therefore felons. The committing age is between 16 and 30 years. The average age is 21 years. [8]

Nevertheless, the New York State Reformatory was, like the juvenile reform schools, attempting to remedy the problem of criminality by means of a behavioral approach.

Both types of institutions, then, sought to remedy a cultural flaw, a failure in the process of transmitting the standards and norms of acceptable social behavior. The Elmira Reformatory hoped "to recover the criminals one by one from the turbulent, predatory class," and make them into "orderly, industrious citizens." The fact that inmates were in the reformatory proved that they had some flaw in their character. Brockway asserted that "imprisoned felons are defective; their crimes show this. They

were out of adjustment with their environment rather than that
their environment was exceptionally unfavorable for their good
behavior." Thus, like the houses of refuge, the reform schools, and
the children's aid societies, the New York State Reformatory at
Elmira was trying to remedy cultural flaws. In many respects its
approach was similar to that of the early congregate institutions
for juvenile delinquents with their stress on the efficiency of education as a means of transmitting values and mores. The Elmira
Reformatory, however, was less concerned with transmitting cultural values as such and sought, instead, to develop the habits of
acceptable behavior. Thus, the Elmira Reformatory illustrated a
growing awareness and application of what would later be called
behavioral psychology.[9]

III

Mary Carpenter, the Englishwoman who had devoted her life to
the reformation of juvenile delinquents and the prevention of
juvenile delinquency, visited the United States in 1873 and studied
American prisons and reformatories. She found them organized
almost exclusively on the congregate system and having the character of "juvenile gaols." The use of the family system in juvenile
reformatories was growing, however, and at least one significant
modification of that system had appeared in the United States.[10]

In 1890 a New York businessman, William R. George, took a
group of the city's slum children to his farm near Freeville, New
York, for the summer. The excursion, which had been aided by
the Fresh Air Fund of the *New York Tribune*, was for the purpose
of giving the children a taste of wholesome country life. George
continued these excursions for the next four summers, but became increasingly discouraged by the behavior of the children.
"Little by little," George recalled,

> I came to the conclusion that the work was doing harm rather
> than good. I noted, reluctantly, that my young people were
> started on a false plane, that one and all of them were reckoning
> their good time according to the amount of clothing and general

produce that they might be able to take back to the city upon
their return. I felt certain that they were claiming charity as a
right; that each day that they lived under that system they
were being pauperized.

George decided to make his young "guests" pay with work for
what they received and issued a series of rules for conduct. There
would be no smoking, gambling, stealing, or fighting, he said, but
George found these rules easier to issue than to enforce. He decided to institute a system of jury trial for violation of the rules,
and he gave the court the power to assess fines of labor for offenses.[11]

George had hired adult supervisors to oversee the activity of
the children, but one day one of them fell ill, and so George appointed "Banjo," one of the older boys, in the supervisor's place.
Banjo proved to be a better leader than the adult, and George
kept him at the job. That winter George decided to extend the
principle of self-government to his "visitors," and at the end of
the next summer he made the arrangement a year-long operation.
He allowed the boys to make and enforce their own laws, and in
addition he required them to work for their food. The resulting
system he called the "George Junior Republic." This new approach, begun in 1895, proved more successful than any previous
system, but there were still too many adults. In 1896 all the adults
were removed from the structure of the Republic except George,
who remained as permanent president. The next year he stepped
aside, and boys held all the offices in the Republic.[12]

The George Junior Republic was a community of boys, having
a President, a Senate, a House of Representatives, and various administrative officials. The laws of the State of New York were the
laws of the Republic, except where they had been amended by
the Republic's legislature. George retained control of all property
and wealth. The boys worked for half a day and spent the remainder in school. George paid them in special Republic money
for their labor, and with it the boys had to pay for their food
and lodging. They lived in cottages, whose accommodations ranged
in quality from the low of the "Beanery" to the luxury of the

"Waldorf." If a boy lost his money or spent it foolishly, he had to go to the jail for food and lodging. The next day he had to break rocks for three hours to pay for his meal.[13]

Nearly everything at the Republic was done on the contract system. Entrepreneurs would sign contracts with George for a certain amount of work, round up a gang of laborers—who had to be paid out of the proceeds of the contract—and then the entrepreneur would supervise the work. Even school lessons made use of the system. The teacher would offer a contract for an assignment or report, and then a group of boys would contract to prepare it. There would be fines for discrepancies or if the completed work were not neat and legible.[14]

The Republic concentrated on older boys; citizenship in the Republic was limited to boys from sixteen to twenty-one years old. Clearly, George hoped to create a miniature version of society, which functioned in exact correlation to the tenents of the self-help gospel. Hard work and frugality led to ease and comfort, while laziness and unwise spending led to a harsh life and even punishment. The fact that offenses against the laws of the Republic drew the same punishment as lack of money indicated that the equation of poverty and crime in late nineteenth-century America remained a viable assumption. George believed that his boys learned three things at the Republic: the necessity and dignity of labor, respect for the law, and the duties of a responsible citizen. The boys learned these lessons well, he would argue, because they learned them from practical experience.[15]

Although a good many of the boys at the George Republic were committed there by the courts, there were some who had been brought by their parents. Unlike other institutions such as the New York Juvenile Asylum, the George Junior Republic accepted boys of all kinds. "There are bad boys," George once said, "mighty bad ones, too, and the badder they are the better I like to get them in the Republic." He explained that "the boy who has sufficient energy and impetus to be aggressively bad has in him the stuff from which good public citizens are made. We take the misspent energy and transform it to serve some useful end, by means of the boy being responsible for his own badness, and the gradual training of his moral nature to the ideas of Democracy." In time George came to have imitators, and by 1910 similar institutions had appeared in Maryland, Pennsylvania, New Jersey, Connecticut, and California.[16]

The question of the age of juvenile delinquents remains a perplexing one, and there is considerable variation as to the ages to which juvenile jurisdiction applies today. When the New York House of Refuge appeared, its supporters regarded juveniles as children under the age of twenty-one for boys and eighteen for girls, but they soon learned that older boys were much more difficult to reform than the younger ones. Consequently, later institutions such as the New York Juvenile Asylum and Brace's Children's Aid Society sought to distinguish between older and younger juvenile delinquents and confine their attention to the younger groups. Thus the older offenders found themselves treated as adults in criminal matters, although in civil law they remained infants who were not responsible for their contracts. The George Junior Republic and the New York State Reformatory at Elmira were two institutions which appeared specifically for these forgotten young people.

The George Junior Republic was a radically different experiment in the effort to find ways to transmit American culture to those whose actions made it clear that they had not learned acceptable forms of behavior. George's solution was to create a microcosm of American society in which the values of the self-help gospel were strongly reinforced. The Elmira Reformatory sought by slightly different means to inculcate the same values. At the George Junior Republic, proper behavior—hard work—led to tangible rewards; at Elmira, proper behavior—cooperation—led to the inmate's release. In both places the inmates "learned" a more acceptable social behavior than they had previously demonstrated.

Such an emphasis on external behavior contrasted significantly with earlier emphases on the spiritual nature of man and the need for penitence and moral regeneration. Under the old system, before a convict could be said to have reformed he was expected to show some signs of repentance. The new system only asked the convict to cooperate. In effect the new system shows that American society had come to rely more on empirical observation, in this case the observation of human behavior, than on religion.

10

The Ladies of Chicago and the Creation of the Juvenile Court

In one of the regular courtrooms of the County Court Building in Chicago, a new and unusual court had been meeting since the first of July, 1899. This new court, the Juvenile Court of Cook County, met twice a week, and on those days the room was usually jammed. Sometimes it was so crowded that the people spilled out into the corridor and pressed beyond the low rail at the front. Those waiting were all adults: anxious mothers and fathers, probation officers, one or two reporters, witnesses, and an occasional curious spectator. The children whose cases were to be heard remained in a clerk's room at the rear. They came in one by one escorted by an officer of the court as the clerk called their cases.

The Juvenile Court heard from sixty to eighty cases a day; consequently the judge could devote only a little time to each child. The court heard dependency cases in the morning and delinquency cases in the afternoon. To the casual visitor the physical arrangement of the room, the somewhat formal procedure, and the officers seemed no different from any other court; but if the visitor remained he would notice several significant differences. All of the cases concerned children, and when the judge talked to the children, his manner was quite different from that of the judges of the criminal courts. A visitor to the court observed that when the judge "talks with the little dependents or delinquents, he is not avenging Justice, with the scales in one hand and the sword in the other. He calls the youngster up beside him, pats him on the head, and in quite the ordinary tone of voice asks 'why did you do this son?' " [1]

Just over three years after the Illinois Juvenile Court law had gone into effect, the first judge of that court, Richard S. Tuthill, recalled the way he conducted that court. "I have always felt and endeavored to act in each case," he said, "as I would were it my own son who was before me in my library at home, charged with some misconduct." First the judge talked briefly with the child and tried to convince him that the court's purpose was not "to punish but rather to befriend and help." The court represented "the good people of the state" who were interested in his future. The judge hoped that the child also paid attention to his remarks, since he would be more sympathetic to the purpose of the proceedings if he understood what was going on. "The point of the inquiry," the judge continued, was "not to find out whether . . . [the child] has done an act which in an adult, would be a crime, and to punish him for that." Instead the judge tried to determine from the facts surrounding a supposed offense whether or not the child before him was "in a condition of delinquency." If he was, then the state could "enter upon the exercise of its parental care over the child." The judge placed most of the delinquents who came before him on probation; that is, they returned to their homes but found their activities supervised by an officer of the court.[2]

When the backers of the first juvenile court began their efforts, their main concern had been to keep juvenile delinquents from coming into contact with adult criminals. The law which established the juvenile court did a great deal more than that. It provided for a new and unique institution—clearly the most important agency to deal with juvenile delinquents created in the nineteenth century.

II

By 1890 more than a million people lived in Chicago. Ten years
before fewer than half that number had been there. The parents
of most of the population (77.9 per cent) had been born outside
the United States. Almost every foreign country imaginable had
its representatives there, but the larger groups were the Germans,
the Irish, the Scandinavians, the Scots, and the English. Substantial numbers of Italians, Poles, Slovaks, Czechs, and Greeks
also made their home in Chicago. A good many of the foreign-
born had come from the countryside, and they faced the double
difficulties of city life and a strange culture. Their children often
found themselves split between two cultures, the generalized
American culture of the school and the old-world values of their
parents.[3]

The cultural conflict faced by the child of immigrant parents
sometimes forced the child into delinquency. Jane Addams wrote
of a Polish boy "whose earnings were all given to his father who
gruffly refused all requests for pocket money." At Christmas his
two little sisters begged him for presents, and he tried to steal a
manicure set and a string of beads. The house detective caught
him before he left the store. These strict, old-world miserly
parents not only took all the money their working sons and daughters earned; they also sent the younger children out to pick up
coal from the railroad tracks or grain from the cars. The parents,
who had no criminal intentions, were honestly ignorant of American law and could not understand why their children were arrested. Many delinquent children became so because they abandoned their homes. They left because of their parents' strict ways
and because there was no fun at home. Then there were the
gangs of immigrant youth whose contempt for their parents found
expression in defiant and anti-social activities. When the children
learned English and the parents did not, the parents became
dependent on their children in the new society. Sometimes this
situation contributed to the delinquent behavior, because it gave

the young "an undue sense of their own importance and a false security" that they could "take care of themselves." [4]

In the 1890's most of the juveniles arrested by the police in Chicago were the children of immigrants, but the children of American-born parents also found the temptations of a large and growing city difficult to resist. The city itself was a cheerless, monotonous place, and the diversions and amusements it offered served more to encourage delinquent behavior than to prevent it. In *Youth and the City Streets* Jane Addams commented on the "inveterate demand of youth that life shall afford a large element of excitement." She continued, "May we not assume that this love of excitement, this desire for adventure is basic and will be evinced by each generation of city boys as a challenge to their elders." But the love of excitement had few free legal outlets in Chicago, and boys often found themselves branded as delinquents as a result of their pursuit of excitement. There were other factors in the city as well, the very conditions of life itself, which encouraged juvenile law-breaking. A probation officer, whose duties required her to know how her young charges lived, wrote about those conditions. "Here sandwiched between the brothel and the saloon, underneath the same roof, are stairways and dark passages leading to tenements where children are housed but not homed. They flit in and out, see sights and hear sounds," she continued, "that would startle you and burden your hearts. These are the children who hear a thousand calls to vice where they listen to the merest whisperings of virtue." [5]

In Chicago in the last decade of the nineteenth century there were for all practical purposes no specialized institutions for juvenile delinquents. When the police caught a child violating the law, they treated him just as they would treat an adult. They took the young offender to a neighborhood police court, where a magistrate set bail. If the youngster could not provide the bail money, he went to a cell in the police station to await his trial before a police justice. In the cells of the police station no effort was made to separate children from criminals of all types. Most of the offenses committed by juveniles fell into the category of petty crimes. In such cases the police justices usually assessed a small fine or a brief period of imprisonment in the City House of Correction or Bridewell. Because of a child's age, however, the police justice often simply let him go. If the offense committed by a juvenile were serious, his case might be referred to the grand jury for indictment. Boys held over for the grand jury were sent to the Cook County Jail, where there was a separate department for them and a school. Every month about fifteen cases involving children went to the grand jury. According to an assistant state's attorney, most of the offenses charged against juveniles were cases of "burglary, petty depredations upon freight cars, candy or bake shops, or stealing pigeons or rabbits from barns, hoodlum acts that, in the country, would be considered boyish pranks rather than a crime." Because of the youth of the accused who came before it, the grand jury regularly refused to indict 75 per cent of the juvenile cases which it heard.[6]

The leniency on the part of the police justices and the grand jury had an unfortunate effect, however. The boy who had been turned loose had learned that he could probably escape prosecution or punishment for his offense because of his youth. His stay at the police station had brought him in contact with adult criminals, and he had probably picked up a certain amount of "badness," which "he curled under his tongue as a choice morsel." After his release he "retailed it to his companions, thus spreading the infection and starting other youths on the same path of crime in which he had himself left several footprints." Once a child found himself in the City Bridewell it was still possible for him to escape the full punishment. About one-third of the boys sent to the Bridewell secured "pardons" through the machinations of an alderman. These pardons were usually political favors and depended on the influence of the boy's parents.[7]

Chicago's children were not completely forgotten or ignored, but it seemed that way. When the British journalist, William T. Stead, wrote in *If Christ Came to Chicago* about the visit he had made there in 1893, he placed America's second city "very near the bottom" in the protection of juvenile offenders from the contamination of adult offenders. "There is very little reverence for children in Chicago," he remarked. "Messenger boys not more than fourteen years of age, go in and out of the police cells every hour of the night gaining an intimacy with the drunken and debased classes, which can hardly be said to tend towards edification." Furthermore "mere lads of the same age make a regular tour through the houses of ill-fame, selling newspapers on Fourth Avenue." Indeed it was not "thought undesirable that such young children should be introduced so early to the abominations of a great city." Nevertheless some Chicagoans were trying to halt the increase in delinquency. Stead praised the efforts of the Waif's Mission to eliminate juvenile vagrancy. The Chicago Visitation and Aid Society, a Catholic charity, likewise worked with the children of the streets. In 1891 the Visitation and Aid Society drew up a bill designed to legalize more active and far-reaching efforts by private agencies in behalf of troubled children. Representative Joseph O'Donnell introduced the bill, House No. 433, in February, 1891, and it was referred to the Judiciary Committee. Awkwardly labeled "a bill for an act to authorize corporations not for pecuniary profit to manage, care and provide for children who may be abandoned, neglected, destitute or subjected to perverted training," it provided for the commitment of such children to child-saving agencies under the supervision of the county courts. The bill failed to become a law.[8]

The Chicago Woman's Club also tried to do something about juvenile delinquency—particularly about the increase that seemed apparent as the end of the nineteenth century approached. In 1888 the Club addressed a petition calling for the enforcement of the 1883 Illinois compulsory education law. They cited "the appalling increase of crime among youth, the large numbers of vagrant children, and the employment of child labor in the city of Chicago" as part of a situation "fraught with danger to the commonwealth" which had resulted from the board's failure to compel children to attend school.[9]

The Woman's Club had long worked to improve conditions in the Cook County Jail and the House of Correction. The members persuaded the authorities to add matrons to the jail staff and took over the maintenance of a jail school for boys which Mrs. Dennison Groves had established. In 1892 the Jail Committee of the Woman's Club had recommended the creation of a separate court for children, but this recommendation did not lead to any real effort by the Club to secure a juvenile court. The Club did help to secure a manual training school—later called the John Worthy School—in the House of Correction. This school was the only facility to which juvenile delinquent boys could be sentenced in the city of Chicago, and it was located within an adult penal institution. Compared with large eastern cities like New York and Boston, the facilities provided for the treatment of juvenile delinquents in Chicago in the 1890's were very inadequate.[10]

The education and child labor reformers, people like Florence Kelley, for example, in Chicago persuaded the Illinois legislature to pass a new compulsory education law in 1889. When the Chicago Board of Education enforced this law in the 1890's, a number of "incorrigible" children came into the schools, but the schools soon expelled them because of their unruliness. The critics of the Board said that the plight of these children showed the effects of the failure to enforce the earlier compulsory education law, and the superintendent recommended the creation of a special "parental" school for the young miscreants who were unfit for the regular schools. The 1892 report of the Chicago Board of Education contained an argument in favor of such a school. "The statistics of the Police Court, the County Jail and Bridewell," the Board said, "show a large number of children who annually become violators of the law, and are placed under arrest." These children become public charges, "supported at public expense in a building built by public taxes and they are cared for and watched by paid officers." The children "have become criminals and a charge upon the city or county by somebody's neglect." In conclusion the Board recommended a new and specialized institution where delinquent and neglected children could receive "training and instruction that will lead them to habits of cleanliness, order, submission to authority, and a useful life." This continued to be the position of the Chicago Board of Education until 1902, when the Chicago Parental School opened.[11]

The handling of juvenile delinquents in Chicago involved the use of all the regular penal machinery provided by the laws of the State of Illinois. For all practical purposes Illinois criminal law treated children over ten years of age as adults. If a young person between the ages of ten and sixteen was detected in a violation of the law, he would be taken to a police court where the police justice could do one of three things with him: release him outright, fine him, or transfer him to the county jail to be presented to the grand jury. If the justice assessed a fine, and the boy could not pay, he had to serve out his fine in the Cook County House of Correction or Bridewell. At the House of Correction there was a separate boys' department which included the John Worthy School. If the boy were transferred to the jail he also found a boys' department and a school. The grand jury might indict a youngster and have him bound over for trial in the regular county courts; and these courts, if they found the boy guilty of a felony, could sentence him to the Illinois State Reform School at Pontiac. The only institution or agency not designed for adults and not used for the handling of adults in this entire process was the Reform School at Pontiac. It was, however, little more than a juvenile prison. It was organized on the congregate principle, and by law received only convicted felons under the age of sixteen. The separate departments for boys in the Cook County Jail and the House of Correction were simply divisions within the regular adult institutions.[12]

In 1895 Mrs. Lucy L. Flower, a leading member of the Woman's Club of Chicago, went to Massachusetts to study that state's approaches to the problem of juvenile delinquency. She paid particular attention to the probation system which had been in operation for more than twenty-five years, and when she returned she began an effort to secure similar legislation for Illinois. After a series of meetings to study the laws of other states pertaining to children, a committee of the Chicago Woman's Club drew up a bill which provided for a separate children's court and probation for juvenile offenders. Because the legal advisers to the Woman's

Club thought this bill was unconstitutional, it was never presented to the Legislature.

The Woman's Club did not give up on its efforts, and the members found a number of allies—the Illinois State Board of Charities, various prominent citizens, and the principal child-helping societies in the city of Chicago. The Chicago Bar Association agreed to help draft a better juvenile court bill. "Neither the State, the county nor city," the Cook County grand jury said in May, 1898, "has provided a suitable or proper place where, under humane and intelligent guidance, these little offenders can be helped along their rough paths." Although the grand jury did not recommend the creation of a separate court for children, it did conclude: "Any plan of improvement which does not include the speedy examination of a boy who has offended against the law, or is homeless, by a proper court . . . will fail to bring about the improvement that is so urgently needed." [13]

Shortly after the grand jury issued its condemnation of the institutions for delinquent boys in Cook County, the Chicago Woman's Club renewed its efforts to improve the John Worthy School. At a February, 1897, meeting the members of the Club decided to appeal to the Mayor of Chicago to help them have the cells removed from the school. Angry because the City Council had already appropriated money to plan the school on a dormitory system, the ladies resolved to try "feminine persuasion" first on the Mayor, and if that failed to use "argumentation." Less than a week after this meeting the Woman's Club sent a petition about the John Worthy School to the Mayor. The petition recited the deficiencies of that school and argued that the children "in the city's care" ought to be "placed under elevating and not demoralizing influences." The ladies also felt that the children should be "handled as children and not as men" and that the children should be completely separated from adult offenders. The Woman's Club also decided to send delegates to the school regularly and to report on the conditions, "improved or otherwise."

In part because of the ladies' agitation the city of Chicago built new quarters on the grounds of the Bridewell for the John Worthy

School. The new building contained cells as well as dormitories, and as if to flaunt this fact in the faces of the members of the Woman's Club, the words "Cell House" were carved over one of the doors. The boys were transferred into the new building on June 30, 1899, and on the occasion there was a brief ceremony. At the conclusion of the dedication service the boys marched off "with folded arms" to their classrooms while singing "Just Break the News to Mother." [14]

III

The Chicago Woman's Club continued to push for a separate court for children. The entire program of the meeting of the Illinois State Conference of Charities held in November, 1898, was devoted to "the children of the State"; and several speakers, among them Frederick Howard Wines and Hastings H. Hart, advocated a special children's court. The delegates adopted a resolution instructing the Conference's committee on legislation to coordinate and support the various efforts to secure new laws favorable to children. The most important project then underway was the Woman's Club idea for a juvenile court. The project received added support when the Chicago Bar Association appointed a committee to consider drafting a bill for a children's court. The committee, which met for the first time in December, 1898, included Judge Harvey B. Hurd as chairman and Mrs. Lucy L. Flower of the Chicago Woman's Club, Miss Julia Lathrop of the State Board of Charities and Hull House, Timothy D. Hurley of the Visitation and Aid Society, and the prospective sponsor of the bill in the Legislature. The committee chose Hart as its secretary, and he prepared the first draft of the bill. Judge Hurd then revised the bill to make it legally acceptable, and the committee presented it to the public as the "Chicago Bar Association Bill." To explain the bill and win additional support for it, Mrs. Flower held a luncheon for the judges of the various Chicago courts in January, 1899.

A month later, February 7, 1899, Representative John C. Newcomer introduced the bill in the Illinois House of Representatives, where it was assigned to the Judiciary Committee. The bill, which was introduced in the Senate a week later, had no important opposition there; but the House Judiciary Committee hesitated to approve it. The Senate and House Judiciary Committees met in joint session to hear testimony on the bill; and Judge Harvey Hurd, Ephraim Banning of the Illinois State Board of Charities, and Timothy Hurley appeared to explain the proposed legislation. Finally, the Senate passed the bill and sent it to the House; the House voted to consider it out of regular order, and on the last day of the session, the bill passed. Governor John Tanner signed it on April 21, 1899, and the Juvenile Court Act became law on July 1, 1899.[15]

This new law, "an act to regulate the treatment and control of dependent, neglected and delinquent children," was the most important law pertaining to juvenile delinquents in the nineteenth century. Indeed, it remains the single most influential law concerning juvenile delinquents in the United States. It marked the end of the essentially penal official approach to juvenile delinquency and the beginning of the flexible "scientific" and preventive approach. The first section of the Act contained a standard and rather brief definition of juvenile delinquency. A "delinquent child" was "any child under the age of sixteen years" who violated "any law of this State or any city or village ordinance." The Act guaranteed the right of trial by jury, but a jury had to be requested. The Act gave jurisdiction to circuit and county courts, except in "counties having over 500,000 population," where it provided for a separate "Juvenile Court" with a separate docket and record and a specially assigned judge.[16]

Cases ordinarily would come before the court's having jurisdiction not by the usual procedure of arrest and arraignment, but through petitions. "Any respectable person," according to the act, "being resident in the county, having knoweldge of a child in his county who appears to be either neglected, dependent or delinquent, may file with the clerk of a court having jurisdiction in the matter a petition in writing, setting forth the facts, verified by affidavit." The court would then issue a summons ordering the parents or guardians of the child named in the petition to appear in court. When the police arrested a child under sixteen and took him before the magistrate, the magistrate was supposed to transfer the child to the juvenile court.[17]

The act gave the court broad powers to deal with both dependent and delinquent children. It could place dependent and neglected children in institutions or with individuals, who, in turn, could place the child in a suitable family home. It could place delinquent children in "the care and guardianship of a probation officer duly appointed by the court," and the child could then remain in his own home, "subject to the visitation of the probation officer." If the child's home were unsuitable, the court could place him in a foster home either permanently or temporarily. It could also "commit the child, if a boy to a training school for boys, or if a girl, to an industrial school for girls." In addition the court could send boys over ten to the State reformatory or girls over ten to the State Home for Juvenile Female Offenders. It could commit children to institutions only until they reached their majority.

Part of the Act pertained to institutions or agencies which received dependent and delinquent children. It required them to employ an agent to supervise and assist children paroled from the institutions. The Act also placed all such institutions under the supervision of the Illinois Board of State Commissioners of Public Charities. The State Board was supposed to visit and inspect the institution, and the institutions were supposed to send annual reports of their operations to the Board. Judges of courts having jurisdiction under the Act could send children only to institutions certified by the State Board.

The Act also regulated child-placing operations like that of the New York Children's Aid Society. It authorized the State Board to require guarantees before allowing out-of-state agencies to place children in Illinois, and it further prohibited the placement of children in Illinois who had "contagious or incurable" disease, or "any deformity," or who were "feeble of mind" or "of vicious char-

acter." Children who became public charges within five years of
their placement in Illinois were to be returned to the placing
agency, and families who accepted children from agencies which
had not complied with the law were to be fined.

The Illinois Juvenile Court Act was a comprehensive law on
most aspects of child welfare, and it incorporated the most recent
legislation on that topic. As such, it was not revolutionary—the
section on the creation of a juvenile court differed only slightly
from the laws of Massachusetts establishing separate trials for
young offenders. What did make the Illinois law important was
the last section:

> This act shall be liberally construed to the end that its purpose
> may be carried out, to wit: That the care, custody and discipline
> of a child shall approximate as nearly as may be that which
> should be given by its parents, and in all cases where it can
> properly be done the child placed in an improved family home
> and become a member of the family by legal adoption or
> otherwise.

This was on the one hand a clear statement that the juvenile
court would be an unusual legal institution. The act specifically
instructed the judge to construe its provisions "liberally." The
judge and the court were supposed to be flexible—perhaps in-
novative—and to work for the best interests of the child. And the
act defined the best interests of the child as being a "family
home," preferably that of his parents if their home was suitable.
The Illinois Juvenile Court Act was the last of nineteenth-century
America's innovations in the care of troubled children. Its provisions drew on a century of experience. The law's uniqueness
came from its spirit of experimentalism which contradicted the
rigid provision of the laws pertaining to juvenile delinquents in
most of the century. The law's provisions about the family home
embodied Charles Loring Brace's stress on the importance of the
family. Emphatically the law expressed the idea that the juvenile
delinquent deserved treatment separate and different from that
accorded adult criminals.

A Massachusetts law of 1870 had first embodied the principle of separate trials for juvenile offenders, and New York passed a similar act in 1892. Pennsylvania followed in 1893, but the law was held to be unconstitutional before it could go into effect. The main purpose behind the Illinois law had been to create a comprehensive, state-supervised child-caring system which would compare with that already in existence in Massachusetts. The Illinois law, however, went further and created a new institution, the juvenile court—an institution which applied the informal procedure and rules of equity jurisdiction to all children's cases. There was nothing new about following equity rules in the cases of *neglected* and *dependent* children. What was unique about the Illinois Juvenile Court Act was its application of equity jurisdiction to *delinquent* children.[18]

Among early writers on the juvenile court, there was a debate about its legal origins. Most of them traced the special powers of the juvenile court back to the English court of chancery, but a few regarded the court, when it dealt with juvenile delinquents, as being essentially a modification of the criminal courts. According to the majority view, the jurisdiction of the juvenile court was derived from the power of the state as *parens patriae,* that the state was the ultimate guardian and protector of all children under its control. This parental power of the state over its children passed to the juvenile court from two earlier courts. The power of *parens patriae* had been granted to the English court of chancery by law and had been established in American state courts of various types. Traditionally these state courts exercised this power in overseeing the property of minors, and some authorities believed that the jurisdiction of the court with respect to minors covered only those children with property. In 1849, however, an Illinois court ruled that equity jurisdiction extended to the "person of all minors" not just to their property. In effect the juvenile court inherited the equity jurisdiction over children from the English court of chancery by way of the state courts.[19]

When appellate courts ruled on the constitutionality of juvenile courts, they based their decisions on the chancery origins of the juvenile court's jurisdiction. The most notable case involving the constitutionality of a juvenile court was *Commonwealth v Fisher* in which the appellant challenged Pennsylvania's juvenile court law. Fisher had argued that the Pennsylvania law provided "different punishments for the same offense by a classification of individuals," but the court held that the law was "not for the punishment of offenders, but for the salvation of children." The state through the effect of the law contemplated the salvation of all children which was "the duty of the state in the absence of proper parental care or disregard of it by wayward children." Fisher had also claimed that this juvenile court was a new court, but the appellate court ruled that "it is a mere convenient designation of the court of quarter sessions to call it, when caring for children, a juvenile court, but no such court, as an independent tribunal, is created." The law did not provide for the criminal trial of a delinquent child but rather created an agency designed to prevent such a trial. "The act," said the appellate court, "is but an exercise by the state of its supreme power over the welfare of its children." Thus the power of this juvenile court to act in the interests of children is derived from *parens patriae* power of the state.[20]

The chancery origin of the juvenile court's jurisdiction over dependent children was clear, but the extension of the court's jurisdiction to delinquent children did not come entirely from the chancery practice. In part the assignment of delinquent children to the juvenile court came about as a result of the failure of the criminal courts to deal satisfactorily with youthful offenders. With respect to juvenile delinquents, the main point of the juvenile court law was that they should be separated at all times from adult offenders. This provision represented no real departure from the purposes and procedures of the criminal courts. A second provision of the law, the idea that the juvenile court should attempt to rescue delinquent children, came from two sources. On the one hand it represented the extension of the chancery idea to delinquent children, and on the other it was the logical next step in the growth during the nineteenth century of institutions exclusively for youthful offenders. Such institutions, as the century progressed, became more specialized and individualized in their treatment of juvenile delinquents. The juvenile court was the most individualized and specialized of all nineteenth-century institutions for juvenile delinquents. Thus the delinquent jurisdiction of the juvenile court was the result of an inspired combination of three principal sources: the power of *parens patriae,* which came originally from English court of chancery, the clear failure of the criminal courts in their treatment of juvenile delinquents, and the well-established commitment of the state to provide some kind of separate, specialized treatment for youthful offenders.[21]

IV

The Cook County Juvenile Court began its operations in a special room in the County Court Building on July 1, 1899, with Judge Richard S. Tuthill presiding. There were still a good many details to work out. The juvenile court law prohibited the confinement of children under twelve in police stations, and it was clear that the spirit of the law extended this principle of separation to all juvenile delinquents. Since the court could not be kept in continuous session, some place to detain children awaiting their appearance in court had to be found. The *Chicago Tribune* had noticed this deficiency in an editorial on June 26, 1899, remarking that "the care of hysterical or unruly girls from 14 to 16 years of age and of vicious boys of even fewer years is often a most trying matter." A Chicago child-helping charity, the Illinois Industrial Association, offered to house juvenile offenders temporarily for twenty-five cents a day, and a conference of top city and county officials accepted this arrangement and agreed to split the cost.

Dependent children at first were kept in a building at the county hospital, also used for the temporary care of the insane. Soon after the opening of the juvenile court, however, the Illinois Industrial Association obtained a lot with a large house in the front and a barn at the rear. The members of the association converted the house into quarters for dependent children and delinquent girls, and remodeled the barn to serve the delinquent boys.

In 1903 the Juvenile Court Committee of the Chicago Woman's Club took over the management of the Detention Home.[22]

As the juvenile court began its operations, Judge Tuthill found that the most useful way of dealing with delinquent children was probation. Probation—the supervision of an offender in his own home by an officer or agent of the court—was the distinctive feature of the system of child care which Mrs. Flower had gone to Massachusetts to study. One of the most important reasons for her support of the juvenile court law was to make sure that Illinois would have probation for juvenile delinquents. Probation was not new, even in Chicago in 1899. Some time before the juvenile court law went into effect Mrs. Alzina P. Stevens, a resident at Hull House, had begun working informally as a probation officer under an arrangement whereby the sergeant at a police station near Hull House allowed her to take charge of children charged with minor offenses. While Mrs. Stevens seems to have undertaken this work on her own, she could have been following the long-established system of probation in Massachusetts.[23]

The origins of the Massachusetts probation system can be traced to the efforts of an ordinary shoemaker, John Augustus, who in 1829, at the age of forty-four, moved to Boston. He lived quietly, prospered modestly, and attracted no particular notice. In August, 1841, he went to one of Boston's municipal courts and noticed "a ragged and wretched looking man," who had been arrested for being "a common drunkard." Augustus belonged to a temperance society, and perhaps that prompted him to go over and talk to the man. The man promised to reform, and Augustus persuaded the judge to place him under his responsibility. Three weeks later Augustus and the man returned to court, and the former drunkard's improved appearance and record of sobriety so impressed the judge that he fined the man one cent and costs. Thus John Augustus began his career as a probation officer. At first he took responsibility only for drunkards, but in 1843 he began to perform the same service for persons charged with other offenses. Three of the offenders Augustus helped in 1843 were juvenile delinquents, an eleven-year-old boy and two little girls.[24]

By 1846 Augustus and the judges of courts had worked out a standard plan for dealing with juvenile offenders. Augustus would ask the court to suspend the final disposition of a case involving a delinquent child. He tried to get the judge to postpone closing a case as long as possible in order "to test the promises of these youth [sic] to behave well in the future," but the prosecutor often pressed for an earlier conclusion of the cases. Once the children's cases were postponed, Augustus encouraged them to reform. "If at the expiration of a certain period," he wrote, "a good report was given of their behavior during the time they had been on probation, their sentences were very light." This system received a full trial in 1847, when Augustus accepted responsibility for nineteen boys. Once a month Augustus would go to court and report on the boys' behavior. At the end of the probation period Augustus and twelve of the boys returned to court for the final disposition of their cases. "The scene formed a striking and highly pleasant contrast with their appearance when first arraigned. The judge expressed much pleasure as well as surprise at their appearance, and remarked that the object of the law had been accomplished." The judge fined each boy ten cents, and Augustus claimed that "this incident proved conclusively that this class of boys could be saved from crime and punishment, by the plan which I had marked out, and this was admitted by the judge in both [the Police and the Municipal] Courts." Thus, well before the Civil War, John Augustus began juvenile probation, a way of dealing with juvenile delinquents which would become one of the most important elements of the juvenile court. By 1852 he had supervised the probation of 116 boys under the age of sixteen. "I have always endeavored to send these persons to school, or some place of employment," Augustus explained. About 80 per cent of them had avoided further trouble with the police, "but had only half of them done well," Augustus said, "the result would have been truly encouraging."

John Augustus died in 1859, but the worth of his system of probation had been established, and for the next ten years other volunteers carried on the work until the Commonwealth of Massachusetts brought the practice under its control and supervision. In 1868 the Massachusetts State Board of Charities investigated the two state reform schools and recommended "a modification of the laws relating to the commitment of juvenile offenders." In 1869 the Massachusetts General Court passed an act which directed the Governor to appoint "an agent to visit all children maintained wholly or in part by the Commonwealth, or who have been indentured, given in adoption or placed in charge of any person by the authorities of any state institution." This officer, the State Visiting Agent, was in effect the supervisor for all children who had come under the care of the state of Massachusetts. He was also a probation officer. The act provided that the Agent or his deputy should appear "in behalf of the child" at all hearings held for the purpose of committing children to the state reform schools.[25]

In 1870 the General Court modified the duties of the State Visiting Agent and placed him under the control of the State Board of Charities. This law also provided for the separate trial of juvenile offenders. Outside of Boston, children under sixteen were to be tried before the probate judge, but in Boston the law said that "all boys and girls under sixteen years of age, complained of for any offense before any municipal court, shall have the complaints against them heard and determined by themselves, separate from the general and ordinary criminal business of said courts." The State Visiting Agent found that his probation duties kept him busy. In 1871 the Agent or his deputy appeared in 1,463 cases involving children under seventeen. Of those children 1,169 were found guilty and the agent arranged to have 584 of them "placed out in families on probation." [26]

The system of separate trials and probation for juvenile offenders was running smoothly by the time Mrs. Flower visited Massachusetts. When a juvenile offender came to court, he rarely encountered adult criminals. Most of the cases concerning juveniles were heard in the afternoon after the judge had disposed of the adult criminal cases. Usually the judge examined the child privately in an anteroom with only the State Visiting Agent or his deputy present. Since the Agent was there "on behalf of the child," the court often simply accepted the agent's recommendation in disposing of a case. Frequently the judge placed delinquent children "on probation" and ordered them to avoid "bad company and observe a curfew." The Visiting Agent served as a probation officer and periodically checked on the probationer's behavior. Although the Massachusetts system of probation seemed to be successful, only two other states, Michigan and California, had passed probation laws when the Cook County Juvenile Court was created in 1899.[27]

There was no lack of cases at the juvenile court in Chicago, and among the cases, there was no lack of variety. Within the first month of the court's operation there were two instances of breaking and entering. On July 10, 1899, two nine-year-old boys broke into an ice cream factory. A week later two boys, aged fifteen and sixteen, broke into a soda water plant. Later, the police brought in five "homeless" boys and charged them with "burglary." Two boys held up a man and robbed him of ten dollars. On July 7, two boys appeared before the court accused of being pickpockets.[28]

Although Judge Tuthill had a number of options available to him in the disposition of delinquent cases, he usually preferred probation. Probation, however, required probation officers. The juvenile court law had authorized the court to "appoint or designate one or more discreet persons of good character to serve as probation officers during the pleasure of the court," but it had also indicated that the probation officers were "to receive no compensation from the public treasury." The court had to depend on charity to furnish a detention home, and it would also have to depend on volunteers to perform its most important work.[29]

The principle that volunteers would do the work of charity was well established, and the idea that social work was a profession had only begun to take root when the Illinois juvenile court law was passed. There were other reasons, too, why the law expressly prohibited the use of tax funds for the salaries of probation officers. Anxious to pass the law with its essential features intact, the supporters probably had this provision inserted to assure the legislature that the juvenile court would not be expensive, and it seemed likely that the charities of Chicago would be able to furnish the necessary volunteers—there was, for example, the work of Mrs. Stevens from Hull House. Indeed, since Mrs. Stevens had some experience in probation, Judge Tuthill appointed her as the court's first probation officer. Mrs. Flower arranged to have some of her friends pay Mrs. Stevens's salary, but it soon became obvious that the court needed more officers. The Juvenile Court Committee of the Chicago Woman's Club assumed the responsibility of paying the salaries of the probation officers, and within the first year of the court's operation, there were six such officers. Among them were agents of two charities—the Children's Home and Aid Society and the Visitation and Aid Society. In addition to these "voluntary" officers, several policemen were assigned to the juvenile court as probation officers. Timothy D. Hurley, of the Visitation and Aid Society, became the Chief Probation Officer.[30]

The juvenile court law provided that probation officers were to "make such investigations as may be required by the court; to be present in court to represent the interests of the child when the case is heard; to furnish the court such information and assistance as the judge may require; and to take such charge of any child before and after trial as may be directed by the court." These instructions were too general and too vague to function as guidelines for probation officers, and so Judge Tuthill wrote out his own instructions. The officers were to have in mind a list of "considerations in the order named." First was "the welfare and interests of the child." The Judge wrote, "It is the desire of the Court to save the child from neglect and cruelty; also to save it from the danger of becoming a criminal or dependent." The Judge put "the welfare of the community" in second place, and in his remarks on that consideration made the same point that nearly every other backer of special treatment for juvenile offenders had made: "The most practical way of lessening the burdens of taxations and the loss of property through the ravages of crime is by the prevention of pauperism and crime. Experience proves that the easiest and most effective way of doing this is by taking hold

of the children while they are young—the younger the better."
In third place was "the intellect and feelings of parents and relatives." The Judge said, "It is right and necessary that parental
affection should be respected as far as this can be done without
sacrificing the best interests of the child and without exposing the
community to unnecessary damage." After these general considerations, Judge Tuthill moved on to more practical matters. The
purpose of the probation officer's investigation of a case was to
"assist the court in deciding what ought to be done." Judge Tuthill
wanted to know "the character, disposition and tendencies, and
school record of the child" as well as the character of the parents
and the quality of the child's home and environment. He would
use this information in deciding whether to leave a child with
his parents, place him in a foster home, or commit him to an institution. On the work of supervision by a probation officer, Judge
Tuthill wrote simply that "the probation officer will be expected to
maintain a special oversight of the child either by personal visits
or by written report from parents or custodian." [31]

During the first year of the juvenile court's operations, Judge
Tuthill heard the cases of 1,466 delinquent children. Only 116 of
them were girls. The most common offense was "stealing"—that
is, taking or the attempting to take property, and 645 boys appeared in court accused of that offense. The only other offenses
with more than 100 boys' cases in the first year were "incorrigibility" and "disorderly conduct," offenses that covered a multitude
of acts. According to an early study of the juvenile court, "incorrigibility" was a word "apparently coined of despair" and used
to cover "such misdemeanors as loitering about the streets and
using vulgar language . . . refusing either to work or to go to
school, roaming the street late at night . . . keeping bad company, refusing to obey parents, and staying away from home."
Equally vague, "disorderly conduct" covered many of the same
offenses.

The most common offenses of girls were "incorrigibility," "immorality," and "disorderly conduct." For girls incorrigibility and
disorderly conduct usually meant staying out late, going to dances,

or associating with "vicious persons." Immorality meant some sort of sex offense, but in order to "protect the good name" of many of the girls who appeared before the juvenile court they were listed as being incorrigible or disorderly. Often "immorality" was reserved for girls found in houses of prostitution. Nevertheless, 80 per cent of the delinquent girls who appeared before the court were there because their virtue was "in peril" if it had not already been lost. According to Jane Addams, "the little girls brought into the juvenile court are usually daughters of those poorest immigrant families living in the worst type of city tenements, who are frequently forced to take in boarders in order to pay the rent. A surprising number of little girls have first become involved in wrongdoing through the men in their own households." [32]

Generally parents, acting in response to a summons, brought their children to court; rarely were the police involved. Usually children remained in their own homes until their cases were heard, but a child who seemed likely to escape or was found out on the streets late at night was usually sent to the Detention Home. A case started when someone—a neighbor or even a parent —filed a petition with the court. Often as a result of their investigation probation officers settled the matter without involving the machinery of the juvenile court. Sometimes the judge himself handled complaints outside the regular procedures of the court. Only about one-fourth of the complaints resulted in a child's appearance in court. Once a case came before the court it was rarely dismissed. According to Judge Merritt W. Pinckney, who became the judge of the juvenile court in 1908, most of the cases were simply continued and never brought to trial. "All that the youngster, girl or boy needs," he said, "is a little fatherly advice, and a lecture, if you please,—sometimes fairly severe—warning the boy that he must do differently and the repetition of the practice that has brought the child into court will inevitably mean that he would either be put on probation or sent to an institution." [33]

The juvenile court, like most of its nineteenth-century predecessors, sought to treat juvenile delinquency by manipulating the delinquent's environment. Of necessity the court assumed that most juvenile delinquents were the product of their surroundings rather than their heredity. "My observation of delinquent children," said Judge Tuthill,

> has convinced me that the percentage of those who are in no respect abnormal in their moral nature is not much if any larger than among the children of well-to-do and honest parents. Their faults are not due to any hereditary point but to bad environment. A bad home, a bad father and more surely a bad mother, [—] want of proper parental care [—] would make delinquents of the children of any of us. Character is of slow growth. Like the body, it is built up imperceptibly. To the formation of a good character in any child, kindly admonition, wholesome example, constant watchfulness and an infinite patience are absolute essentials[:] children, like men and women, are creatures of habit. Bad habits, like weeds, will grow in any soil. To prevent such noxious growth must needs be the care of every parent. . . . The trouble of the delinquent is that he has had no such care.

Obviously, when the judge committed a delinquent to an institution, he had radically altered that child's environment. Putting a child on probation was also an effort to modify his environment. The supervision and guidance of the probation officer added new elements to the child's surroundings and also brought a measure of control and judgment into the child's life.[34]

Before placing a child on probation the judge gave him a "kindly admonition and warning" that if he returned to "his former misconduct" or did not "gain the approval of the probation officer," he would be "otherwise dealt with." Parents and relatives were expected to help in the process of reforming the delinquent, and the judge warned them about the consequences of negligence. Children placed on probation usually came from homes where the environment was "ineffective," so that probation was basically a form of "judicial guardianship" whereby the state, acting through the court and the probation officer, provided the discipline and

guidance missing in the delinquent's home. According to one
probation officer,

> the probation process in essence, is a process of education by
> constructive friendship. It presupposes an intense personal in-
> terest; it presupposes a perception of a child's needs in such a
> way that the child may be more securely set upon his feet by
> throwing about him every constructive force the community has
> to offer. . . . The process does not require theories; it does not
> require book knowledge. It must never be in any degree senti-
> mental, patronizing or amateurish. It requires sympathy, but,
> good humor, patience and above all a thorough knowledge of
> the needs of child life and the manifold ways in which to meet
> them.

The probation officer in addition to his attempt to modify a delinquent's surroundings through his supervision also underlined
the juvenile court's environmentalism in his work as an investigator. He studied the conditions of the child's life, and recommended
changes which would, he hoped, prevent the child from becoming
a criminal or a dependent. This stress on environmentalism simply
followed a well-established approach; for, although the social
sciences, particularly criminology and psychology, had already
begun to emphasize the need for the study of the heredity and
the psychology of criminals, these disciplines were as yet not
sufficiently developed to aid the court.[35]

The court's environmentalism can be seen clearly in its procedure, which was deliberately informal. Generally the judge
ignored the rules of evidence applicable in criminal trials. According to Judge Tuthill, the purpose of having a delinquent in
the juvenile court was "not to find out whether he has done an
act which in an adult would be a crime, and to punish him for
that; such facts are considered merely as evidence tending to show
whether the boy is *in a condition of delinquency,* so that the state
ought to enter upon the exercise of its parental care over the
child." Echoing this attitude, one early writer on juvenile courts
characterized the juvenile delinquents as "the product of social
conditions that were no fault of his." The problem for the judge of
a juvenile court, then, was not to decide what the child had done

—and then fix his punishment according to law—but to decide why the child was there and what could be done to prevent him from coming back. The judge's options were limited, however; he could only alter the delinquent's surroundings. He could do nothing about the child's heredity, and he had no way of knowing about his psychology. Even if the judge could have learned about the delinquent's psychology, he had no knowledge of what to do about it.[36]

Most of the boys and girls who came before the juvenile court (more than 70 per cent) were the children of immigrants, which strongly suggests that their delinquency was a consequence of their foreign culture. One of the difficulties facing the judge of the juvenile court was that the bad environment of the child before him was often the result of a cultural conflict. That is, the child was delinquent because his parents did not fully understand the values and mores of American society. Consequently, the court had to try to assist the process of assimilation of many children of foreign-born parents. The main role assigned to the juvenile court was that of children's guardian, but the fact that most of those children suffered from a lack of understanding of American culture meant that the juvenile court became, more or less without design, an agency of assimilation.[37]

The juvenile court did not, however, develop any specialized techniques to cope with this extension of its function. According to Julian W. Mack, who served as the juvenile court judge in Chicago from 1904 to 1907, "the Juvenile Court deals with each child as a distinct individual examining into its entire past, and then determining, not what is the best thing to do for children, but simply and solely, what is the best thing to do for little John Brown." This approach was more than a methodology; it represented the essence of the juvenile court philosophy. The whole purpose of the court was to deal with the individual juvenile delinquent on an individual basis. This philosophy was what made the juvenile court unique; it was what distinguished the hearings of the Chicago juvenile court from the separate trials of juvenile offenders in Massachusetts and New York. Those courts, despite the fact that they heard children's cases apart from adult cases and usually followed an informal procedure, were still criminal courts. They sought primarily, not to do what was best for the individual child before them, but to determine whether or not the child had committed the particular offense with which he was charged. In all criminal courts, once the guilt or innocence of the accused had been decided, the law restricted the judge's discretion much more than it did in the juvenile court. In principle the law provided equal punishment for all guilty persons, and therefore the court could not tailor its actions to individuals. Indeed, judges of criminal courts often dismissed the cases of juvenile delinquents, not for lack of evidence, but because of the judge's reluctance to assess the penalties prescribed by law on children.[38]

In their efforts to find the right remedy for each child, the judges of the Cook County Juvenile Court ran into a number of problems. If, for example, the judge decided to commit a delinquent boy to an institution, the only place he could send him was to the John Worthy School at the Bridewell. Judge Tuthill complained that the John Worthy School was "not an adequate or indeed a proper place for the reformation or reclamation" of delinquent boys. The main difficulty with it was its limited capacity. "It is impossible," Judge Tuthill said, "to keep boys in it for a period sufficiently long to give time for the destruction of bad habits and for the cultivation of good habits. Every day the court is compelled to release boys whom the reports show have been making satisfactory progress in order to give place to others." Other disadvantages of the John Worthy School were its location, separated from the adult sections of the Bridewell only by a wall, and its lack of facilities for outdoor recreation. Judge Tuthill thought the State of Illinois should build an agricultural home for delinquent boys, and in words reminiscent of Charles Loring Brace, he praised the virtues of country life:

> From personal experience as a boy brought up on a farm in Southern Illinois, I can authoritively [sic] declare that there is nothing so enchanting to a boy as country life; tumbling in the

rich grass, smelling the new mown hay, and the rich earth turned up by the shining plow share; climbing trees; making grape vine swings in them, and swinging so high that heaven itself seems almost in reach.

The boys that the judge did send to the John Worthy School often derived little benefit from their short stay there, and, despite the court's efforts to supervise them through probation, they often returned to court having committed new offenses.[39]

The vagueness and narrowness of the definition of juvenile delinquency in the juvenile court law was another problem which faced the Cook County Juvenile Court. The law clearly stated that a juvenile delinquent was "any child under the age of 16 years who violates any law of this state or any city or village ordinance." If the court procedure had been derived from this definition, the juvenile court would have been close to a criminal court, for its first effort would have been to determine if the accused child had violated a law. The court did not in fact operate that way. Most of the court's supporters agreed on the need for a clearer definition of the meaning of "a condition of delinquency." A committee including Mrs. Flower, Julia Lathrop, Judge Tuthill, Timothy Hurley, Hastings H. Hart, and Judge Harvey Hurd met to draw up an amendment to the juvenile court law. In explaining its action the committee said:

> The lack of a good definition of delinquency in the present law is apparent and the amendment is intended to include all children that are in need of government and care. Heretofore they were supposed to have committed a crime or misdemeanor. Under the present law and proposed amendments the child and its parents are brought into court and the inquiry is as to all the surroundings and what is for the child's highest and best interests.

The amendment proposed by the committee passed the Illinois Legislature and became law on May 11, 1901.[40]

This amendment changed the juvenile court law in two ways. It added a section on the responsibilities of parents empowering the juvenile court to investigate the parents of a delinquent or dependent child and to order them to provide the child with a proper home. Second and more important, it modified considerably the definition of juvenile delinquency. A delinquent child was not only one who had broken the law but also one "who is incorrigible; or who knowingly associates with thieves, vicious or immoral persons; or who is growing up in idleness and crime; or who knowingly frequents a house of ill-fame; or who knowingly patronizes any policy shop or place where any gaming device is, or shall be operated." This broader definition was not an innovation nationally, a similar law having been passed ten years before in New York at the urging of the Society for the Prevention of Cruelty to Children. The New York law, however, was still being applied in 1901 by criminal courts. The new definition, besides being broader than the old, was also vaguer, for it enacted into law the term "incorrigible," which had no precise meaning and which required the judge to determine if the accused child knew the character of the place where he had gone or the moral quality of the people with whom he associated. He could be judged "in a condition of delinquency" for actions which, if committed by an adult, occasioned no illegality.[41]

When the juvenile court first appeared, its backers hailed it as a great innovation in the treatment of troubled children, and some even claimed that it would be the chief means of solving all of society's problems. Once the court had been given a fair chance to demonstrate its capabilities, however, it became clear that it was no panacea. Not long after the juvenile court began operating, criticism appeared. An officer of the Society for the Prevention of Cruelty to Children in New York charged that probation, instead of aiding delinquent children, had only resulted in "an unusual increase of arrests, many for very frivolous offences." In response to this criticism a Chicagoan admitted that "the enthusiasm among charitable people which has followed the inauguration of our Juvenile Court has doubtless led us into some extremes. The operation of the Juvenile Court Law has been so plainly beneficial that persons whose discretion may not be of the soundest have here and there failed to observe the strict limitations which must be set upon it." [42]

However, the claims made by supporters of the juvenile court did not abate under such criticism. In fact it seemed only to stir up more defenders of the court. In 1904 Charles R. Henderson, a sociologist at the University of Chicago, told the delegates at the National Conference of Charities and Correction that

> the records of these courts and the stories of the probation officers must soon arouse the administrators of cities, of school and park boards, of churches, of philanthropists and patriotic men of wealth to a supreme and prolonged effort to transform the environment; to make the houses and streets clean and wholesome; to provide playgrounds; to see that the natural energies of youth are turned from destructive to constructive activities, and that the mind and soul are everywhere surrounded by pure, delightful and inspiring suggestions.

Such ideas, despite their moral merit, merely repeated the old claims of the earlier supporters of the court. Consequently *The Survey*, a weekly published by the New York Charity Organization Society, felt it necessary to remind its readers that

> many enthusiasts have almost made a fetish of the juvenile court, thinking it a complete solvent for the whole problem of delinquent children, and failing to realize that after all it is still a corrective agency of the state, dealing with the results of conditions which should as far as possible be prevented. Such well-meaning but superficial people hold the court to an impossible standard of perfection, and are misled by criticism of its administration when among the thousands of well handled cases their attention is focused on half a dozen children who have not had the best treatment on probation or in an institution.

The debate over the function of the juvenile court continued without any decision, but other, more specific criticisms also appeared.[43]

A county judge in Colorado charged that the juvenile court had been created by "men and women more earnest than competent," and he rejected the idea that the juvenile court was not primarily concerned with determining the guilt or innocence of the children before it. "The true function of a court," he wrote, "is to determine judicially the facts at issue before it. . . . Investigations of the lives, environments, or heredity of delinquents, the infliction of punishment, and the supervision of probation institutionalize the courts and are repugnant to every tenet of the science of law." Juvenile courts were not only wrong in theory; according to the judge they were also ineffective: "They have found themselves unable to dispose of any simple case to the certain satisfaction of those most interested in it." As a result "juvenile courts are held in suspicion by the layman, in contempt by the lawyer, and regarded with a sense of weakness by the judge." This criticism charged the court with having gone too far from the traditions of the criminal law. Others thought that it had not gone far enough. Bernard Flexner, a lawyer and an early authority on juvenile courts, argued that "we need to get away more completely from the criminal terminology still employed"; and Charles R. Henderson wrote that "the juvenile court has not yet entirely sloughed off the marks of its origin in the criminal courts. . . ." What disturbed Flexner was the court's statistics. "With striking inconsistency," he wrote, "we institute a proceeding in chancery with the idea dominant that we want to protect the child, that we want no stigma attached to it; and yet we publish elaborate reports dealing with every phase of crime, from idling and loitering to the worse offences against public morality." That the juvenile court was controversial shows that it had aroused public opinion; that other states and foreign countries rapidly created their own juvenile courts shows that it answered a pressing social need.[44]

V

The creation of the juvenile court marked the end of the evolution of institutions for juvenile delinquents in nineteenth-century America. The penal process may be thought of as a combination of procedures and institutions arranged along a line, with an offense at one end and punishment or some form of probation at the other. In between are discovery or reporting of the offense, arrest, in-

carceration while awaiting trial or bail, and trial. The evolution
of institutions for juvenile delinquents began with the establishment of the New York House of Refuge, which was designed to
modify the punishment given to juvenile offenders by providing
specialized and separate treatment for them once they had been
convicted. The concentration was, however, still on the punishment end of the penal process. When Charles Loring Brace
founded the New York Children's Aid Society, he concentrated
at the other end. He sought to prevent the offense, that is, to prevent juvenile delinquency by working with potentially delinquent
children. John Augustus, through his informal practice of probation, tried to modify the middle of the penal process and to
eliminate the final step, punishment. When Massachusetts placed
the practice of probation under state control in 1870, it also provided for separate trials of juvenile delinquents. Thus by the end
of the third quarter of the nineteenth century, reformers had tried
to alter all but two of the steps along the penal line. Arrest continued to be the same for juveniles as for adults, and children were
still detained in police stations awaiting trial.

The modifications and alterations which reformers had won for
the treatment of juvenile delinquents were for the most part
changes in scale rather than substance. The New York House of
Refuge was basically a juvenile prison. Sending children to the
West, and providing cheap but not free lodging houses for newsboys, amounted to expecting little children to respond to the same
values as adults. Adults followed the lure of "manifest destiny"
and the ideal of the self-made man when they went west; and
charity, whether given to men or boys, encouraged pauperism.
The separate trials for juvenile offenders did mean that children
and adult criminals would not see each other in court, but the
courts themselves remained fact-finding criminal tribunals. In
short, most of the institutions which nineteenth-century Americans established for juvenile delinquents were basically junior
versions of similar institutions for adults.

The juvenile court was different. Not only did the laws which
established it eliminate the imprisonment of children awaiting

trial in police stations, and end for all practical purposes the arrest of juveniles by the police, but it also changed the purposes of a trial. The judge in juvenile court was more concerned with what was best for the individual child before him than with whether or not that child had committed an offense. Here then was a new institution designed specifically for children. The only institution for adults like it was the court of chancery, and it had become, for the most part, a distant memory.

The creation of the juvenile court meant that society no longer regarded the juvenile delinquent as a miniature adult who broke the law because he had chosen of his own free will to do so, nor as an object to be studied, classified, and lamented over. Now society could see him as a child, immature and in need of help more than anything else. Society saw, too, that the term "juvenile delinquent," for all of its usefulness in describing a child who had broken the law, was very imprecise. There was a great difference between a boy out after curfew and Jesse Pomeroy, yet both of them were "juvenile delinquents." Clearly the method of the criminal law, which defined categories of offenses and prescribed set penalties, could not rationally be applied to all juvenile delinquents. The juvenile court remedied this difficulty by being flexible and by seeking to know as much as possible about the individual child: his character, what kind of family he had, the quality of his neighborhood, his habits, his schoolwork, everything. Unfortunately probation officers could furnish only external facts about a child. The court could not know whether the child was medically sound or not, nor could it know anything of the child's psychology. To treat each child as an individual the court had to know about these areas, too. But the social sciences had not kept pace with the development of social institutions. Superficially, the juvenile court seemed to be an ideal vehicle for the application of the teachings of the social sciences to America's troubled youth. When the court came into existence, however, there was little the social sciences could offer.

11

Cesare Lombroso and G. Stanley Hall: Scientific America Considers Her Wayward Children

The dry white skull lay on the table before the most learned criminologists in the world. They had come to Paris in August, 1889, for the Second International Conference on Criminal Anthropology. Among the delegates were Cesare Lombroso, founder of the discipline; Gabriel Tarde, French jurist; Dr. Moriz Benedikt, prominent Austrian psychiatrist; and Thomas Wilson, curator of prehistoric anthropology at the Smithsonian Institution, who represented the United States. The skull had once held the brain of Charlotte Corday, the famous killer of Marat during the French Revolution; it quickly became the main bone of contention at the Conference. Because of the depth of the skull's occipital fossettes (small hollows in one of the posterior bones), one of Lombroso's followers presented it as an illustration of the "born criminal." To the Italians, for whom the name of Charlotte Corday had no special meaning, this was the skull of "a common vulgar impulsive murderess" and as such it had merit chiefly as a scientific artifact. Prince Roland Bonaparte had preserved the skull and testified to its authenticity. To Frenchmen, however, Charlotte Corday was a "heroine who rid the world of a monster." [1]

Lombroso led the debate with a defense of his view that physi-

cal abnormalities, including irregularities of the skull, characterized what he called the born criminal. Two of his colleagues,
Baron Garofalo, the president of the Criminal Tribunal of Naples,
and Enrico Ferri, a professor at the University of Rome, also defended the view that the skull was that of a criminal. Despite the
impressive credentials of Lombroso and his disciples, the French
criminologists did not hesitate to challenge the claim of the Italians. Charlotte Corday was a national heroine, and the whole
basis of the French school, which stressed the social origins of
crime, had been attacked. Gabriel Tarde led the counterattack
against the Italian position. When Tarde finished, Dr. Manouvrier,
a professor in the School of Anthropology in Paris, joined the debate and charged that the ideas of the Italian school had been
derived from the discredited discipline of phrenology. Crime,
Manouvrier implied, was primarily a matter of sociology and
statistics.[2]

The debate over Charlotte Corday's skull revealed the outlines
of a relatively new social science, criminology, which had two
branches, criminal anthropology or the Italian school, and criminal sociology or the French school. Modern criminology began
with the publication of Lombroso's *L'Uomo Delinquente* (Criminal Man) in 1876. Lombroso had collected the data for his study
of criminal man during a four-year period when he conducted
anthropological studies on the inmates of Italian prisons. He
thought that there was a correlation between physiology and human behavior, and therefore he expected to find—and claimed to
have found—that criminals had a higher percentage of physical
anomalies than the normal population. Such anomalies consisted
of irregularities of the skull, the brain, and the face as well as
abnormalities of the sense organs. Other anomalies were various
kinds of physical handicaps, such as underdeveloped legs or infantilism of genitalia. Lombroso contended that when he found a
considerable number of physical anomalies in any one individual,
he would also find behavioral problems. Persons with a great
many anomalies usually lacked moral awareness and full character development. They tended to be irritable, vain, and eager

for revenge. To Lombroso habitual criminals seemed uncivilized, atavistic, a throwback to earlier and more primitive societies. To explain the appearance of the almost savage habitual criminal, Lombroso developed the concept that the habitual criminal was a biological type who had failed to evolve as fully as normal men. In Lombroso's view not all criminals could be classified as habitual; those who turned to crime more or less by accident or from the pressure of circumstances, he called occasional criminals. Since the habitual criminal represented a special type of the human race, he became—especially in popular terminology—the born criminal.[3]

In contrast to the Italian school, French criminologists denied the existence of a criminal type or born criminal. Instead of concentrating on man, they studied society and relied heavily on statistics. Crime, they believed, resulted from the criminal's inability to resist the pressures and temptations of modern life. According to Gabriel Tarde, "the offense is an act emanating not from the living being, but from the personal individual such as society alone can make him and cause him to increase in number in its image." To the extent that they did study man, French criminologists were more interested in his psychology and character than in his physical appearance. Tarde thought that "the character of the criminal is already much easier to trace with precision than is his physical type." Unlike Lombroso and the Italians, however, the French criminologists did not make direct scientific observations of the physical characteristics of individuals; nor did they develop an experimental, laboratory-oriented methodology. For their data they relied on statistics, following an established French approach to social problems.[4]

The first significant analysis of criminal statistics appeared in 1829 in Adolphe Quételet's *Recherches statistiques sur le royaume des Pays-Bas,* in which he discussed the distribution of crime by age and sex group and the ratio of condemned to accused among criminals. More important than his brief treatise was Quételet's *Recherches sur le penchant au crime aux différents âges,* which appeared two years later. In this longer work he discussed the

patterns of the numbers of crimes. "There is a budget which we
pay with a frightful regularity," he wrote, "it is that of prisons,
chains and the scaffold." Quételet, who taught mathematics,
physics, and astronomy at various institutions of higher learning
in Belgium, believed that the regularities he found in moral
statistics (crime, suicide, and marriage) compared with the laws
of physics, and he emphasized the importance of social factors
in causing crime. "The crimes which are annually committed," he
wrote in 1835, "seem to be a necessary result of our social organization. . . . Society prepares the crime and the guilty is only the
instrument by which it is accomplished." [5]

Modern authorities generally date the origin of sociology from
the publication of Auguste Comte's *Cours de philosophie positive*
(6 vols., Paris, 1830–42) in which he argued for the primacy of
the scientific mode of thinking. "Each of our leading conceptions
—each branch of our knowledge," he wrote, "passes successively
through three different theoretical conceptions: the Theological,
or fictitious; the Metaphysical, or abstract; and the Scientific, or
positive." In the last stage "the mind has given over the vain
search after Absolute notions, the origin and destruction of the
universe, and the causes of phenomena, and applies itself to the
study of their laws—that is their invariable relations of succession
and resemblance." Among the sciences Comte saw a natural hier-
archy and evolution which began with mathematics, and moved
up through astronomy, physics, chemistry, and biology to the
highest which was social physics, or sociology. Comte had written
his first book in order to outline how the new science of sociology
would develop. It would, he believed, discover laws of society
comparable in their value with the laws of physics. Comte rejected the ideas which underlay Quételet's moral statistics, however, because they were based on the theory of probability and
were therefore too imprecise. Nevertheless, Comte and Quételet
together could be called the founders of the French school of
criminology, or criminal sociology. [6]

The writings and debates of the early criminologists helped to
found the discipline, but they were almost unknown in the United

States. Americans were less interested in theory than Europeans, and even when the social sciences did begin to develop in the United States, they were heavily practical in their orientation. Until about 1890 American "social scientists" were gentlemanly amateurs, philanthropists, and charity workers who attended the annual meetings of the American Social Science Association and the National Conference of Charities and Correction.

II

The American Social Science Association, modeled after a similar British organization, appeared in 1865. It held annual meetings at which members read papers on a wide variety of topics. The Association met in four sections: Education, Health, Finance, and Jurisprudence. The finance section, or the division of social economy as it came to be called, sponsored the creation of a new agency, the "Conference of Boards and Charities," for members of the State Boards of Charities. In 1879 this conference severed its connection with the American Social Science Association and changed its name to the National Conference of Charities and Corrections.[7]

Until the 1890's, the American Social Science Association and the National Conference of Charities and Corrections were the most important social science establishments in the United States. For the most part the delegates to the annual meetings of these bodies (Americans generally) paid little attention to the theories of European social scientists. The papers at the meetings emphasized a practical, reformist approach to social problems, which in effect implied a rejection of the more deterministic European theories. Nevertheless, the proceedings of these meetings—the papers and the discussions—provide an insight into the thinking of American "social scientists" during the late nineteenth century.[8]

Throughout its existence, the National Conference of Charities and Corrections devoted a great deal of time to children. The members discussed the practical problems of the child in trouble, of the delinquent child, of the orphan, and of the immigrant child.

Rarely, however, did the papers or the discussions touch on theories or principles, and even when they did they remained essentially practical in their orientation. At the 1885 meeting of the National Conference of Charities and Corrections, William T. Harris, who had been the superintendent of schools in St. Louis and who would become the United States Commissioner of Education in 1889, presented a paper on "Compulsory Education in Relation to Crime and Social Morals." Harris defined crime as an attack on society and explained that one characteristic of a criminal was that he ignored his fellow man. This same trait, Harris continued, could be found in children. "It is clear," he said, "that man can live in society and constitute a social whole only so far as individuals are educated out of their natural animal condition, and made to respect social forms more highly than mere animal impulses." While the need for education to civilize man is accepted, Harris went on, "much of the education into a respect for social forms and usages is given by the family and before the age of schooling." Here Harris underlined the insight that had inspired the family system at the *Rauhe Haus* in Germany and the placing-out system of the New York Children's Aid Society. "The family," Harris said, "builds up within the child's mind the structures of his moral character, making for him a second nature of moral habit and custom, whose limits and boundaries he regards as of supreme moment." Harris, however, did not suggest that a child's education was complete with the moral training he received at home. The school in addition to the formal instruction it provided, gave the child discipline, which implied training in punctuality, silence, and industry. Besides the school and the family, Harris added, society also educates its citizens through such agencies as the state, work, and religion. Crime results when these agencies fail in their task of socializing the individual. Thus William T. Harris said in effect that one of the best ways to reduce crime and juvenile delinquency was to make sure that society's socializing agencies functioned more efficiently.[9]

In 1886 J. C. Hite, the superintendent of the Ohio Boys' Industrial School, presented a paper on "Moral Evolution in Re-

formatories" and told the delegates that children who become
wayward, almost in every instance, are those whose characters
have become weakened by the strong influences of evil surroundings. He went on to say "It is a mistaken idea that all boys
who are placed in reformatories are worse by inheritance than
the average boy." Hite had touched on a theme widely debated
in late nineteenth-century social science circles: which was more
important in the shaping of character, heredity or environment?
Occasionally, a speaker would try to include both heredity and
environment in his explanation of children's deviant behavior.
Robert W. Hill, a minister from Salem, Oregon, told the 1887 annual meeting of the National Conference that "diseased and enfeebled parents beget diseased and enfeebled children," but
quickly added that "not many young children have the power to
distinguish good from evil, and the ordinary surroundings of the
children of poverty have a tendency to diminish rather than to
add to the innate power of discernment in this regard."

The delegates to the National Conference could see no acceptable way to overcome the handicap of bad heredity. Therefore,
they stressed the importance of environmental factors for problem
children and juvenile delinquents. "Every delinquent child," said
Peter Caldwell, the superintendent of the Louisville Industrial
School of Reform, "is a living indictment of society's neglect and
indifference; and when he becomes old enough to realize the full
consequence of his neglect, it cannot be surprising that he should
feel justified in warring against his kind by way of getting even."
Speaking just after Caldwell at the 1898 meeting of the Conference, James Allison, the superintendent of the House of Refuge
in Cincinnati, agreed that environment caused deviant behavior—
in Allison's words "moral disease." Allison also thought that "under
the regimen of evil companions and a bad home, the dependent
needs only the opportunity to become delinquent, and the delinquent is such simply because of the deficiency in him of a moral
sense which has failed its proper development." [10]

At times, however, delegates did stress the importance of heredity as a cause of crime or pauperism. In 1888 Oscar McCulloch

traced the genealogy of a family he called the "tribe of Ishmael." He found a long and statistically abnormal history of disease, crime, and poverty in that one family. McCulloch's study, important as it was, was less significant and less well known than an earlier study by Richard Dugdale, a member of the executive committee of the New York Prison Association. In 1874 the Association asked Dugdale to inspect some of the state's county jails. During his travels he came across a remarkable family, which he described in "The Jukes," an appendix to his report to the Prison Association in 1875. An unusually large number of the members of this family through several generations were either insane, criminals, or prostitutes. Two years later Dugdale published the story of the Jukes separately with the subtitle, "A Study in Crime, Pauperism, Disease, and Heredity." At the beginning of the book Dugdale explained that he was trying to determine which was more important in causing crime, heredity or environment. Dugdale displayed an impressive array of data and analysis and concluded that "the tendency of heredity is to produce an environment which perpetuates that heredity; thus the licentious parent makes an example which greatly aids in fixing habits of debauchery in the child. The correction is change in environment." Dugdale's book, which was probably the most important American contribution to criminology in the nineteenth century, proved so inconclusive about heredity and environment that further debate and discussion on that issue were the result. His study also marked the beginning of the application of the scientific method to the study of crime in the United States. It was, however, premature.[11]

III

The dominant mode of thought among American intellectuals in the late nineteenth century was evolutionary. Generally speaking, this mode could be labeled social Darwinism, and it had two sides. There was a conservative, individualistic attitude which embraced the concept of laissez-faire as its social philosophy and which professed a fatalistic satisfaction with the slow but inevitable progress of evolution. The other side was a modification of this view; it accepted the primacy of evolution but denied man's helplessness in the face of evolution. Chief among the exponents of this second view, or "reform Darwinism," was Lester Frank Ward, whom American sociologists somewhat reluctantly claim as the founder of the science of society in the United States. Ward merits the label of founder because of the publication of his *Dynamic Sociology* in 1883. American sociologists are slow to acknowledge any real debt to Ward because his book was too cosmic, too materialistic, and tied too much to an evolutionary philosophy. As a result, the book had little significant influence in the creation of the discipline of sociology in the United States. Ward had the misfortune to fall between two academic departments. Most sociologists regard him as a social philosopher, while most philosophers regard him as a sociologist. In addition, Ward probably made his greatest contributions to knowledge in two other fields, geology and paleobotany. Nevertheless, Ward is important in the history of social science in the United States; he provides the link between the eclectic deliberations of the American Social Science Association and the creation of the academic discipline of sociology. In addition, Ward provided criticism of the negative anti-reform views of social Darwinists, like those of William Graham Sumner and Herbert Spencer, and he later became the president of the American Sociological Association.[12]

In 1882 Herbert Spencer visited the United States (his books would sell an impressive 368,755 volumes by 1903) where he was feted as a great scholar—as the sage of the century. The climax of his American tour came with a dinner at Delmónico's in New York. The dinner had been arranged by his American publisher, Edward L. Youmans, who also edited *Popular Science Monthly*. A substantial number of American intellectuals attended the dinner and afterwards vied with one another in their tributes to Spencer. Clearly Herbert Spencer was one of the most popular Englishmen to visit the United States.

More important than Spencer's popularity, however, was his

apparent domination of American thought. His ideas, first expressed in *Social Statics* which was published in 1851, provided an elaborate theoretical justification for the doctrine of laissez-faire. Spencer saw society as analogous to life itself. Society was basically an organism, and it evolved from a lower to a higher state through a process which Spencer called "equilibration." His analysis of social evolution also depended on an analogy with physics. The process of equilibration could be likened to the physical principle of the conservation of energy: it was a self-defeating force; ultimately society would come to the end of its process of evolution and at the same time reach a state of perfection. This process and ultimate result, Spencer asserted, was an inexorable law. Thus to Spencer and his disciples progress was inevitable; to eliminate the problems of society one had only to wait for evolution to take care of them. Reform and charity were not only useless; they were dangerous. In fact they constituted an "absurd effort to make the world over," as William Graham Sumner expressed it. Such activities, by ameliorating the conditions of the weaker members of society actually delayed progress. The great engine of evolution was competition, and the principle of "the survival of the fittest"—borrowed from Malthus and reinforced by Darwin's use of it—explained how competition led to progress.[13]

Social Darwinism had obvious implications for businessmen in the period of ruthless competition which characterized the expansion of the American economy during the late nineteenth century. Social Darwinism might have cast a pall of gloom over American reformers, philanthropists, and charity workers had they accepted it; but they, in their optimism, took a different view. It would be impossible to estimate the degree to which Americans accepted the ideas of Spencer and Sumner, but it seems clear that many Americans did accept the idea of evolution as the mode of change, whether the change was biological or social. Reformers, however, disagreed with Sumner that their activity was a waste of time and argued by implication through their continued efforts that human resourcefulness could shape the course of evolution.

Lester Frank Ward's *Dynamic Sociology* furnished the best exposition of the view that man could, by controlling his environment, alter and shape the process of evolution. Indeed, Ward contended it was man's duty to try to control evolution, and that a new discipline, sociology, would be necessary to undertake the task. "Before the science of society can be truly founded," Ward wrote, "another advance must be made, and the actively dynamic stage reached in which social phenomena shall be contemplated as capable of intelligent control by society itself in its own interest." [14]

During the last decade of the nineteenth century social science seemed literally to burst on the American scene. Academic sociology—a discipline related to Ward's ideas, but derived basically from European theories—appeared early in the decade. By the turn of the century both psychology and criminology were a part of American social science. In addition social reform was attempting to become more scientific and more professional. Finally, the settlement house, a new institution imported from England, sought to combine social science and social reform. All of these developments marked the beginning of a profound change in the way nineteenth-century Americans responded to the challenge of juvenile delinquency.

Academic sociology developed in the United States because of the efforts of three men: Albion W. Small, Franklin H. Giddings, and Edward A. Ross. Small created the first department of sociology in the United States at the University of Chicago in 1893. Giddings had already begun teaching a graduate course in sociology at Bryn Mawr in 1890. Three years later he moved to Columbia University to become the chairman of the newly created department of sociology there. Ross, who was one of the early great lecturers in sociology, began teaching at Stanford in 1893. To these men rather than to Ward goes the credit for founding the discipline of sociology in the United States. [15]

At the same time the people who staffed charity and relief agencies, philanthropists, members of state boards of charities, and administrators of prisons and reformatories were also seeking to turn their work into a profession. The managers of city charities had already begun to label the activities of their agencies "scientific philanthropy" because the charities were supposedly employing scientific methods of investigating their clients and giving relief. Volunteers did most of the work in these societies, and it was difficult for the charities to develop and maintain a systematic method of handling their cases. As a result, one of the officers of the Boston Associated Charities, Miss Zilpha Smith, organized classes for the social workers of her city. In 1892 she explained to the National Conference of Charities and Corrections that charity work had become so complicated that it required training before it could be practiced. A year later at the Chicago World's Fair, Anna L. Dawes read a paper in which she supported Miss Smith's view of the problems involved in social work and called for training schools for volunteers in philanthropy and charity. These early pleas stressed the practical aspects of social work, but in 1897 Mary Richmond, whose *Social Diagnosis* would later set the standards for training in philanthropy and charity, told the National Conference of Charities and Corrections that social workers needed a professional education similar to that given to medical students. In 1898 the New York Charity Organization Society began a special summer course in the methods of philanthropy, which proved to be the beginning of a national movement in social work education. In 1903 the University of Chicago created the Institute of Social Science, and in the following year the New York School of Philanthropy began offering a full-year course.[16]

In the late 1870's a young lecturer in Balliol College, Oxford, Arnold Toynbee, began living with and talking to the workmen who made their homes in East London. It seemed to Toynbee that the two classes, university students and working men, despite their vastly different lives, had a great deal to give each other. Gradually, Toynbee persuaded some students to join him in his efforts to understand and aid the working men, but before he could institutionalize his work he died in 1883 at the age of thirty-one. After his death Canon Samuel G. Barnett, the pastor of the parish of St. Jude's Whitechapel, led a movement to create an educational institution for working people in memory of Toynbee's efforts. The young men that Toynbee had attracted to his work joined with the Canon and moved into a house in the working men's district. In honor of the founder of the movement they called the building Toynbee Hall.

The young men who came to live in Toynbee Hall thought that their superior knowledge and culture—which they possessed because of their upper-class background—would be of benefit to the poor people who lived around them. Such an idea, although clearly patronizing, seemed less offensive to British tradition than it might have seemed in the United States. Stanton Coit lived at Toynbee Hall for three months in 1886 and resolved to create a similar institution in his native New York. In 1887 Coit established the Neighborhood Guild, the first settlement house in the United States. A second house, College Settlement, appeared in New York two years later in 1889—the same year in which Jane Addams launched Hull House, probably the best-known settlement house of all.[17]

Settlement houses provided a number of services for their neighborhoods. They established clubs for people of all ages, opened playgrounds for children, and in general served as community centers. They also served as social laboratories for both academic sociologists and students at the new social work schools. When Florence Kelley, one of the most active female reformers in the country, came to Hull House in 1891, she started and supervised a series of scientific social investigations of the Hull House neighborhood. Out of these studies came *Hull House Maps and Papers, a Presentation of Nationalities and Wages in a Congested District of Chicago, Together with Comments and Essays and Problems Growing out of Social Conditions*, published in 1895. In 1894 Graham Taylor, a Congregational minister inspired by Toynbee Hall and Hull House, founded another settlement, Chicago Commons. More than Hull House, it was a center for the study of society, and students came there from several universities to investigate all kinds of social problems. Taylor became a leader in the movement to unify the social sciences and social work, and in 1903 he and Julia Lathrop, a resident at Hull House, helped to found the Social Science Center for Practical Training in Philanthropic and Social Work at the University of Chicago.[18]

In 1899 Jane Addams in "The Subtle Problems of Charity," which appeared in *Atlantic Monthly,* added her own insight to the growing demand for a truly scientific approach to social problems. Volunteer workers tried to apply their own standards of morality to the families with whom they worked, and as a result they simply did not understand the poor. The problem of child labor provided an example of this sort of failure to understand. "It is not that the charity visitor of another day was less wise than other people," Miss Addams wrote, "but that she had fixed her mind so long upon the indicated lameness of her family that she was eager to seize any crutch, however weak, which might enable them to get on. She failed to see that the boy who attempts prematurely to support his widowed mother may lower wages, add an illiterate member to the community, and arrest the development of a capable working man." In conclusion Jane Addams recommended a more scientific approach to charity which would understand and consider "human motives . . . with an open mind and a scientific conscience." [19]

By 1900 social science, whether academic sociology or the scientific study of social reform, was clearly established. Charity workers and academicians alike expected sociology to provide new insights into the causes of social problems and furnish new methods of alleviating those problems. The workers and academicians expected similar results from psychology and criminology.

A frequent visitor to Hull House and close friend of Jane Addams was the chairman of the University of Chicago's Department of Philosophy, Psychology, and Pedagogy, John Dewey. In 1895 he became a member of the settlement's board of trustees, and he remained closely involved with the affairs of Hull House for a number of years. Dewey's main reason for coming to Hull House, however, was to talk to Jane Addams. He valued her insights and criticisms of his ideas. It was especially fitting that Dewey should be connected with Hull House because his thought reflected a unification of social reform and social science just as the activities of the settlement did. Where the activities of Hull House showed the growing interdependence of sociology and social reform, Dewey's ideas indicated the close relationship between psychology and reform. In effect Dewey's work supplied a remedy for the main defect in the writing of Lester Frank Ward. Ward had argued that man should control social evolution, but he had been vague on how man could do this, and his understanding of psychology had been inadequate. To understand John Dewey's importance in the history of social science in nineteenth-century America a brief review of the history of psychology is necessary.[20]

Like sociology, psychology developed in the United States in part as a response to the provocative intellectual challenge of the idea of evolution. So important was this response that some authorities argue that in the late nineteenth century, a "new" psychology appeared. The founder was Wilhelm Wundt, a German psychologist, who became the leader of a "school" of psychology and attracted students from all over the world—including a number of Americans. Wundt's emphasis on the laboratory and on the experimental method of determining psychological propositions distinguished his work from that of other psychologists.

The founder of the new psychology in the United States was William James, who is probably better known for his philosophical ideas than for his psychology. Along with most other Americans in the late nineteenth century, James had been influenced by Darwinism and evolution, but like Ward and Dewey, he rebelled at Herbert Spencer's extreme determinism. James is regarded as the American founder of modern psychology because he used a laboratory in his teaching of the subject at Harvard and because he published the first significant textbook in the field in the United States, *The Principles of Psychology*, which appeared in 1890.[21]

One of James's influential students was G. Stanley Hall. In any consideration of the relationship between social science and juvenile delinquency Hall is especially significant because he was interested in the psychology of young people. Hall had studied philosophy in Germany after graduating from Williams College in 1867. He then taught at Antioch College for four years. Impressed with Wundt's new psychology, he decided to return to Germany for further study but lack of funds and the offer of a teaching position at Harvard delayed his trip. While at Harvard, Hall studied psychology with James and received the first doctorate in psychology in the United States. He finally went to Germany in 1878 and became Wundt's first American student.[22]

Hall returned to the United States in 1880. He lectured for a year at Harvard on pedagogy and then took a position at Johns Hopkins. There he created a psychological laboratory which was so much more comprehensive in its activities than James's that some authorities have called it the first in the United States. Among Hall's students at Johns Hopkins was John Dewey. In 1887 Hall founded the *American Journal of Psychology*, the first of its kind in the United States. The next year he moved to Worcester, Massachusetts, to become the president of newly created Clark University, and took the *Journal* and the laboratory idea with him.[23]

Evolution and Darwinism were as important in Hall's thinking as they were in the ideas of Ward, James, and Dewey. Indeed, Hall's psychology was essentially evolutionary, although he called it "genetic psychology." Hall's interest in human evolution led him to study the psychology of adolescents, the result of which was the publication in 1904 of a two-volume study entitled *Adolescence: Its Psychology, and Its Relations to Physiology, Anthropology, Sociology, Sex, Crime, Religion, and Education*. In the preface Hall explained that his method of studying psychology was eclectic; it was a combination of observation, description, and induction.

"In all civilized lands," Hall wrote, "criminal statistics show two sad and significant facts: First, that there is a marked increase of crime at the ages of twelve to fourteen, not in crimes of one, but of all kinds." Hall also pointed out that "adolescence is preeminently the criminal age when most first commitments occur and most vicious careers begin." He complained that "the

proportion of juvenile delinquents seems to be everywhere increasing." He thought that juvenile crime reflected a youth's difficulty in adjusting to his environment:

> The young offender soon comes to feel himself an enemy of
> society; to regard legitimate business as legalized theft and
> robbery; religion as a cloak for hypocrisy; clergymen as paid to
> preach or labor with prisoners; doctors kill or cure as if for
> their interest; lawyers are licensed robbers or running knaves;
> purity is a mere pretense; the world is ruled by selfishness; the
> courts or justice shops are shams; and those who prey upon the
> weaker sides of human nature know foibles of even the good
> only too well. The seasoned young criminal feels himself superior
> to the plodder who labors legitimately because he lacks the wit
> or adroitness to do otherwise.

Hall also thought that children were "more or less morally blind"
and that adolescents were "essentially antisocial." Adults usually
did not appreciate "the irresponsibility and even neurasthenia
incidental to this stage of development" and failed to see that
difficult children were often "victims of circumstances or of im-
maturity," who deserved not so much condemnation as "pity and
hope."

Hall condemned strict punishment as a means of reforming
juvenile delinquents. "The antiquated practice of fixing a minimum
penalty for each offense," he wrote, "should be banished from all
penal codes for children and offenders in early adolescence, and
the largest discretion given to the court." He also recommended
a more scientific approach to the problem of juvenile delinquency.
He argued that "the greatest need of the penologist and the
criminologist is the further study, by expert methods, of individual cases and their relations to the social environment. We
must fathom and explore the deeper strata of the soul, personal
and collective, to make our knowledge really preventive, and
recognize the function of the psychologist, pedagogue, and the
physician which should be far more prominent for youth than
for older offenders." When William A. Healy, one of James's students, accepted a position as the psychologist for the Juvenile

Psychopathic Institute in connection with the Cook County Juvenile Court in Chicago, Hall's recommendation became a reality.[24]

IV

G. Stanley Hall is important in the history of American psychology primarily because he imported the new psychology from Germany and used it to analyze the problems of youth, but he also inspired the first American efforts to apply the teachings and techniques of criminal anthropology to juvenile delinquents. These efforts came in the work of George Dawson and Maximilian P. E. Groszmann, two Clark University students. Although they were the first Americans to apply criminal anthropology to juvenile delinquents, they were not the first to notice this new discipline. In 1887 a physician at the Bloomingdale Asylum for the Insane in New York, William Noyes, read a paper, "The Criminal Type," at the American Social Science Association. Noyes's paper was the first American discussion of criminal anthropology, but this new discipline did not gain wide acceptance in the United States until the first decade of the twentieth century. After Noyes the next American writing on criminal anthropology was Thomas Wilson, the curator of prehistoric anthropology at the Smithsonian, whose report on the Second International Congress of Criminal Anthropology—the famous Paris Conference of 1889—appeared in the 1890 Annual Report of the Smithsonian.[25]

When Robert E. Fletcher, the retiring president of the Anthropological Society of Washington, wrote an article on "The New School of Criminal Anthropology," he listed no American works in his discussion of the literature of the discipline. Fletcher's article, which was a cogent summary of the main trends in both the Italian and French schools of criminology, provided a definition of criminal anthropology for Americans. It was "the study of the being, who in consequence of physical conformation, hereditary taint, or surroundings of vice, poverty, and ill example, yields to temptation and begins a career of crime." [26]

During the 1890's most of the studies on criminal anthropology published in the United States merely rehashed the ideas of European theorists like Lombroso and Tarde. Typical of these writings was an article by E. S. Morse which appeared in *Popular Science Monthly*. "The important truth to realize," Morse wrote, "is that overwhelming and incontestable evidence shows that the criminal as a type, not only exists, but that his criminal taints are transmitted, and that this transmission may run through many generations. It is proved by voluminous evidence that children are born criminals." Morse's solution was to prevent the criminal and impoverished classes from reproducing themselves. Morse's article was representative of the "heredity causes crime" school, while a good example of the "society causes crime" school is furnished by an article in the *Annals of the American Academy of Political and Social Science* written by Carroll D. Wright, one of America's leading labor statisticians. Wright did not deny the existence of a "born criminal," but he insisted that economic conditions often forced men into crime.[27]

The individuals responsible for the introduction of criminal anthropology into the United States were prison physicians, the most important of whom was Dr. Hamilton D. Wey, the medical officer of the New York Reformatory at Elmira. Wey did not accept all of the conclusions of the Italian school of criminology, but in general he accepted its basic tenets. He believed that society did contain a criminal element, but he rejected Lombroso's idea that the criminal type could be explained by the concept of atavism. "Is it not a more correct anthropology," Wey asked,

> to regard criminals rather as "sports"—using the term in its zoological significance, a variation suddenly or singularly, from the normal type of structure, usually of transient character, or not perpetuated? An animal or plant, or one of its parts, that exhibits or is the result of spontaneous variations from the normal type?

In effect Wey rejected the notion of the existence of a criminal type and also the idea, inherent in the misreadings of the *Jukes*, that acquired criminality could be inherited. However, another prison physician, W. A. M'Corn of the Wisconsin State Prison, claimed that he rarely found prisoners without some kind of skull deformity, and the physician at the Illinois State Reformatory at Pontiac, A. B. Middleton, also claimed to have found enough physical anomalies among the inmates there to provide strong support for Lombroso's theories.[28]

In spite of the observations of these prison physicians it was not until the chaplain at the San Quentin Prison, August Drähms, published *The Criminal* in 1900 that Lombroso could acknowledge that his ideas had been fairly presented in the United States. "I have not had the good fortune for some time," he wrote in the introduction to Drähm's book, "to find an author who so thoroughly understands my ideas, and is able to express them with so much clearness, as the author of this book." *The Criminal* was the first book by an American to attempt a biological, anthropological, and social approach to the problem of crime, and the only exception Lombroso took to it was "where the author holds that 'the American criminal differs in physiognomical type from his European contemporary.'" Drähms wrote that "there is no such thing as a criminal type in the anthropological sense; there is, nevertheless, a distinctively criminalistic element susceptible of classification." Drähms thought that the criminal could be classified in three main categories: the instinctive criminal, the habitual criminal, and the single offender. The main purpose of *The Criminal* was to develop a sound scientific basis for those classifications.[29]

The second important work on criminology by an American was Frances Kellor's *Experimental Sociology*, which was published in 1901. Miss Kellor, a graduate student in sociology at the University of Chicago, described her book as "a study of methods of investigation of delinquents and their treatment, together with such suggestions for the prevention of criminality as has resulted from it." She summarized the findings of the European criminologists, but her primary purpose was to demonstrate the need for a scientific laboratory to investigate the individual criminal. The investigations of such a laboratory, she believed, would provide a better understanding of crime. They could also be used to modify the treatment given to prisoners and increase the efficiency of reformatory efforts. Although Miss Kellor tried to avoid the division between the French and Italian schools of criminology, her training and methodology placed her definitely on the side of criminal sociology. She contended that Americans were "interested chiefly in determining the causes of crime in order to secure reformatory and preventive measures." Consequently, Americans were not much interested in anthropological measurements, which "alone threw no light upon cause." While Drähms's *The Criminal* is the best American book of the turn of the century propounding the ideas of the Italian school, Miss Kellor's *Experimental Sociology* is the best book written in the same period by an American presenting the theories of the French school.[30]

The Italian school received added support when G. Frank Lydston, a professor of criminal anthropology at the University of Chicago, published *The Diseases of Society* in 1909. Like Kellor, Lydston tried to balance social and anthropological interpretations of crime, but he thought that criminologists ought to study "the remote influences which produce criminality in general." He also asserted that "criminality is largely atavism, whether the atavism be social, moral or physical." Lydston thought that atavism was "the dynamic of crime," but he placed it in a larger context than Lombroso had: "All of the evolutionary factors that tend to produce the criminal—comprised by heredity, atavism, and environment, in their various divagations and interrelations—are potent in proportion to the age of the given social system." [31]

Lydston is an appropriate figure with which to conclude the discussion of criminology in the United States. He accepted the main conclusions of both schools of the new discipline, and like Ward, Sumner, and Spencer, stressed evolution as the principle of social development. Also, Lydston, like most of the early American criminologists, Wey, M'Corn, and Middleton, was a physician. By the time he wrote, criminologists had begun to settle their differences, and the French and Italian schools had become the "positivistic school" which stressed anthropological research. Lombroso's theories dominated the field, but Americans never fully accepted his deterministic views. With the growth of academic sociology and the movement toward the professionalization of social reform, Americans had other disciplines with which they could modify the findings of the positivist school of criminology. One of the main reasons why Americans did not like the views of Lombroso was that they seemed to say that nothing could be done about reforming criminals. In particular social reformers did not like the implication that their work was useless. Some Americans, however, accepted Lombroso's theories and tried to use them in experimental studies.

V

The early efforts of criminologists to study juvenile delinquents are important for two reasons. The research of these scientists caused them to move away from the deterministic views of Lombroso, but more importantly, the research showed the trend toward increasing individualization in the study of juvenile delinquents, a trend parallel to that of creating more individualistic institutions for juvenile delinquents.

By the end of the nineteenth century, criminal law was itself changing; it had passed through three phases and was moving into a fourth. The idea of revenge for individual injuries dominated the earliest stage, concepts of greater security for individuals and society accompanied by repression for offenses characterized the second period. The main ideas of the third era—which began in the eighteenth century—were the reformation of the criminal and a rational approach to punishment. The new period, the fourth, which followed the appearance of the discipline of criminology, stressed the possibility of preventing crime. To prevent crime, criminologists believed, one must first study the individual criminal and determine why he committed his act. Then it might be possible to prevent similar individuals under similar conditions from committing crimes. At this point in their theories criminologists found that Americans could agree with them. The best way to prevent crime in adults, some Americans had been arguing since the early years of the century, was to reform juvenile offenders. In *L'Uomo Delinquente* Lombroso praised the New York Children's Aid Society because it was an example of a preventive approach to the problem of juvenile crime. The two Clark University students, George Dawson and Maximilian Groszmann, working with G. Stanley Hall, studied juvenile delinquents in order to gain some insights into the adult criminal.[32]

Dawson's study, entitled "A Study of Youthful Degeneracy," appeared in *Pedagogical Seminary*, a journal founded by Hall in 1896. Dawson aligned himself with the positivist school in criminology and argued that "all the graver forms of crime undoubtedly spring directly or indirectly from constitutional peculiarities that are transmissable." To place his study in a theoretical framework, Dawson adopted the concept of degeneracy, the idea that arrested human development could be inherited, and claimed that this concept would "bring crime, insanity, idiocy, and pauperism within the domain of the law." In effect, Dawson set out to measure Charles Loring Brace's "dangerous classes" scientifically.

Dawson examined sixty juvenile delinquents at the Lyman School (formerly the Massachusetts State Reform School for Boys) and at the Massachusetts State Industrial School for Girls. He took anthropomorphic head measurements, observed the children's physical anomalies, their sensory perceptions, and their mental reactions. In addition he surveyed the children's family life and home environment. For purposes of comparison he used a control group of children from the Worcester, Massachusetts, public schools. He found that the delinquent children had smaller heads than the control group and that in general the health of the delinquent children was poorer. The delinquents seemed to have wider faces, and Dawson thought this indicated either infantilism or that the delinquent children belonged to a lower race. Dawson also found asymmetrical ears, large lower jaws, prognathous jaws, and a great many other appearance defects. When he administered mental tests, he found that the delinquent children not only did poorly but did not respond well to the testing situation. The delinquent children, particularly the boys, were inattentive, restless, and worked sporadically. Dawson saw this behavior as further evidence that juvenile delinquents had infantile minds.

In his conclusion Dawson claimed that he had found what he set out to prove—that is, that many juvenile delinquents were degenerates. "In them," he wrote, "some, at least, of the forces of development are acting retrogressively." Thus, he concluded, American juvenile delinquents belonged to a world-wide criminal class:

> Like tens of thousands of their kind throughout the world, they will spend their lives in state institutions or under police surveillance. They are out of harmony with their environments; and are, far more than is usually appreciated, *incapable* of meeting the demands of a civilization that exists only by assimilating the good and eliminating the bad.

Delinquent children could not help having committed their offenses because of their bad heredity and because of their degraded parents, most of whom were "intemperate, improvident or criminal." Thus bad heredity and degraded parents were the remote causes of juvenile delinquency; the immediate cause was usually the urging of a friend or companion. The delinquents' offenses, "their truant expeditions, their tobacco habits, their thefts, were usually joint affairs; and frequently the boys said that they had been influenced into wrong doing by those who were older and more experienced in evil." [33]

Dawson had made basic anthropological measurements of delinquent children, had interpreted his data in the light of the concept of degeneracy, and had placed American juvenile delinquents in a world-wide criminal class. He had not, however, closely integrated his findings with the teaching of the positivist school of criminology. Writing three years after Dawson, Maximilian Groszmann attempted to do just that. "Psychology and anthropology must be our guides," he wrote, "they prove that the thing needed is not so much a strict penal system for the *punishment* of offenders, as creative measures for the extirpation of *defects* which, under the now existing social conditions, appear as criminal tendencies, but which were not so considered in past ages; defects which indicate, in the majority of cases, arrested development." Like Dawson, Groszmann believed that crime was "an anomalous condition—a degeneration of the perfect type," but where Dawson labeled the minds of juvenile delinquents "infantile," Groszmann referred to criminality as "a savage condition of the mind."

Groszmann emphasized the idea that the criminal was a throwback to an earlier stage in man's evolution. The criminal class belonged to "a social stratum which has never been reached by the progress of civilization, whose psychic development had come to a standstill many generations ago, or who were continually lagging behind." Groszmann believed that embryology summarized phylogeny and argued that "we recapitulate, in a certain abbreviated form, during the years of embryonal life and childhood, our entire family history, from the dawn of human existence, in consecutive culture-epochs; and in the same measure as the younger years reproduce the earliest stages of human civilization, we pass consecutively through stages of greater differentiation . . . and at puberty, the family traits proper will assert themselves with especial vigor." This belief led Groszmann to conclude that "it is probably due to some form of arrested development during the pubertal stage, or to some unchecked impulse to realize in action the demoniac promptings of adolescent fancy, that we have so large a percentage of criminals of pubescent age."

During the 1890's the French and Italian schools had begun to draw together into the positivist approach to criminology, which had begun to emphasize the importance of social factors in causing crime. Groszmann's work also showed this tendency to blend the teachings of the two earlier schools. For example, he cited "fatigue" as an important factor causing juvenile crime. Fatigue, in Groszmann's view, reduced reasoning power to "an animal level." More important than fatigue—or any other social factor—were the schools. According to Groszmann,

> Our present so-called educational system deserves this name only in a very modest measure. It stimulates the intellect at the expense of character; it develops shrewdness rather than wisdom.

It implies more drill than development; it grafts upon the real nature of the child an artificial, conventional substance. Often it conflicts with the most fundamental instincts, and thus causes an instability of character, a vacillation of will impulses, as will become sadly manifest in moments of trial and temptation. Much in our present education is artificial, mechanical, arbitrary; and its product is only too frequently a living conventional lie.

To help prevent juvenile criminality Groszmann recommended several reforms. He called for an intelligent temperance crusade and specialized schools for deficient children. He also thought that existing schools should be more responsive to the true nature of children and teach by example rather than by mechanical drill. In addition he believed that if women's work was lightened, the education of children would automatically improve.[34]

Like Groszmann, Benjamin Reece, the author of an article on education and crime in *Popular Science Monthly*, criticized the effectiveness of American schools in preventing crime. In fact he thought that the schools actually increased crime. Taking his data from the Tenth Census he wrote that "we are confronted by facts which reveal a condition of decreasing illiteracy and increasing crime." He cited figures which showed that in the decade ending in 1880 the population had increased by 30 per cent, while illiteracy increased by only 10 per cent. In the same period crime increased by 82 per cent. These three percentages led the author to conclude that crime increased as illiteracy decreased. By way of further proof he cited the case of South Carolina; it had the highest rate of illiteracy in the country and the lowest crime rate. Reece thought that the link between the crime rate and the rate of illiteracy was the growing wealth of the country. He seemed to be saying that if there is more to steal, criminals will try to steal more often. "Do not the facts disclose by our social statistics," he asked, "cause it to appear that, in the adjustment of our schools, we have gone too far in our aim for material advancement and development of wealth, and that we are correspondingly losing in the direction of moral growth and culture?" [35]

Statistics can be misleading and they can be misread. According to another writer on education and crime, the Reverend A. W. Gould, Reece had both misread his figures and had been misled by them. Gould pointed out that an increase in the number of reported criminals may, in fact, indicate a decline in the crime rate. "The gradual elevation in the standard of life, and the intervention of the courts in cases which were formerly decided by the bullet or the knife," Gould wrote, "occasions a rapid increase in the number of criminals." Reece had failed to consider carefully his use of South Carolina as an example, Gould continued. Reece was right about the rate of illiteracy and low crime rate, and he had indicated that most of South Carolina's criminals were black, but he had simply asserted that most of the Negroes in South Carolina were educated. Having said this, Reece overlooked an important point: of 826 inmates in South Carolina's prisons, 570 were black; the illiteracy rate for Negroes was three times that for whites. Therefore, Reece's contention that the schools actually increased crime was absurd.[36]

While Reece and Gould were debating the relationship between the schools and crime, the view of Dawson and Groszmann that American juvenile delinquents belonged to a world-wide criminal class did not go unchallenged. Enoch Stoddard, a physician and a member of the New York State Board of Charities, disagreed with their reliance on an evolutionary explanation of children's crime. In a paper entitled "Juvenile Delinquency and the Failures in Present Reformatory Methods," which was published in the thirty-first *Annual Report* of the New York State Board of Charities, Stoddard wrote that "it would seem that heredity has been credited with too much power as a determining factor, and circumstances and environment with too little." In particular, Stoddard wanted to emphasize "the possibly greater influence of environment in the earliest stages of physical and mental evolution in determining the future character of the individual." He thought that the early stages of child development were especially significant for juvenile offenders:

> The mental abnormalities of the juvenile delinquent are mainly defective intellect, obtuseness of feeling for others and defective

will power. These juveniles are offenders quite as much on
account of stupidity as through any formed design to transgress established rules. Those especially displaying an absence of
feeling are children who have never enjoyed the inspiration of
parental affection and the developing influences of home life;
but have either been placed in hard and unsympathetic conditions, or have known institutions as their only parent. From
among these came our most desperate and dangerous criminals.

In effect, Stoddard had attacked the basic ideas of the positivist
school of criminology, but his main purpose was to criticize the
treatment given most juvenile offenders after conviction.

Stoddard thought that juvenile reformatories were still too much
like prisons and that their approach was far too repressive. He
favored a gentler treatment, which would stress reformation. He
also advocated a better system of classification of delinquents—a
system which would be based on a "scientific examination" of
young offenders. Such an examination would make greater "individualization" of treatment possible. Thus Stoddard should be
included among American psychologists, physicians, and students
of juvenile delinquency who advocated a more individualistic approach to the problems of the child offender. They wanted an
understanding of the causes of juvenile delinquency, and they expected the methods of science to be the principal means of understanding those causes. These men also advocated a more rational
and flexible approach in the treatment of juvenile delinquents.[37]

Stoddard's emphasis on environmental factors and Reece's use
of statistics reflected a growing trend among Americans to look
for the hard facts about social problems. This trend is well illustrated by the statistical tables of the Tenth Census. Table CXXXII,
"Inmates of Reformatories of the United States in 1880," listed
11,648 such inmates, a total which indicated the population of
"reformatories" on June 1, 1880. Of that number 1,248 were non-
white, and 9,258 were male. A similar tabulation in the Eleventh
Census showed 14,846 such inmates, 11,535 of whom were male.
Beyond the listing of such totals, the compilers of the Tenth

Census made little effort to study juvenile crime statistically. The 1890 Census, however, did relate the number of inmates in "reformatories" to the total population for both the Tenth and Eleventh Censuses. In 1880 the ratio was 229 offenders per million population, and in 1890 the ratio was 237 per million population. The Eleventh Census also included other calculations. For example it indicated that 95.3 per cent of all inmates in reformatories were literate, but 97 per cent had no trade. It also contained tables in which broad categories of offenses committed were listed: 6,930 offenses were "against society," and 4,515 were "against property." The remaining miscellaneous offenses included "destitution" and "exposure to criminal contagion." [38]

For any kind of statistical analysis of juvenile delinquency in nineteenth-century America, however, the census returns are far from satisfactory. In the introductory note to the "Report on the Defective, Dependent and Delinquent Classes . . ." of the Tenth Census, the compiler of that volume, Frederick Howard Wines, confessed that he was "not certain whether the enumeration of prisoners in the census hitherto has included the inmates of juvenile reformatories or not." Thus the earliest census returns which might be used are those of the Tenth Census in 1880. Those returns, however, are of little practical use. Counting inmates of penal institutions on a given day is in itself of questionable value for purposes of discussing crime rates or any other meaningful statistic relating to crime. The total reached by that method says nothing about the number of persons arrested, the number convicted, or the number convicted but not sentenced. Furthermore, it reveals nothing about the number of crimes reported, or the number of crimes committed but not reported. Even if there was an increase in the number of prisoners in penal institutions over a ten-year period, that fact by itself bears no clear relation to the crime rate. It could indicate only that the police were more vigilant, that judges were more strict in assessing penalties, or that more penal facilities were available. Although the Eleventh Census did contain some analysis of the total number of inmates, the

returns for 1890 had been collected on the same basis as the returns for the Tenth Census. Consequently, one cannot use the
census returns of the nineteenth century for a statistical analysis
of juvenile delinquency in that century.[39]

There were other figures on juvenile institutions—the statistics
compiled by the U.S. Bureau of Education and included in the
Annual Report of the Commissioner of Education, but these
figures are even less satisfactory than the data of the Census because they are even less controlled. Where the Census figures
included the total number of inmates in reformatories on a given
day, the tables in the Education *Reports* provide no indication as
to how the figures were derived. At first glance the Education
statistics and the Census returns are remarkably close. The 1890
Census reported 14,846 inmates in "reformatories" on June 1, 1890,
and the 1889–90 *Report* of the Commissioner of Education listed
14,734 "pupils" in "reform schools." The Education *Reports*, however, did not attempt to define "reform schools," and their total
included inmates in institutions such as truant schools which were
not included in the Census returns. The Education totals, while
they did include returns from truant schools, did not have returns
from all of the country's reform schools. The 1889–90 *Report*, for
example, does not have any listing of the Western House of Refuge
in Rochester, New York. The totals in the Education *Reports*
apparently were collected by the Bureau of Education more or
less at the whim of the reporting institutions without any statistical
control. Consequently, the totals of "pupils" in the Education *Reports* are virtually meaningless. Indeed, Table 2 of the tables on
reform schools in 1889–90 *Report* of the Commissioner of Education is labeled "statistics of reform schools for 1889–90 or there-
abouts." [40]

In spite of the irrelevance of the census statistics on juvenile
delinquency and the inaccuracy of the returns in the *Annual
Reports* of the Commissioner of Education, many Americans took
these figures to mean that juvenile crime was increasing in the
United States. Indeed, they probably were right, but proof of the
correctness of their view is unavailable.

VI

The tremendous growth of American cities in the period after the Civil War greatly intensified the social problems, and among the most important of those problems was that of juvenile delinquency. Children literally swarmed in the streets. Some of them were law-breakers, but many of them were simply society's cast-offs—neglected or dependent young people who lived from day to day by begging, stealing, or trickery. To the conservative mind of that era these immature people were a serious threat to society. Lacking basic skills and sometimes even the rudiments of an education, they seemed destined to grow up as desperate criminals of the worst sort. There appeared to be an inexhaustible supply of them, since many of them were the children of the throngs of immigrants who daily poured into American cities. Consequently, as fast as Charles Loring Brace shipped these children to the West, more appeared to take their place. Thus the social problems—juvenile delinquency, adult crime, disease, unemployment, ghetto housing, and many others—of the city intensified to such a degree that the old individualistic and philanthropic efforts to alleviate them proved inadequate. Americans, looking for relief of the pressures on the cities, expected the social sciences to find new and more efficient ways of attacking these problems.

The rise of social science in the United States prepared the way for Americans to study the individual delinquent and to try to understand his psychology. The new scientific investigators, consciously relating their efforts to the work of doctors, considered juvenile delinquency to be a social disease—a disease with its own pathology and one that might even be biologically determined. These investigators, instead of regarding the delinquent as a proper object for either punishment or pity, saw him primarily as a subject to be studied. Without the work of the social scientists in convincing the public of the need for an individual approach to deviant people, however, the task of winning public support for the extension of the juvenile court would have been much more difficult.

The juvenile court idea spread rapidly, and by 1910 most large American cities had one. The early juvenile court was not the product of the work of scientists, but rather the creation of the practical-minded, problem-solving people who had been working with juvenile delinquents all along. Since it was soon evident that the knowledge of such people was simply not adequate to deal with some of the children, the techniques, teachings, and methods of the social sciences were added to its approaches to individual delinquents.

12

Ben Lindsey and William A. Healy: The Extension of the Juvenile Court

At the turn of the century the exterior of the county courthouse in Denver was hardly inspiring. It was an old stone building in the middle of a square surrounded by trees and lawns that turned brown in the winter. Among the trees were fountains that usually did not work. Like so many other courthouses, the one in Denver was crowned with "Justice"; but this statue stood atop a dirty, soot-covered building. Perhaps significantly, lightning had struck the figure, leaving only a stump in place of the scales.

The room where the county court met, for all the broken symbolism and faded elegance, was the busiest in the state, and early in 1901 a new judge sat on the bench. He did not fit the stereotype for judges at all. He was young and without the portliness which supposedly conveyed dignity. Judge Ben Lindsey, who was just over five feet tall and weighed less than one hundred pounds, later recalled his feelings on coming to this court: "The mills of Justice began to grind and I was there to see that everything in the hopper passed truly between the stones. Sitting behind a desk that looked as if it had been designed as a wooden sepulchre, I acted as a public umpire. . . ."

Jury trials were the worst. "I was no more than a judicial automaton on a dais," Lindsey wrote. One winter afternoon he sat listening to a case that involved a claim on some furniture in a warehouse. One of the assistants to the District Attorney came up to the bench and asked the judge if he could interrupt his proceedings to hear a larceny case that would not take long. Lindsey agreed, and the attorney returned with a little boy accused of stealing coal from the railroad tracks. A railroad detective testified, and it was clear that the boy had no defense. Judge Lindsey found him guilty and sentenced him to the State Reform School.

The Judge nodded to the counsel for the warehouse case, and later recalled, "he rose—and was greeted with the most soul-piercing scream of agony that I ever heard." It came from the boy's mother who had just comprehended that the proceedings meant that she would lose her boy. She continued to scream, and the bailiffs dragged her out of the courtroom into the hall. Lindsey adjourned the court for the day and retreated into his chambers, but could still hear the woman screaming. The woman's screams had attracted two reporters who came to the Judge and asked him what he was going to do about it. Lindsey called the District Attorney, and together they agreed to suspend the boy's sentence, although they doubted the legality of this course. When the boy was returned to his mother, she at last stopped screaming.

Troubled about the legality of the suspended sentence and concerned about the conditions under which the law in Denver dealt with juveniles, Lindsey began investigating. He visited the home of the boy whose sentence he had suspended and found the family living "in a filthy shack" with the father too ill to work. The boy was "not a criminal, not a bad boy, merely a boy." Another case involving children hardened Lindsey's resolve to do something about the treatment given juvenile delinquents in Denver. One morning a court officer brought three little boys before the judge on a charge of burglary. One of the boys protested against the charge. "Judge," he said, "we ain't no burglars." The boys had been looking for watermelons in railroad cars. "Did you get any watermelons?" Lindsey asked. "No," said the boy, "but we got into a box-car, and found a box that had figs painted on it, and we each took out and drank a bottle of the stuff, and it was California fig syrup, and I think, Judge, we have been punished enough." More boys came to Lindsey's court, and he discovered that officers of the court who depended on fees instead of a salary brought in children when their income fell short.

Lindsey soon learned about other aspects of the treatment typically given juvenile delinquents in Denver: "I found boys in the county jail locked up with men of the vilest immorality, listening to obscene stories, subject to the most degrading personal indignities, and taking lessons in a high school of vice with all the receptive eagerness of innocence." Lindsey also searched the laws of Colorado to find something to justify not only his suspension of sentence but also to provide some better means of handling children accused of crimes. He found the answer in the Colorado School Law of 1899. Section Four provided that

> Every child between the ages of 8 and 14 years, and every child between the ages of 14 and 16 years who can not read and write the English language or not engaged in some regular employment, who is an habitual truant from school and is incorrigible, vicious or immoral in conduct, or who habitually wanders about the streets and public places during school hours, having no business or lawful occupation, shall be deemed a juvenile disorderly person, and subject to the provisions of this act.

The law further provided that the county court had jurisdiction over "juvenile disorderly persons" and it could commit them to the "boys' industrial school or the girls' industrial school or to some other juvenile reformatory." Furthermore the act sanctioned Lindsey's conduct: "Any order of commitment may be suspended by the judge of the county court during such time as the child may regularly attend school and properly conduct itself." The law was intended primarily to support school discipline, but Lindsey saw it as a way to establish a juvenile court.[1]

Lindsey recruited probation officers from among the school system's truant officers, and began hearing children's cases separately from the rest of the business of the county court. He had created a juvenile court by means of imaginative legal improvisation. After he learned of the Chicago court, he became the leading promoter of juvenile courts in the United States. In the meantime the Chicago juvenile Court did not stand still. While Ben Lindsey traveled throughout the country speaking for the extension of juvenile courts, the ladies of Chicago created the Juvenile Psychopathic Institute and hired William A. Healy, the first psychologist to be associated with a juvenile court. Thus, while Ben Lindsey sought to expand the number of juvenile courts in the United States, William A. Healy was one of the first men to expand the functions of the court.

II

Benjamin Barr Lindsey was born on November 25, 1869, in Jackson, Tennessee, where his father worked as a telegrapher for Western Union. The discovery of gold in Colorado and the offer of a job with a new railroad in Denver led Ben's father to move to that western city. The rest of the family came out later, arriving in Denver in 1880. Two years later Ben and his brother, Chal, went to Notre Dame to study in the "minim" department for younger boys. The Lindsey boys had to leave South Bend, however, when their father lost his job in Denver. They returned to Jackson, Tennessee, in 1884, while their mother and father remained in Denver. Ben then enrolled in Southwestern Baptist University in Jackson, where he found little sympathy for the views he had learned at Notre Dame. "I soon found myself overcome in numbers, if not in argument," he recalled, "since the Pope had no other champions among the Baptist fundamentalists. . . . I found my solace in the debating society, the Apollonians, which furnished me an outlet for other than religious controversies." When Lindsey defended the Irish in a debate and won, he decided to become a lawyer, "because that profession seemed to me to offer opportunity to express the burning passion within me to fight for justice." After three years in Jackson, the Lindsey boys returned to Denver. Ben got a job in a land office, and his brother started working for a lawyer. Since Ben wanted to be a lawyer, he and his brother traded jobs.

In 1894 at the age of twenty-five Ben Lindsey was admitted to the bar, and soon after he entered partnership with Frederick A. Parks, another young lawyer. One of their first cases, a malpractice suit against a prominent Denver surgeon, ended with a hung jury, and the young men suspected that a juror had been bribed. When two other cases ended in a similar fashion, Lindsey and Parks decided to enter politics and change the law regarding jury decisions in liability cases. Lindsey was a Democrat and Parks a Silver Republican. They decided that Parks, being the more magnetic, should run for the State Senate in 1898. Parks won the election and took his seat. Lindsey and Parks had prepared three bills, one of which provided that only a three-fourths vote by a jury could decide a liability case. The other two bills were a workmen's compensation law, and a measure that would provide compensation for pain and suffering in personal liability cases. The three-fourths bill passed the Legislature, but the Supreme Court declared it unconstitutional. In the election Lindsey worked for the "fusion" ticket of Democrats and Silver Republicans and helped to secure the election of Charles S. Thomas, a Democrat, as Governor of Colorado. Thomas rewarded Lindsey's efforts by appointing the young lawyer as public administrator of Arapahoe County (Denver). According to Lindsey, this position "brought me an invaluable experience out of which I later developed a new application of the old chancery court practice in my work in the Juvenile and Family Relations Court in Denver."

Lindsey continued to work in politics, and in 1900 his partner urged him to try for the Democratic nomination for District Attorney. Parks wanted to put Lindsey in a position to increase the income of their fledgling firm; Lindsey refused to go along. The partnership dissolved, and Lindsey did not get the nomination. He became a member of the State Executive Committee for the Democratic party and helped to secure a victory for the Democrats in Colorado in 1900. As a consequence of the election, Governor Thomas appointed Judge R. W. Steele of the County Court to the

Supreme Court, and the County Commissioners chose Lindsey to fill the vacancy.[2]

Lindsey assumed his duties as County Judge on January 1, 1901, and shortly afterward heard his first case involving a juvenile. He talked to various civic groups and persuaded the school authorities to allow him to use truant officers as probation officers. He also developed a standardized procedure to deal with children accused of criminal offenses. The child, instead of being charged with a crime, was brought before the County Judge and "informed against . . . as a disorderly juvenile person." The Judge then issued a warrant, but the court officers usually did not serve the warrants, and instead merely told the child's parents to appear in court at a certain time. When the case came up, Lindsey did not hold a formal trial. He talked with the boy and then decided if the boy could be put on probation. "We never release a boy upon probation," Lindsey later explained,

> until he is impressed with the idea that he must obey. It is explained what the consequences will be if he does not obey and keep his word. It is kindly but firmly impressed why all this is so, and why after all he is the one we are most interested in and that it is *for* him we are working and not *against* him. We want him to work *with* us and not *against* us. He must, to do this, obey in the home, in the school, and of course, he must obey the laws of the land and respect the rights of others.

The Judge then talked to the parents and inquired about home conditions, after which he explained the terms of probation. Typically, Lindsey sentenced a boy to the State Industrial School, but suspended the sentence so long as the boy's behavior was satisfactory. Lindsey then ordered the boy to report at the next "juvenile court day." [3]

Lindsey usually held juvenile court days every other Saturday. Boys under fourteen had to bring written reports from their teacher about their conduct and progress. When a boy had been placed on probation, Lindsey usually wrote to his teacher or employer and explained what the court was trying to do. For example, he wrote to a Miss Ames, a teacher in one of the Denver schools, that one of her pupils "was before me today on the charge of truancy. I have suspended sentence in his case on his promise to attend school regularly and to be a good boy. I will greatly appreciate it if you will kindly send me a report each week or two as to his attendance and behavior, for I desire to be advised as to his conduct." Boys over fourteen who were not in school met the Judge in his office on Saturday evenings. When boys were neither employed nor in school, the Court helped them to find jobs. Typical of Lindsey's efforts to obtain jobs for boys was a letter he wrote in January, 1902, to W. P. McPhee, a Denver businessman. "From time to time in connection with our work here in the juvenile court division of this institution known as the County Court," Lindsey said, "we have to help some poor boy get a job." He went on to note that "it occurred to me that possibly you might have occasion to employ boys in this big establishment of yours, and if so I would consider it a favor if you would let me know, either now or any future time, as we generally have somebody on the list we are trying to help." [4]

Juvenile court days began at nine on Saturday mornings when all the boys whose cases were pending assembled in the courtroom. Usually there were about two hundred boys present. Before the proceedings began the boys received copies of approved magazines such as *The American Boy, Men of Tomorrow,* and *Success.* Lindsey had persuaded the publishers to give him reduced rates and had asked his friends to support this effort. In September, 1902, for example, he wrote to R. H. Malone that

> in our juvenile court here we have a number of ways of assisting the wayward youths about here. One of them is to provide them with good literature, which is doing much to break up the habit of dime novel reading and the like. . . . I am asking a few of my personal friends to stand this expense as a sort of public service which I think is as worthy as many of the charities you are no doubt called on to aid.

For these Saturday sessions the courtroom altered. The tables for counsel were removed and replaced by chairs; the room took on the appearance of a classroom. Judge Lindsey sat at a table among the boys, and he opened the proceedings with a short talk. "I usually spend fifteen minutes in talking to these boys," he explained,

> generally taking as a title for the discourse some subject that immediately gains the boy's heart and attention. For instance, "snitching" means to "peach" or "tell," a term known to every boy from the wealthiest to the poorest, and the best to the worst. Some splendid lessons may be instilled under this title— the difference between a tattle-tale, the sissy boy, the goody boy, a manly boy, a real boy, accessory before and after the fact in the commission of crime, guilty knowledge, with a few stories woven in—lessons which gain a tremendous hold upon a boy and leave him with many lessons which I find have positive good effect.

Lindsey tried to avoid a preaching tone. "I talk to them very much as if I were one of them discussing some ordinary boy's troubles. . . ." He stressed the positive approach of the juvenile court and told the boys that the court's purpose was to help them.

Occasionally during these talks Lindsey would discuss boys who had not kept the terms of their probation. "I am compelled to tell them with sorrow, rather than with anger," he later wrote, "of some boy too weak to do right, to keep his word, to be square, and with a hope that I may strengthen him to be square and to be strong and because I love him and not because I hate him or am angry at him, I must send him to the Industrial School." When Lindsey had finished his talk, the boys filed up to his table and presented their reports. "I read the report of each boy," he later wrote, "with comment thereon, praising up before the other boys and individually and if the entire number have good reports, a general word of praise for all. Any boy in this crowd who hasn't a good report is made to feel the effects of it in a way that you may readily appreciate. His pride is simply hurt that he does not come up to the others, which is the secret of more in boy life than we can well appreciate. If handled rightly, this is a wonderful leverage for good." Those with unsatisfactory reports waited for a private interview with the judge. In these interviews Lindsey tried to make friends with the boys. "Personal influence, touch and association with some of the worst boy burglars and thieves that ever infested any city," he recalled, "have produced such remarkable reformation that policemen, principals of schools and parents have professed in many cases to be amazed." Lindsey had talked with hundreds of boys in his chambers around his table "as one boy would talk to another, on an equal footing, and their confidence and frankness has been as refreshing as it has been enlightening."

The working boys came to the judge's office at 7:30 in the evening on juvenile court Saturday. "They bring no written statements from their employers as a rule," Lindsey explained, because "some of the boys feel sensitive about having their employers constantly advised that they are under surveillance or restraint of any kind." The employers usually cooperated with the court, and Lindsey reported that "they even take a more special interest in a boy for that reason, and I find through our good offices, which are often invoked, are more patient and charitable with the faults of such boys. . . ." In the judge's office, Lindsey said, "we have a sort of boys' club meeting . . . in which I am free and easy with all of them, inquire about their work, their pay, their prospects of advancement, give them an encouraging word, . . . and often write as many as a dozen letters for those who are out of employment. . . ."

One of the unusual aspects of Lindsey's court procedure was his insistence on cleanliness. He had showers installed in the court building and sent every "dirty" boy who appeared in his court to the basement to take a bath. The showers were also available on juvenile court Saturdays.

Lindsey recognized that his juvenile court—as based on the school law—was on somewhat dubious legal ground. When the County Attorney of El Paso County, Colorado, wrote to him about his procedures, he admitted that "it may be that we are stretching this law a little. . . . But," Lindsey continued, "it has worked well in hundreds of cases here, and we believe our course is not only legal, but fully justified by the best modern methods of dealing with juveniles." Lindsey then described a recent case to the attorney to illustrate the court's methods:

> A few days ago, a young man had a bicycle stolen from him by a boy thirteen years old. This young man went to the Justice Court to swear out a complaint against the boy for grand larceny, and I believe also burglary, as the boy had broken into a barn to get the wheel. The Justice simply sent the young man to the district attorney, and the district attorney filed an information in this court against the boy, charging him with being a juvenile disorderly person. It was the child's first offense, and he was thus saved the stigma of being convicted of burglary. He was put on our parole list and reports here regularly once every two weeks.

Such a system, Lindsey argued, not only saved the county money by eliminating the expense of a preliminary hearing, it also was more effective. Of five hundred boys who had appeared before Lindsey's court, less than fifty went to the State Industrial School.

During his early work with children, Lindsey developed a very successful, if informal system. It worked well because Lindsey had the time and the willingness to be patient with the children who came before him. In a letter written to William Sprague, a publisher, Lindsey noted that "it is astonishing how much good there is in some boys apparently of criminal tendencies, if you can only reach the boy in the right way." Lindsey approached boys in a positive way. His work in securing jobs for them convinced them that he was on their side. In April, 1902, for example, he told Sprague that "in the last two months we have obtained very good positions for over 30 boys, out of the reform school, or who have been convicted in this court, and I believe that nine-tenths of them under the system we have here are going to come out all right, and the result will be better for the state and better for the boy than following the old methods of punishment." In fact Lindsey's system proved so effective that some boys even turned themselves in. In January, 1903, he noted that.

> we have had in this court over fifty voluntary delinquents during the last year who have belonged to the same gangs of boys

who were actually brought here, but who have come in and confessed to stealing, burglary and very serious offenses, in many cases giving details, when we have placed them upon the probation list with the understanding that if the offense is repeated they shall be prosecuted for what they have confessed to doing. We did not start this, or even suggest it—it simply grew up; . . . the boys came here without any suggestion from us but through the influence of those members of the gang who were brought here.

Clearly, Lindsey had created a bond of trust with his young clientele.

Another aspect of Lindsey's approach was his almost complete informality. Unlike Judge Tuthill in the Cook County Juvenile Court, Lindsey did not hear children's cases from the bench in a regular courtroom. He heard juvenile cases on the "five-o'clock docket," that is, after the conclusion of the regular business of the county court. "These cases are heard in chambers around my table," Lindsey reported, "and a great deal of time given to each, the probation officer being present with his reports, also the parents and only those interested." To secure the boys' cooperation, Lindsey occasionally resorted to a conspiracy of sorts. "I have often said," he told the delegates to the National Conference of Charities and Corrections in 1903,

now fellows look here, if I keep you all out of Golden (this is the town where the Industrial School is located) and you go and swipe something again, why what will folks say? Why, they will just say, "That fool judge up there ought to have sent that kid up. If he had, he wouldn't have swiped anything, and made other people a lot of trouble." Now it is my custom to say, "Kids we are all in the same boat, and if anybody swipes anything again, I am going to get fits, and the first thing you know, you will be getting a new judge up here that will hike you all up." (A little boys' slang, judiciously and wisely used at the psychological moment, has a powerful effect and does more to reach the boy heart than you will imagine. I do not believe, if used with discretion, it has a bad effect.)

Lindsey respected the dignity of the boys he saw. He sometimes talked their language, but he never talked down to them. While he helped boys, they never mistook his help for weakness.[5]

Lindsey claimed that his methods were basically practical. In September, 1904, he sent a copy of the *Report* of the Juvenile Court to G. Stanley Hall and told him that he had ordered a copy of Hall's *Adolescence* for the use of the court. "The methods I have employed here," Lindsey said, "have simply grown up as a result of my observations and experience, and I have up to this time purposely refrained from consulting or studying any sociological works for fear I might embibe [sic] some theory. . . ." Lindsey was glad that he had done so, but indicated that he was now ready to study theoretical works.[6]

Almost by accident Ben Lindsey had created a juvenile court. He did it by bending the law and by persuading other officials, including the District Attorney, to go along. He then used the same persuasive powers on the children who came before his court. His court was informal, even colloquial, and perhaps illegal, but it was also very effective. Its effectiveness came from Lindsey's personality. Other men in similar circumstances had not seen the possibilities in the Colorado School Law, and Lindsey himself, despite his success, began to grow uneasy about the precarious legal foundations of his Juvenile Court.[7]

One of the factors which may have increased Lindsey's concern about the legality of his activity was his discovery of the Illinois Juvenile Court Act. Early in 1902 he came across the *Juvenile Record*, a monthly paper published by the Visitation and Aid Society of Chicago to publicize the Chicago Juvenile Court. The editor of the *Juvenile Record*, Timothy D. Hurley, also served as the Chief Probation Officer for the Chicago Juvenile Court. Lindsey wrote to Hurley and described his own work. Hurley passed Lindsey's letter on to Judge Tuthill who wrote the Colorado Judge that "I assure you it is a great pleasure for me to learn that such valuable work is being performed, with such good results, by you and your associates in Denver." [8]

Matters came to a head at the meeting of the Colorado County Judges Association in the spring of 1902. The judges decided that a separate law for the juvenile court was necessary and directed Lindsey to draw it up. Shortly after that meeting Lindsey attended the National Conference of Charities and Corrections in Detroit as a delegate from Colorado. In Detroit, Lindsey learned more about other state laws pertaining to juveniles and about plans to create new juvenile courts. At about the same time he visited Chicago and inspected Cook County's facilities for juvenile delinquents. These experiences probably influenced Lindsey to press for two new bills: One to put the juvenile court on a sound legal foundation and another to provide punishment for adults who contributed to the delinquency of a minor. In July he sent a copy of the Denver Juvenile Court *Report* to the *Denver Republican* and asked that it be published in order to stimulate public interest in the juvenile court bill.[9]

The Colorado Legislature would not meet until 1903, and in the interim Lindsey mounted a campaign to arouse public interest in and support for a new juvenile court law. He spoke on behalf of the new laws whenever he got an opportunity. He also began a crusade against the proprietors of gambling dens and wine rooms, who openly served children. In April he wrote a letter to Hamilton Armstrong, the Denver Chief of Police:

> On Saturday last we tried in this court among the juvenile cases coming here for disposal two cases in which it appeared that boys of tender age (13 and 14 years) are frequenting a certain gambling house in this city, which these boys tell me is under Lambie's Bakery on Larimer Street . . . I think this is a disgrace to the city and I cannot believe that the place would remain open a moment with the knowledge of yourself in particular, and I therefore ask that you arrest the proprietor and I will do all I can to furnish you with sufficient evidence to convict, as I believe I can.
>
> Another juvenile case tried in this court is that of a young girl whom it seems from the evidence has frequented the saloon of a man by the name of Fitzgerald, and I am informed that no action has been taken against the man. Justice Mayer of the Special Sessions Court of New York, gives it as his opinion that the great majority of juvenile criminals in New York are directly attributable to what he terms two cent pool rooms, and *cheap,*

low saloons. . . . I have myself observed school boys in some
of the pool rooms about town, as I have passed along the street
where such places are located. They lead a boy into the saloon
and the gambling dens . . . and if there is any way to keep
such places clear of juveniles I trust you will see that it is done.

Chief Armstrong referred Lindsey's letter to the Police Board, and
as a result the President of that Board, Frank Adams, came to see
Judge Lindsey. "I made a personal appeal to him," Lindsey recalled. "I told him of what I had seen, of how the young girls and
boys were being sacrificed; and he promised and repeated his
promise, that he would see that the laws were enforced and the
children protected." But an investigation showed that Adams had
not kept his promise. Lindsey then invited the entire Police Board
to come to his courtroom, and he made sure that several reporters
were also there. He accused the commissioners of "neglecting their
duties, of knowingly permitting the dives to ruin children, and of
being personally responsible for much of the appalling immorality"
that came before his court. The newspapers carried accounts of
the meeting on their front pages, and a public outcry compelled
the police to enforce the laws against serving minors in the
saloons and gambling dens.

Lindsey also campaigned against the conditions in the Denver
jails. In this effort, as in the drive against the wine rooms, the
judge had two motives. He wanted to secure a detention home
for juvenile delinquents, and he wanted to keep the juvenile court
in the public eye. "I had found conditions in the jails," he wrote,
"almost as bad as they were in the dives. Boys repeated to me the
obscene stories they had heard there, from the older prisoners,
and described the abominable pollutions that had been committed
on their little bodies." Some of the boys also complained about
mistreatment and abuse from the police. As before, Lindsey went
to Chief Armstrong and to Frank Adams, but they told the judge
that the boys were lying to him. There was no improvement by
the turn of the year when Lindsey's juvenile court bills were
introduced. In the legislature Senator "Billy" Adams, the brother
of the President of the Denver Police Board, led the opposition

to the bills. Lindsey told a reporter about the jail conditions, and the resulting article led the Police Board to denounce Lindsey publicly. Lindsey then promised a full investigation. He invited the Governor of Colorado, the Mayor of Denver, the Police Board, and some of the city's prominent ministers to come to a special hearing in his courtroom. On the morning of the day of the hearing he learned that the subpoenas he had ordered served on boys who had been in jail had not been delivered. He then called on "Mickey," one of the boys who had been in juvenile court, and asked him to bring in as many boys who had been in jail as he could find. By the time the hearing started Mickey had rounded up about twenty of "the worst lot of little jail birds that ever saw the inside of a county court." One of the boys had been in jail twenty times.

The hearing took place in the Judge's chambers and without reporters. There were no reporters because, Lindsey said, "I knew what sort of vice and unprintable testimony was coming." The boys came in one by one, and Lindsey stressed the need for them to tell the truth. The boys told "stories of bestiality that were the more horrible because they were so innocently, so baldly, given. . . . One boy broke down and cried when he told of the vile indecencies that had been committed upon him by the older criminals. . . ." Finally, one of the ministers who could stand no more asked that the proceedings stop. The Governor was particularly impressed and announced that he would support Lindsey's juvenile court bill. The ministers blasted the conditions in the jails in their sermons, the newspapers reported the sermons, and the opposition to Lindsey's bills disappeared.[10]

Lindsey had drafted his bills with care. In September, 1902, he wrote to Hurley and asked for "citations of any cases discussing the constitutional aspect of juvenile courts." He wanted to be sure that the Colorado Juvenile Court law would not be declared unconstitutional. For the most part Lindsey followed the Illinois law. "I think that the Illinois Act is a model that we can all well copy from," he wrote, "although I have serious doubts as to its constitutionality at some points, and these doubts we have attempted to remove in the law which we have prepared for this state." One problem Lindsey noticed in the Illinois law and tried to avoid in his own bill was that "because of the very informality of the proceedings [in a juvenile court] facts might come out which might incriminate the child or others, and thus deprive them of rights with formality of legal proceedings or due process of law." In answer to this problem the Colorado law of 1903 contained the following passage: "A disposition of any child under this act, or any evidence given in any such cause, shall not in any civil, criminal or other cause or proceeding whatever in any court be lawful or proper evidence against such child for any purpose whatever, excepting in subsequent cases against the same child under this act." [11]

Before he submitted the bills to the legislature, Lindsey sent copies to Timothy D. Hurley, the Chief Probation Officer of the Cook County Juvenile Court in Chicago. Hurley made several comments on the juvenile court bill, and Lindsey incorporated some of Hurley's criticisms in the final version of the bill. Hurley objected to the word "conviction" in the first section and Lindsey eliminated the word. Hurley also objected to the use of the word "prosecute" to describe the action taken by the District Attorney's Office against children, and in the final proceedings Lindsey changed this section to read that "all proceedings under this act shall be by information or sworn complaint to be filed by the district attorney as in other cases under the general laws of the State." Hurley also criticized the section of Lindsey's bill which would have made the names of delinquent children and their parents a part of the records of the Colorado State Board of Charities and Corrections. Lindsey added a section which prohibited the disclosure of names. One suggestion Hurley made which Lindsey did not incorporate was to insert a religious section which would require children to be placed out in families of the same faith. Lindsey felt that Colorado laws already covered this point adequately. [12]

The new Colorado Juvenile Court law and the "adult delinquency law" passed the legislature in March, 1903. The Juvenile Court law clearly shows that Lindsey had followed the Illinois Juvenile Court law of 1899 and the 1901 amendment to that law. Like the Illinois law the Colorado law contained a section concerning the manner in which the law should be interpreted:

> This act shall be liberally construed, to the end that its purpose may be carried out, to wit, that the care and custody and discipline of the child shall approximate as nearly as may be that which should be given by its parents, and that as far as practicable any delinquent child shall be treated, not as a criminal, but as misdirected and misguided, and needing aid, encouragement, help and assistance.

The Colorado law also included under the definition of juvenile delinquency all the actions listed in the 1901 Illinois law and several more. According to the Colorado law a child under sixteen who "patronizes or visits any public pool room or bucket shop; or who wanders about the streets in the night time without being on lawful business or occupation; . . . or who habitually uses vile, obscene, vulgar, profane, or indecent language . . ." would be "deemed a juvenile delinquent person." A more notable departure from the Illinois law was the "act to provide for the punishment of persons responsible for or contributing to the delinquency of children," which said that the parents, guardians, or any other person "responsible for, or by any act encouraging, causing or contributing to the delinquency" of a child would, if convicted, be subject to a fine of up to one thousand dollars or imprisonment of up to one year in the county jail. It also provided that the judge could "impose conditions upon any person found guilty under this act, and so long as such person shall comply therewith to the satisfaction of the court the sentence may be suspended." The Cook County Court, although technically not an independent court, was for all practical purposes a separate court which heard only children's cases. The Colorado law gave jurisdiction to the county courts, but directed them to keep separate dockets and records for juvenile cases.[13]

III

Ben Lindsey's true importance comes not so much from his work in Denver or as a Colorado lawmaker as from his efforts to spread juvenile courts throughout the country. Lindsey's work in Denver was extraordinarily effective and did lead to important modifications in the procedures of juvenile courts. To understand Lindsey, his Denver work must be considered, but to place him in proper perspective, he should be seen as the best known juvenile court judge in the world and the leading "evangelist" of juvenile court "gospel." [14]

In 1902 Lindsey began a campaign to support the establishment of juvenile courts throughout the country. He attended the National Conference of Charities and Corrections at Detroit as an official delegate from Colorado. During a discussion on juvenile reformatories, Lindsey launched his effort. "Before I leave this conference," he said, "I desire to impress upon the delegates the necessity of earnest work in your respective states to have your legislatures next winter enact the proper laws to establish juvenile courts." While at this meeting Lindsey adopted a standard approach to audiences. To make his points, he used anecdotes and stories from his experiences at the juvenile court in Denver. During a section meeting on juvenile delinquents, he told the story of "Charlie," who had come before Lindsey's court for the third time. "There was something in Charlie that appealed to me," Lindsey told the delegates,

> The probation officer, who had looked into the case advised that he be sent to the industrial school. I took that boy up into my chambers, and I got acquainted with him; and we got to be good friends. I told him they all wanted me to send him up, and, if I did not and he went wrong again, that I should get into trouble. Charlie saw the point and said, "Give me another chance, and let me be your friend." We shook hands. It was a bond, a contract between us. He went to school, and after two weeks, I got a "fair" report from him. He had not played "hookey" once. The next time he came with a "good" report,

and finally, with an "excellent" report; and he always received
encouragement. I have in mind twenty boys of that kind, who
have been worked in that way, all of whom have stood right
with me.

The point of the story, Lindsey said, was that people who worked
with delinquents should understand them and gain their confidence. "We must find out the particular trouble in each case, and
use everlasting patience," he concluded.[15]

"My dream has been," Lindsey wrote later, "to see a special
court in each city in this country, vested with complete jurisdiction to deal with all these laws and all these questions that
concern the child and the home. . . ." He visited Chicago in
the spring of 1902 on his way to Detroit, and when he returned
to Denver, Lindsey prepared a report on the procedures and
activities of the Denver Juvenile Court and sent it to the *Denver
Republican* for publication. In an accompanying letter he explained that the report was "a plea for the establishment of juvenile courts all over the United States." At the same time Lindsey
began his campaign for a more adequate juvenile court law in
Colorado.[16]

In the fall of 1902 Lindsey began his travels in behalf of the
juvenile court movement and addressed a meeting of the Kansas
Society for the Friendless. As was characteristic of nearly all of
his public addresses, this talk was full of anecdotes and personal
vignettes. In Kansas, Lindsey told the story of a fifteen-year-old
boy "as adept and confirmed a burglar as most adult criminals."
He had escaped from jail and had been in jail five times, but
Lindsey was able to influence him. "I suppose I have spent over
20 solid hours off and on, evenings and Sundays," Lindsey said.
"Why shouldn't I? He has cost the state, by actual records and
figures over $1,000." Lindsey described his operation fully and
argued that it not only saved money—by his calculation his court
in eighteen months had saved the State of Colorado $50,000 but
also helped prevent crime.

Shortly after the juvenile court bill became law in the spring of
1903, Lindsey went to Atlanta to give a paper at the National

Conference of Charities and Corrections. Here again Lindsey described the workings of the Denver Juvenile Court and stressed the effectiveness of his own probation system. "I do not know how to explain what may be done with the juvenile court and its offices better," he said, "than to tell what has been done in the court over which I have the honor to preside and to refer to some of the principles underlying the methods produced." In that same year Lindsey wrote the first of a series of articles for *Charities*, a weekly magazine published by the New York Charity Organization Society and edited by Edward T. Devine and Paul Kellogg. His article was appropriately entitled "Some Experiences in the Juvenile Court of Denver," and like his speeches, it was folksy and full of anecdotes. In it he stated his own measure for evaluating juvenile courts. "If that new method of dealing with juvenile offenders, generally known as the juvenile court and probation system," he wrote, "produces better results than the old method of attempting to correct children through the criminal courts, it is a success. This is the test rather than how many boys or girls it succeeds in correcting." [17]

In 1904 Lindsey went to California to give an address on "The Child and the State" to the California State Conference of Charities and Corrections. This talk, although similar to most of Lindsey's other addresses, was much more philosophical. He quoted G. Stanley Hall, for example, on the psychology of adolescence and then said that "very little time or attention is paid to the boy. Very little thought and intelligence are given to his life and the things that control him." Lindsey also stressed the need for the medical study of individual delinquents. "One-third of the boys who get bad," he said, "have something the matter with them physically. It is the duty of the State to study the boys and to accommodate itself to their needs and necessities while they are going through this period of life." He concluded his remarks with a discussion of the savings that a juvenile court would bring and said, "I hope these facts and these little experiences, my friends . . . will convince you here in San Francisco, as it has [sic] convinced us in Denver, that it is, after all, wiser and less expensive to save children than to punish criminals." [18]

In the fall of 1904 Lindsey prepared an elaborate report on the activities of the Denver Juvenile Court and mailed it to influential reformers throughout the world. He sent copies, for example, to A. E. Winship, the editor of the *Journal of Education*, G. Stanley Hall, Count Leo Tolstoi, Edward L. Thorndike, Julia Lathrop, and Jane Addams. To Tolstoi he wrote: "I shall be greatly complimented and honored if you can find the time to read this booklet, and would value as one of my dearest possessions a word from you as to what you think of the plan as compared to the old method of reforming criminals through jails and penal institutions." Among the responses to the report was a letter from Edward L. Thorndike, who wrote "to express my deep appreciation of the work that you have been doing, and my satisfaction in seeing a report of your work in such form that it can be put into the hands of students." The report itself was a typical Lindsey production. Most of it consisted of anecdotes and case studies which illustrated his system and his principles. Lindsey also included some impressive statistics to show that the juvenile court had been a success and had saved money for the State of Colorado.[19]

For the 1905 meeting of the National Conference of Charities and Corrections, Lindsey served as chairman of the sub-committee on juvenile courts. Lindsey reported at the meeting that in the fall of 1904 he had sent a circular urging "the adoption of juvenile court laws for all the states" to "the daily press, [and to] philanthropic, religious and educational journals" throughout the country. He noted that juvenile courts had received favorable treatment in the press and mentioned both *Charities* and the *Juvenile Record* as being particularly active in their support of the juvenile court movement. The World's Fair at St. Louis had included a juvenile court exhibit, and he quoted from President Roosevelt's message to Congress, on December 6, 1904, in which the President praised the juvenile court. Early in 1905 Lindsey visited Kansas, Nebraska, Illinois, Wisconsin, Indiana, Kentucky, Tennessee, Pennsylvania, New York, New Hampshire, Ohio, Utah, and Washington, D.C. "I had the honor to speak to several legislatures," he said, "some in session, and to some at special meetings called by the members in behalf of children's laws." In Washington he talked to President Roosevelt about the creation of a juvenile court for the nation's capital. In the same year *Charities* published another of Lindsey's articles, "The Boy and the Court; the Colorado Law and its Administration," which was similar to the address he gave to the California Conference of Charities.[20]

During his years as County Judge, Lindsey had often offended the business interests of Denver, and in the election of 1904 they nearly succeeded in removing him. Lindsey had alienated the Democrats with his reforming efforts, and he knew that he had no chance of gaining their nomination. He thought, however, that he would receive the Republican nomination without any difficulty. Only at the last minute did he learn that the Republican leaders were planning to give the nomination for County Judge to someone else. Lindsey mobilized the young Republicans who favored his nomination, and they packed the galleries of the State Convention with Lindsey supporters. The Lindsey backers stampeded the convention and secured his nomination. Lindsey won re-election and soon began campaigning for reform of the state's election laws. This time Lindsey's corporate and political enemies found a new way to attack him. They prepared to separate the juvenile court from the County Court and severely limit the powers of the juvenile court. They knew that if Lindsey were forced to choose between the juvenile court and the County Court that he would remain with the children. Lindsey was able to eliminate the restrictions his enemies would have placed on the juvenile court, but he was unable to prevent the split away from the County Court. The new Colorado law passed in 1907, and the peculiar combination of powers that Lindsey had enjoyed as Judge of the County Court and of the juvenile court came to an end.[21]

As a result of his activities on behalf of the juvenile court movement, Lindsey became a national figure. In 1906 he wrote that "I feel just swamped with the stack of mail and the amount of work I have on hand and hardly know which way to turn. The notoriety which I seem to have attained in the children's work has made me a mark for philanthropic magazines, publications, societies and individuals all over the country. . . ." A delegate to the National Conference of Charities and Corrections which met in Atlanta in 1903 said that Lindsey "*is* the 'children's court' of Denver and has done unique and effective service as a preventive agency. His functions are those ordinarily performed by an investigator, a judge, jury, probation officer, and vender of vernacular." Lindsey's greatest asset was his personality. He was extraordinarily adept at communicating with people. "He understands boy nature," Samuel J. Barrows, the Secretary of the New York Prison Association said of him,

> and he makes boys understand him. He knows their dialect and uses it; he gets their ear, their confidence and their heart. They will tell him stories of their own wrong doing which they have not confessed to their teacher, their pastor or their own parents. He not only gains their confidence, but he gains their affection, so that boys keep straight in order to keep "square with the judge."

The same traits made him equally facile in his 'talks with adults. Lindsey's methods were irregular, but they were practical and produced hundreds of picturesque episodes which greatly aided the juvenile court movement. Lindsey was, because of his talks which were full of warm stories about "his boys," a very memorable figure. Thus Lindsey became nationally known as "the kids' judge," and Lincoln Steffens devoted separate chapters of his *Autobiography* and *Upbuilders* to him. Lindsey made the juvenile court human, he was responsible for the first contributory delinquency law, and he led the effort to spread the juvenile court idea throughout the country.[22]

IV

While Lindsey worked for the establishment of juvenile courts, their numbers grew slowly. By 1905 ten states had passed some sort of juvenile court law. These courts were of two types. Most were similar to the Chicago and Denver courts and used chancery procedure, but some were based entirely on the criminal law and used criminal procedure. The juvenile court idea continued to spread, however. By 1909 twenty-two states had juvenile court laws, and by 1915 forty-six states, three territories, and the District of Columbia had them.[23]

Some of the early juvenile courts developed the same way the Denver Juvenile Court had—informally and on dubious legal foundations. A police judge in Indianapolis, George W. Stubbs, began in the fall of 1901 to set aside one day a week to hear children's cases. In 1902 he went to Chicago to visit and observe the work of the Cook County Juvenile Court. He modified his own procedure as a result, but Indiana did not have a juvenile court law until 1903. In Buffalo, New York, in 1900 Judge Robert Murphy began to use the New York law of 1892 which provided for the separate trial of juveniles, but hesitated to use chancery procedure without legal support. A committee from Buffalo's Charity Organization Society tried to persuade the New York Legislature to pass a state law creating and funding separate juvenile courts (instead of separate trials). This effort failed, but the Buffalo committee was able to create a juvenile court for their city by amending the city charter.[24]

Advocates of a separate court for children in New York City also decided to amend their city's charter rather than seek a new state law to establish a juvenile court. They were successful in that effort and the law took effect in 1901. It provided for a completely separate court called "The Court of Special Sessions, First Division of the City of New York, Children's Part" and further provided that "said children's court shall be held by the several magistrates in rotation. . . ." This court did not use chancery procedure; indeed it was still a criminal court with formal, public hearings and full report of its activities in the press. The State of New York had a probation law, but it applied only to adults; consequently, the New York City Children's Court could not use this device in dealing with the children who came before it. As a result the court often found itself reduced to lecturing the children and releasing them. Otherwise, the court could either fine children or commit them to an institution for juvenile offenders such as the New York House of Refuge.[25]

Most of the new juvenile court laws were based on the Illinois and Colorado laws. Lindsey had helped to secure passage of the Kansas law, for example, and had assisted in the drafting of the Indiana law—just as Timothy Hurley had assisted in the drafting of the Colorado laws. An exception of sorts was the Massachusetts Juvenile Court Law of 1906. It contained the usual passage about liberal construction and added the statement that "proceedings against children under this act shall not be deemed to be criminal proceedings." Nonetheless, the proceedings were *against* the child and not *on behalf* of the child, and the purpose of the proceedings was to determine the child's guilt or innocence.[26]

In general the southern states lagged behind in the creation of juvenile courts just as they had in creating other institutions for juvenile delinquents. One reason for the delay was the rural character of the South. The secretary for the Southern States of the National Child Labor Commission suggested that "the system of family discipline, which has prevailed in the South, embraces the old-fashioned idea that the best juvenile court yet devised is the parental woodshed." However, Baltimore established a juvenile court in 1902, and Atlanta and New Orleans followed in 1904 and 1905. Atlanta resorted to a municipal ordinance, and New Orleans had to depend on volunteer social workers to operate its court.[27]

It was not until 1906 that a juvenile court was established in the nation's capital. A bill to create such a court had been introduced in Congress in 1901, but it did not pass. In 1902 the city's police court judges began holding special sessions for juvenile offenders, and in 1904 President Theodore Roosevelt urged the

creation of a juvenile court in Washington. "In the vital matter
of taking care of children," the President said in his Fourth Annual Message,

> much advantage could be gained by a careful study of what has
> been accomplished in such States as Illinois and Colorado by
> the juvenile courts. The work of the juvenile court is really a
> work of character-building. It is now generally recognized that
> young boys and young girls should not be treated as criminals,
> not even necessarily as needing reformation, but rather as need-
> ing to have their characters formed, and for this end to have
> them tested and developed by a system of probation . . . by
> profiting . . . [from] the experiences of the different states and
> cities in these matters, it would be easy to provide a good code
> for the District of Columbia.

The President's message shows that by 1906 the juvenile court
had gained enormous prestige in the United States. It also shows
that the concern for children, which the children's literature of
the late nineteenth century had helped to stimulate, had now
become national. The President's recommendation of the establishment of a juvenile court for the nation's capital further indicated that the court had become a standard American institution
—neither new nor experimental, an institution accepted by the
public and which every American city could be expected to have.
The law creating a juvenile court in Washington passed in 1906,
but juveniles who offended against federal laws did not always
enjoy similar treatment. Sometimes federal officials took such offenders to state courts, and at other times United States Attorneys
handled juvenile cases informally with what amounted to probation. Nevertheless, it was not until 1932 that Congress provided
for the regular transfer of juvenile offenders to state courts.[28]

V

In March, 1907, Illinois again modified its juvenile court law with
two new statutes. One act provided for paid probation officers and
the other clarified the provisions of the earlier laws and added a

section on the adoption of children which the juvenile court had placed in foster homes. "The state of Illinois made a very elaborate re-draft of their juvenile court law," Ben Lindsey said, but "my own idea is that it embodies a great many details and instructions that are unnecessary. . . ." In August of that year the Chicago Juvenile Court moved into new quarters. The city and county had jointly financed a new, three-story brick building on Ewing Street near Hull House. The juvenile court now held its sessions in a much smaller room; parents and others remained in a large waiting room adjacent to the courtroom. The building also contained detention facilities for neglected and dependent children as well as delinquent children. Since the City of Chicago and Cook County were willing to pay not only for the cost of housing children awaiting a hearing before the juvenile court, but also the salaries of the probation officers, the Juvenile Court Committee of the Chicago Woman's Club lost its reason for being.[29]

In 1906 the women of the Juvenile Court Committee had created the Juvenile Protective League to study the social conditions which caused juvenile delinquency. The demise of the Juvenile Court Committee made it possible for the ladies of Chicago to devote more effort to the study of the causes of juvenile delinquency. They noticed that some of the children who came before the court were repeat offenders, and they felt that these individuals ought to be studied. Jane Addams recalled that "at last it was apparent that many of these children were psychopathic cases and they and other borderline cases needed more skilled care than the most devoted probation officer could give them." The Children's Hospital Society had provided medical examinations at the detention home since 1902, but this procedure had not included all of the children who came before the court and the doctors made no special effort to "study" the children they examined. After the Juvenile Court and the Detention Home moved into their new quarters in 1907, it was possible to examine all of the children who would come before the court. The Juvenile Protective League decided to support the psychological study of juvenile delinquents after Mrs. Ellen Sturges Dummer agreed to

provide the necessary financial support. The League chose Julia
Lathrop of Hull House as the chairman of the committee to find
a qualified psychologist to direct such a study.[30]

Julia Lathrop talked to William James about the requirements
for the position; and he recommended one of his students, Dr.
William A. Healy. Early in 1908 Miss Lathrop wrote to Healy
outlining the requirements for the position. Healy replied that
such a study should result in "a work that may be as classical as
that of Lombroso," but which would be "more scientifically
founded and a thousand times more practically beneficial." Such
a study would take four or five years and would need "a thoroughly experienced and unbiased man working with the best
medical and psychological technique over a prolonged period."
Healy explained that

> the literature must be thoroughly culled, statistics studied, insti-
> tutions at home and, perhaps abroad, visited all to gain the
> strongest possible point of view. Then a very large series of
> cases must be investigated—probably in some measure all by
> the same man in order to get the best values for comparison.
> Taking, for instance, at least 500 cases of really [sic] delin-
> quents from the Juvenile Court and as many patients as pos-
> sible from the clinics and private practice . . . and other cases
> from various institutions, one could then and then only, get
> reliable conclusions. The examination would have to involve all
> possible facts about heredity, environment, antenatal and post-
> natal history, etc. You have already in your work on old Juve-
> nile Court cases surely collected much that would bear on these
> points.

The committee offered the position to Healy, and he accepted it,
beginning work in the spring of 1909.[31]

In March, 1909, the Juvenile Protective League established the
Juvenile Psychopathic Institute with Julia Lathrop as President
and William A. Healy as Director. The executive committee included Jane Addams and the Judge of the Juvenile Court, Julian
W. Mack. The Institute planned

> to undertake . . . an inquiry into the health of delinquent chil-
> dren in order to ascertain as far as possible in what degrees

delinquency is caused or influenced by mental or physical defect or abnormality and with the purpose of suggesting and applying remedies in individual cases whenever practicable as a concurrent part of the inquiry.

In a statement for the press Jane Addams stressed that the new agency would look for the causes of juvenile delinquency. "When a youthful criminal is brought before the Juvenile Court," she said,

> he will be examined by Dr. Healy. The doctor's assistant will follow up this examination by finding out under what conditions this child lives and learn if possible the complete mental and physical history of his ancestors. We then will be in position to know exactly the status of the child's case and how to deal with it.

Healy was well qualified to undertake this work. He had received an M.D. from Rush Medical College at the University of Chicago in 1900 and had served as a physician at the Wisconsin State Hospital for a year. He was an instructor of gynecology at Northwestern for two years, and at the time of his appointment to the Juvenile Psychopathic Institute, he was Professor of Neurological and Mental Disease at the Chicago Polyclinic. He had also done post-graduate work in London, Berlin, and Vienna.[32]

The first major project of the Institute did not appear until 1915, but in 1912 Healy told the delegates at the National Conference of Charities and Corrections that "the need for the individualization of treatment [of juvenile delinquents] has been well recognized by some legal authorities." What had not been so acknowledged was the need for the scientific investigation of individual delinquents. "The study that is necessary," Healy said, "is that of the whole human individual which includes all things that are likely to have influence upon the formation of character and conduct." [33]

In 1915 Healy published *The Individual Delinquent: A Textbook of Diagnosis and Prognosis for All Concerned in Understanding Offenders*. It was an effort to write "a practical textbook" based on an analysis of the cases of 1,000 repeat juvenile offenders. "The prime motive for our research into beginnings and causative factors," Healy wrote, "we have ever felt to be the establishment of scientific laws of predictability upon which all sorts of treatment could be rationally planned." Previous works were useful because of "their marshalling of statistical and individual facts," but Healy said, "our experience is simply that we found the facts too much for the theories." Consequently, Healy discarded all previous theories as to the causes of juvenile delinquency and focused on the individual cases. He argued that this approach was consistent with earlier scientific efforts:

> The idea that the individual must be carefully studied in order that crime may be ameliorated has been steadily growing since the day of Lombroso. The humanitarian efforts of John Howard were evidence of the appreciation of the needs of offenders as individual human beings; the view of Lombroso was that of the scientific man who sees in this field the inexorable laws which govern man's nature and environment. It makes little difference which theoretical view of penology is held; the problem of society ever is to handle a given offender satisfactorily.

Healy and his staff studied each offender from a social, a medical, and a psychological point of view. They compiled a family history, noted the characteristics of each offender's environment and gave each offender a psychological test to evaluate his mental and moral development. They also took basic anthropological measurements; but Healy said that "the high hopes of the leaders of the anthropometric school of criminologists not having been fulfilled, especially with regard to our American population; the detailed work to be done in this field with prospect of valuable results is, according to our best authorities, decidedly limited." Healy did not find that delinquents represented any particular physical type, nor did he find any physical condition that led to delinquency. Thus, he seemed to say that there was no physical way of identifying a juvenile delinquent or a criminal.

What Healy did find was that the causative factors in juvenile delinquency were too complex and interrelated to lead to easy generalization. Since this was true, it would be equally difficult, Healy thought, to generalize about efforts to reform juvenile delinquents, but he said that "the treatment of delinquents is un-warrantably inefficient." Because of the complexity of the causes of delinquency, Healy did not produce a theory but concluded his work with a list of "causes," among which he listed "bad com-panions, adolescent instability, early sex experiences, mental con-flicts, and love of adventure." [34]

In 1915 Healy and his assistant, Augusta F. Bronner, prepared a paper on "Youthful Offenders" which was "a comparative study of two groups, each of 1000 young recidivists." The paper was presented at the Pan American Congress in Washington, D.C., in January, 1916. Healy and Bronner noted that

> "in this country we have severed already, with the advancing socialization of our courts, from the tradition of a set punish-ment for a given offense. . . . But to help the adjudicating au-thorities in their decisions they must not be given a mere bald statement of what the individual is on the physical side and on the mental side from the psychiatric standpoint; there is much more at the foundations of delinquency than that. What are all the main elements which have caused this offender's conduct? What efficient remedies can be offered? To meet these funda-mental issues a broader study is necessary.

They had found that 67.5 per cent of one group and 75 per cent of the other group of delinquents were normal mentally, and only 2 per cent of either group showed any kind of "constitutional inferiority." They concluded: "Our whole work shows nothing more certainly than that no satisfactory study of delinquents, even for practical purposes can be made without building sanely upon the foundations of *all* that goes to make character and conduct." [35]

By 1916 Healy had not produced the theory to replace Lom-broso's, but he approached such a theory in *Mental Conflicts and Misconduct* published in the following year. He had noticed that during his investigations of offenders and during hearings before the juvenile court that "the individual [delinquent] experiences a distinct inner urge towards misdoing—misdoing that often leads to little else than anxious apprehension and other suffering on the part of the misdoer." This "inner driving force" was neither reasonable nor prudent; it was "a reaction to component parts of mental life and to certain prior experiences." The misconduct resulting from this force represented what Healy called "mental conflict." He thought that this concept offered a better way of understanding some delinquents than other theories and that the effort to understand juvenile delinquents through "mental analysis" would be more fruitful in some cases. "It was not long," he explained

> before we were forced to the conclusion that such information as might be obtained by mental testing, physical examination, by learning the main points of development and family history, and by inquiring into companionship and other environmental conditions, was absolutely insufficient to explain the essentials of the development of a marked tendency to delinquency in certain cases. Certain elements of mental life had to be sought out and invoked for explanation, even if practical issues alone were in view.

It seemed to Healy that those delinquents whose misdeeds had resulted from mental conflict had acted against their own desires and "in the face of possible punishment and other suffering."

The method of investigation which Healy and his assistant followed was "mental analysis." It was a technique quite similar to and derived from Freudian psychoanalysis and sought to use the delinquent's memory "to penetrate into the former experiences of mental life." The mental conflict that Healy sought to understand and analyze was a "conflict between two elements of mental life . . . out of harmony with each other." As examples of such disharmonies Healy listed "repression,—when a mental experience, or group of thoughts with an emotional tone or part of such a constellated system of ideas, is pushed back, 'put out of mind,' 'forgotten,' it is said to be repressed"—and "substitution—what occurs when emotional energy, escaped from the repressed parts of a constellation, becomes attached to associated but not unbearable and consequently, not necessarily repressed elements."

Of 2,000 juvenile delinquents considered, Healy and Bronner found 147 "instances where mental conflict was a main cause of the delinquency," but Healy did not say that these findings represented a constant factor: He also emphasized the need for more study of the problems of childhood because "the genesis of delinquent careers often dates back to [the] mental life of childhood." Healy found that there was "no special type" among the cases of mental conflict. There was no correlation with race or nationality, and in general the individuals studied were higher than the average delinquent in over-all abilities. In addition, the environmental circumstances of the cases were very diverse except that almost all of the "misdoers with mental conflicts never have had anyone near to them, particularly in family life, who supplied opportunities for sympathetic confidences." Prognosis for the treatment of delinquents suffering from mental conflict depended on the intelligence of the individual and on "healthy, vigorous mental interests and confidential relationships."

Healy concluded modestly that his book had demonstrated that "the study of mental conflicts is a scientific method of approaching certain problems of misconduct." He had, however, shown clearly that some juvenile delinquents suffered from mental illness and that their offenses came from impulses which they could neither understand nor control. Healy discovered this through the use of psychoanalysis (a term which he did not use in order to avoid offending the disciples of Freud) and as a result showed that the causes of juvenile delinquency were more complex than even he had at first thought. Healy also stressed indirectly the importance of family relationships. "The basis for much prevention of mental conflict," he wrote "is to be found in close confidential relations between parents and children." He continued that "parental relationship is so vitally connected with the emotional life of childhood [that] the suggestion of irregularity in it comes as a grave psychic shock." Thus Healy demonstrated that the insight of Charles Loring Brace, that "the family was God's reformatory," was essentially correct.[36]

From the point of view of psychology *Mental Conflicts* has additional significance. Healy's first major work, *The Individual Delinquent*, while it represented a distinct departure from the earlier pattern of the "scientific" study of juvenile delinquents, was thoroughly in keeping with the psychological methods of the first decade of the twentieth century. That is, its approach was rigidly experimental and empirical and made no use of prior theories or metaphysical considerations. G. Stanley Hall had established this tradition in American psychology through his laboratory work at Johns Hopkins and Clark University. *Mental Conflicts,* however, discards this experimental method in favor of Freudian psychoanalysis. Ironically, Hall arranged for Freud's famous visit to the United States in 1909, which was responsible for greatly extending Freud's influence among American psychologists. But American psychologists reacted to Freud's ideas in a variety of ways, and many of them clung to the positivistic tradition that Hall had established. Healy's *Mental Conflicts* was one of the first American books to demonstrate an application of psychoanalysis in clinical psychology and was the first to use psychoanalysis in connection with the treatment of juvenile delinquents.[37]

Healy, then, was the first scientist to study individual juvenile delinquents and the first scientist to have any significant effect on the treatment of youthful offenders. In 1922 Healy wrote *The Practical Value of Scientific Study of Juvenile Delinquents.* In a letter of transmittal, Julia Lathrop, now the Chief of the Children's Bureau, explained that "the study of the physical and mental qualities of a delinquent child and of his history and surroundings is an approach to the individual and his needs rather than to an offense and its legal penalty." Such a study was in keeping with the whole trend toward individualization of treatment for juvenile offenders—the trend which had led to the creation of the juvenile court.

The juvenile court, Healy thought, was essentially "scientific" in its approach to juvenile delinquency because it focused on the fact that an individual had offended rather than on the fact that society had been injured by an offense. The juvenile court dealt with cause and effect and tried to determine not whether an offense had been committed but why the child had offended and what could be done to help the child. Thus Healy's work and the creation of the juvenile court were parallel developments. The court was a flexible institution designed to treat the individual delinquent, but the court lacked the knowledge of psychology to treat those delinquents who suffered from "mental conflicts." Healy's work illustrated that lack and began the process of the scientific study of individual delinquents. The juvenile court's flexibility made it a far cry from the New York House of Refuge. It was an institution which discarded predetermined and stereotyped methods of dealing with young offenders and concentrated on what was best for the child in each particular case. Similarly, Healy's work represented a genuinely new departure in the scientific study of crime. He started with no predetermined theory and demonstrated that no one theory could adequately explain the phenomena of juvenile delinquency. He also showed that most of the accepted ideas about the "causes" of juvenile delinquency were equally unfruitful. Healy's convincing demonstration that the causes of delinquency were complex marked the end of the evolution of ideas about young offenders in nineteenth-century America.

Before Healy's efforts and before the creation of the juvenile court, Americans had been willing to regard juvenile delinquency as a reasonably simple matter of child law-breaking. They assumed that juvenile delinquency and adult crime alike were largely the result of free choice by the people involved. It is true that some reformers believed that social conditions often drove men and children to crime, but they were unable to influence society's handling of adult criminals. American society, although it did not begin to regard children as children rather than as miniature adults until after the Civil War, did concede that children's character was plastic. Therefore, society was willing to support various institutions for the reformation of juvenile delinquents. These institutions, however, were little more than scaled-down versions of adult penal agencies, and they generally treated their charges by means of an inflexible and highly formalized system which certainly did not recognize the individual characteristics of each inmate. Social scientists who preceded Healy at least had begun to question the "conventional wisdom" of nineteenth-century America with regard to crime and punishment. At first, however, they concentrated on explaining and testing European theories. Groszmann and Dawson, for example, tried to tie the results of their studies of juvenile delinquents to the criminological theories of Lombroso. Only Stoddard anticipated Healy's work when he called for a study of individual delinquents. But Stoddard only called for such a study; Healy was the first to undertake it. Thus the creation of the juvenile court and the efforts of William A. Healy mark the end of a century of development in American society's responses to the challenge of juvenile delinquency.

VI

It is appropriate to conclude this study with the juvenile court and the work of William A. Healy, because the court represented the last and most important institutional development in nineteenth-century America and because Healy's work changed the way scientists studied crime and juvenile delinquency. The juvenile court did not suddenly appear; it was the result of a series of interrelated developments which took place during the three-quarters of a century preceding its creation. The founders of the New York House of Refuge had recognized the need for separate and specialized treatment for juvenile delinquents in 1824. Charles Loring Brace advocated the idea that juvenile delinquents and potential young offenders belonged in good family homes. The juvenile court, through probation, advocated the same idea. That a special court should consider the needs of an individual offender more important than society's needs could not have been promoted when society regarded all offenders as members of a homogeneous group. First, society had to discover its children as children, particularly its delinquent children. The new literature which appeared after the Civil War helped to give society a clearer view of the young people who before that time had suffered from the stereotype in the public mind. This new literature also placed the problems of American society, particularly the problems of the cities, before the American people in a vivid way. Consequently, the new literature not only gave society a clearer view of all its children, it also generated a favorable climate for the reform of American society. The juvenile court was one such reform, and it was typical of the nineteenth-century approach to social ills. It was a practical, common-sense institution designed basically to solve problems.

Throughout the nineteenth century the question of juvenile delinquency—broadly considered as deviant behavior by young people—had a function in American society. Following Durkheim's hypothesis that crime helps a society to define its values and therefore has a purpose, this study shows that juvenile delinquency is similar to crime in this respect. The changing definition of juvenile delinquency in nineteenth-century America indicates that American values also changed. One factor which makes the identification of American values easier was the tendency—until the work of Healy—to generalize about the "causes" and "cures" of juvenile delinquency. By 1825 a juvenile delinquent was a young person under twenty-one who had broken the law, or who was a threat to the community because he was either not in school or not working. The Protestant Ethic must have operated with considerable vigor in early nineteenth-century America if a child could be regarded as a juvenile delinquent because he was "idle." That the Protestant Ethic remained one of the basic American values throughout most of the century is illustrated by the continued activities of the New York Children's Aid Society. Charles Loring Brace often went to the Newsboys' Lodging Houses maintained by the Society (and which charged for services) to talk to the boys about "success" and "self-reliance," and one of the purposes of the placing-out system was to give city young people another chance to make good—in the West.

The institutions which Americans created to reform youthful lawbreakers generally stressed the "necessity and dignity of labor" and devoted half of every day except Sunday to some kind of physical work. Sometimes they used the products of the inmates' labor to help support the institution. The children spent the remainder of their waking hours in school, a fact which illustrates the American faith not only in the effectiveness of education but also the idea that education was for everyone. Indeed, America's faith in education was so great that for a time early in the nineteenth century many Americans assumed that education alone was sufficient to transmit the country's democratic culture to its children. Since the curricula of houses of refuge and reform schools represented the bare essentials of the educational system, they reveal some of the ideas Americans had about their culture. Thus Americans thought that every citizen should be able to read and write and use simple arithmetic; that he should know something about history and geography, particularly that of his own country, and that he should be strongly religious and preferably Protestant. The system used in houses of refuge and reform schools applied to the whole child as early nineteenth-century Americans saw him. Labor disciplined the body, school work disciplined the mind, and religion inspired and disciplined the soul. The treatment in houses of refuge and reform schools indicated that the officers of those institutions regarded their inmates as children who belonged to the class of people who broke the law. They had broken the law, the officials seemed to have thought, because they had not worked enough or learned enough or because they had not been to church. They were deviants, then, because they had not fully absorbed American culture.

Charles Loring Brace's major contribution was that he saw that the family rather than the school transmitted the values of a society—the essential elements of that society's culture. This idea was not new with Brace; he borrowed it from Horace Bushnell, who was his pastor in Hartford, from Johann Wichern at the *Rauhe Haus*, and from English and French institutions based on the *Rauhe Haus*; but Brace was the first American to apply this insight to juvenile delinquents. Brace's placing-out system shows that Americans were beginning to see children as individuals. The *Annual Reports* of the Children's Aid Society always contained the stories of particular children the Society had sent west—of course, they were always success stories. They illustrate not only the continued viability of the Protestant Ethic and the self-help ideal, but also a growing humanitarianism. It was only a beginning, and often it was a case of one stereotype replacing another. While "lo, the poor children" was kinder than the view of children as miniature adults, it was no more accurate and certainly not much more individualistic. Brace's work also illustrated the "agrarian myth"—the view that life on the farm was to be preferred to life in the evil city. And the agrarian myth had elements of truth. During the years after the Civil War American cities grew so rapidly that they were truly evil places that often brutalized and corrupted men. The problems of the cities mounted so rapidly that it seemed as if the individual would be lost in them. But it was an individual's plight (that of little Mary Ellen) which led to the creation of the Society for the Prevention of Cruelty to Children; and the movements for charity organization and "scientific philanthropy" were efforts to deal with welfare cases on an individual basis. The fact that charity volunteers wanted their work to be "scientific" is one illustration of the growing prestige of science in American society in the late nineteenth century. When the social sciences appeared, however, the reformers and charity workers regarded them with dismay. They seemed to indicate—particularly in the area of criminology—that reform was a waste of time. But the reformers did not stop trying to solve society's problems. Their continued activity illustrates another aspect of American culture: while Americans may have raised science over theology in the late nineteenth century, they were not really interested in scientific theories as such. They were still more concerned with practical problems, and for the most part, they preferred common-sense approaches. The juvenile court grew out of such an approach; ironically it was the first truly scientific institution for juvenile delinquents. There was further irony in the fact that William Healy, who worked closely with the Cook County Juvenile Court in Chicago, indicated that the problem of juvenile delinquency could not be understood through the use of all-inclusive theories.

The growth of American cities in the nineteenth century forced their residents to face the problem of youthful misbehavior and

crime. In trying to meet the continuing challenge of juvenile delinquency, nineteenth-century Americans set up a variety of
agencies, reform schools, foster home placement, juvenile courts,
systems of probation, and psychopathic clinics, which today form
the basic structure with which Americans try to solve the problem
of juvenile delinquency. They also learned to see their wayward
children as individuals with particular difficulties who needed
more individualized treatment. Thus, out of the squalor and filth
of the cities, out of the pressures generated by the rapid and un-
controlled expansion of these cities, came significant institutions,
and a growing awareness on the part of society of children as
people, complex valuable individuals.

Notes

PREFACE

1. Anthony M. Platt, *The Child Savers: The Invention of Delinquency* (Chicago: Univ. of Chicago Pr., 1969); Robert S. Pickett, *House of Refuge, Origins of Juvenile Reform in New York State, 1815–1857* (Syracuse, New York: Syracuse Univ. Pr., 1969).

CHAPTER 1

1. The account of Jesse Pomeroy's crimes and trial may be found in the *Boston Daily Globe*, July 20–23 and Dec. 9–11, 1874.
2. Not to be confused with the Juvenile Court, which first appeared in Chicago in 1899; see below, Chapter 10.
3. Page Smith, *As a City upon a Hill: The Town in American History* (New York: Alfred A. Knopf, 1966), pp. 128–29.
4. Emile Durkheim, *The Rules of Sociological Method,* translated by Sarah A. Soloway and John H. Mueller (Glencoe, Ill.: The Free Press, 1950; 1st published in 1895), p. 70; Durkheim, *The Division of Labor in Society,* translated by George Simpson (Glencoe, Ill.: The Free Press, 1949), p. 102; Kai T. Erickson, *Wayward Puritans: A Study in the Sociology of Deviance* (New York: John Wiley, 1966), pp. 4–7, 14, 20, 22.

CHAPTER 2

1. Paul Samuel Reinsch, "English Common Law in the Early American Colonies, "Univ. of Wisconsin, *Bulletin,* No. 31 (Studies in Economics, Political Science and History, Vol. II, 1899), 8, 58.
2. Max Farrand, ed., *The Book of the General Laws and Liberties*

(Cambridge, Mass.: Harvard Univ. Pr., 1929), viii; Charles M. Andrews, *The Colonial Period of American History*, 4 vols. (New Haven: Yale Univ. Pr., 1934), I, 455–57; William Whitmore, ed., *The Colonial Laws of Massachusetts. Reprinted from the Edition of 1660, with the Supplements to 1672* (Boston: Rockwell and Churchill, 1889), p. 129; Andrews, *Colonial Period*, I, 458; Arthur P. Scott, *Criminal Law in Colonial Virginia* (Chicago: University of Chicago Pr., 1930), p. 27; Edmund S. Morgan, *The Puritan Family: Essays on Religion, and Domestic Relations in Seventeenth Century New England* (Boston: Trustees of the Public Library, 1944), p. 38. I have not altered the spelling of quotations throughout this work, but for purposes of clarity, I have changed the capitalization.

3. Monica Mary Kiefer, *American Children Through Their Books, 1700–1835* (Philadelphia: Univ. of Pennsylvania Pr., 1948), pp. 7, 31; Nathaniel B. Shurtleff, ed., *Records of the Governor and Company of the Massachusetts Bay Colony in New England* (Boston: William White, 1853–1854), II, 7; *Massachusetts Colonial Laws*, pp. 136–37; Morgan, *Puritan Family*, p. 29, 48.

4. *Massachusetts Colonial Laws*, pp. 189, 211.

5. William H. Whitmore, ed., *The Colonial Laws of Massachusetts. Reprinted from the Edition of 1672, with the Supplements through 1686* (Boston: Rockwell and Churchill, 1887), pp. 27, 235–36.

6. Perry Miller, *Errand into the Wilderness* (New York: Harper and Row, 1956), p. 1; Kiefer, *Children Through Books*, p. 8; Shurtleff, *Records of Gov. and Co.*, II, 6–7; Samuel Eliot Morison, *The Intellectual Life of Colonial New England*, 2d ed. (New York: New York Univ. Pr., 1956), p. 66; Robert Middlekauff, *Ancients and Axioms: Secondary Education in Eighteenth Century New England* (New Haven: Yale Univ. Pr., 1963), pp. 6–7.

7. David M. Schneider, *The History of Public Welfare in New York State, 1609–1866* (Chicago: Univ. of Chicago Pr., 1938), p. 33; *Charter to William Penn, and Laws of the Province of Pennsylvania Passed Between 1687 and 1700, Preceded by the Duke of York's Laws . . .* , comp. and ed. by George Staughton, *et al.* (Harrisburg: L. S. Hart, 1879), p. 19.

8. Andrews, *Colonial Period*, III, 298, 306; Penna., *Colonial Laws*, p. 142; Hubert W. Fitzroy, "The Punishment of Crime in Provincial Pennsylvania," *Pennsylvania Magazine of History*, LX (1936), 246.

9. "Articles, Laws, and Orders, Divine, Politique, and Martiall for the Colony of Virginia," in Peter Force, collector, *Tracts and other Papers Relating to the Origin, Settlement and Progress of the Colonies in North America, from the Discovery of the Country to the Year 1776* (Washington: W. Q. Force, 1844), III; Andrews, *Colonial Period*, I, 188; see also William Walter Hening, comp., *The Statutes at Large; Being a Collection of All the Laws of Vir-*

ginia, From the First Session of the Legislature in the Year 1619 (New York: Printed for the Editor by R & W & G Bartow, 1823), I.

10. "Poor Children to be sent to Virginia," *Virginia Magazine of History and Biography,* VI (Jan. 1899), 232; Hening, *Statutes,* I, 157, 336; Edmund S. Morgan, *Virginians at Home: Family Life in the Eighteenth Century* (Williamsburg, Va.: Colonial Williamsburg, 1952), pp. 8–22.

11. "Indentures of Apprentices," New-York Historical Society, *Collections for the Year 1909* (New York, 1910), p. 113; Morgan, *Puritan Family,* p. 37; Morgan, *Virginians,* p. 23.

12. Marcello Maestro, *Voltaire and Beccaria as Reformers of Criminal Law* (New York: Columbia Univ. Pr., 1942), p. 50.

13. Charles Louis de Montesquieu, *Spirit of the Laws* (New York: Hafner, 1949), pp. 34, 89; Maestro, *Voltaire and Beccaria,* p. 50; Cesare Beccarria, *An Essay on Crimes and Punishments,* facsimile ed. (Albany ʾ W. C. Little and Co., 1819), pp. 29–30, 74, 148–61.

14. Derek L. ʾʾov. d, *The English Prisons: Their Past and Their Future* (ʾ ndoʾ Methuen, 1960), pp. 6–8, 9; William Hepworth Dixon, *Joʾ ard: A Memoir* (London: Jackson and Walford, 1854), pp. 60, 109–18.

15. John Howard, *The State of Prisons,* Everyman's Lib. ed. (London: J. M. Dent, 1929), p. 16; D. L. Howard, *English Prisons,* p. 9.

16. Orlando F. Lewis, *The Development of American Prisons and Prison Customs, 1776–1845, with Special Reference to Early Institutions in the State of New York* (New York: The Prison Ass'n. of New York, 1922), p. 13; quoted in Harry Elmer Barnes, "The Historical Origins of the Prison System in America," *Journal of the American Institute of Criminal Law and Criminology,* XII (May 1921), 44; Lewis, *American Prisons,* pp. 16–17, 25–26; Barnes, *J. of Am. Inst. of Crim. Law,* XII, 48–49.

17. Harry Elmer Barnes, *The Repression of Crime* (New York: George H. Doran Co., 1926), pp. 98–102; Barnes, *J. of Am. Inst. of Crim. Law,* XII, 46.

18. Barnes, *Repression of Crime,* pp. 105–7; Arthur A. Ekirch, "Thomas Eddy and the Beginnings of Prison Reform in New York State," *New York History,* XXIV (July 1943), 381–83; Barnes, *Repression of Crime,* pp. 107–10; Harry Elmer Barnes, "The Origins of Prison Reform in New York State," New York State Historical Association, *Quarterly Journal,* II (April 1921), 94–95; Alice Felt Tyler, *Freedom's Ferment; Phases of American Social History from the Colonial Period to the Outbreak of the Civil War* (New York: Harper & Row, 1962), pp. 274, 278.

CHAPTER 3

1. Isaac Collins to James W. Gerard, March 4, 1850, in New York House of Refuge, *Thirtieth Annual Report* (1855), p. 73: Gerard

to Collins, March 6, 1850, *ibid.*, p. 75; "Reminiscences of James W. Gerard, Esq.," in *Proceedings of the First Convention of Managers and Superintendents of Houses of Refuge and Schools of Reform in the United States of America, Held in the City of New York, on the Twelfth, Thirteenth and Fourteenth Days of May, 1857* (New York: Wynkoop, Hallenbeck & Thomas, 1857), pp. 75–78; "Extracts from the Annual Report of the Society for the Prevention of Pauperism in the City of New York for the Year, 1822," *ibid.*, pp. 79–82.

2. Constance McLaughlin Green, *American Cities in the Growth of the Nation* (London: Univ. of London, Athlone Pr., 1957), p. 9.
3. Bradford Kenny Pierce, *A Half-Century with Juvenile Delinquents, or The House of Refuge and its Times* (New York: D. Appleton and Co., 1869), pp. 32–42; Grace Abbott, *The Child and the State*, 2 vols. (Chicago: Univ. of Chicago Pr., 1938), II, 345–46; Samuel L. Knapp, *The Life of Thomas Eddy; Comprising an Extensive Correspondence with many of the most Distinguished Philanthropists and Philosophers of this and other Countries* (New York: Connel and Cooke, 1834), p. 23.
4. Edouard Ducpetiaux, *Des Progrès et de l'état actuel de la réform pénitentiaire et des institutions préventives, aux Etats-Unis, en France, en Suisse, en Angleterre et en Belgique* (Bruxelles: Hauman, Cattari and Co., 1838), p. 323; Henry Barnard, *Reformatory Education; Papers on Preventative, Correctional, and Reformatory Institutions in Different Countries . . .*, 3 vols. (Hartford, Conn.: F. C. Brownell, 1857), III, 295; John Griscom, *A Year in Europe: Comprising a Journal of Observations in England, France, Switzerland, the North of Italy and Holland, In 1818 and 1819*, 2 vols. (New York: Collins and Co., 1823), I, 121–23.
5. Charles A. Bennett, *A History of Manual and Industrial Education up to 1870* (Peoria, Ill.: Manual Arts Press, 1926), pp. 111, 112, 131–35; Barnard, *Reformatory Education*, pp. 34–35, 55.
6. Griscom, *A Year in Europe*, pp. 384–400.
7. Quoted in Abbott, *Child and State*, II, 346.
8. Peirce, *Half-Century*, pp. 32–42; Abbott, *Child and State*, II, 345–46. The actions of the New York City Common Council relevant to the creation of the New York House of Refuge may be found in New York, Common Council of the City of New York, *Minutes of the Common Council of New York* (New York: Published by the City of New York, 1917), V, 641; VII, 65; X, 467–68, 556, 747; XI, 722. See also *New York Spectator*, Jan. 23, 1824; and Charles G. Sommers, *Memoir of the Rev. John Stanford, D.D.* (New York: Swards, Stanford and Co., 1835), pp. 272–77.
9. Society for the Prevention of Pauperism in the City of New York, *Report on the Expediency of Erecting an Institution for the Re-*

formation of Juvenile Delinquents (New York: Mahlon Day, 1823), title page; Peirce, *Half-Century,* pp. 45–48.

10. Society for the Prevention of Pauperism, *Report on Expediency,* pp. 3–36; *New York Spectator,* Dec. 25, 1823, Jan. 23, 1824.

11. *Minutes of Common Council,* XIII, 538, 578–81; "Daybook No. 1," New York House of Refuge Records, Manuscript Collections, Carnegie Library, Syracuse University. Hereafter, these records will be cited as NYHR.

12. *New York Spectator,* Feb. 3, March 30, 1824; New York Legislature, Senate, *Journal* (1824) App. A., p. 96.

13. *New York Spectator,* March 30, 1824; *Minutes of Common Council,* XIII, 648; Abbott, *Child and State,* II, 351.

14. New York, *Laws of 1824,* c 126.

15. "Case Histories No. 1," NYHR.

16. Society for the Reformation of Juvenile Delinquents in the City of New York, First Annual Report (1825) in New York, Legislature, House, *Documents Relative to a House of Refuge* (New York: Mahlon Day, 1832), pp. 38, 42–49; hereafter the Society is cited as SRJD.

17. "Daily Journal, No. 1," NYHR, Jan. 28, March 13, 1825; "Case Histories No. 1," NYHR.

18. "Minutes of the Acting Committee, No. 1," NYHR, April 30, 1825; "Daily Journal, No. 1," NYHR, Oct. 4, 1825, Sept. 22, 1826.

19. "Minutes of the Acting Committee, No. 1," NYHR, May 10, May 21, 1825; "Daily Journal No. 1," NYHR, April 14, 1825 [March ?] 1826; For a sketch of the new building see SRJD, *Fifth Annual Report* (1830), frontispiece.

20. "Daily Journal, No. 1," NYHR, April 25, 1825, May 26, July 11, July 12, July 19, July 28, 1826.

21. *Ibid.,* Aug. 8, 1825, Aug. 13, 1826, Jan. 1, 1827.

22. SRJD, *Second Annual Report* (1826), in *Documents Relative to a House of Refuge,* p. 80. See below, Chapter 10.

23. *Documents Relative to a House of Refuge,* pp. 106–8.

24. "Daily Journal, No. 1," NYHR, Sept. 5, Dec. 18, Dec. 21, Dec. 24, 1826.

25. SRJD, Sixth Annual Report (1831), in *Documents Relative to a House of Refuge,* pp. 219–52; Elijah Devoe, *The Refuge System, or, Prison Discipline Applied to Juvenile Delinquents* (New York: J. R. M'Gown, 1848), pp. 36, 46, 56; SRJD, *Seventh Annual Report* (1832), in *Documents Relative to a House of Refuge,* pp. 253–302.

26. "Daily Journal, No. 1," NYHR, July 22, Aug. 6, 1826, Oct. 16, 1827.

27. SRJD, *Fourth Annual Report* (1829), in *Documents Relative to a House of Refuge,* pp. 179–80; SRJD, *Fifth Annual Report* (1830); Homer Folks, *Care of Destitute, Neglected, and Delinquent Children* (New York: Macmillan, 1902), p. 203.

28. Josiah Quincy, *A Municipal History of the Town and City of Boston, during Two Centuries* (1630–1830) (Boston: Little and Brown, 1852), pp. 35–106.

29. Massachusetts, "Laws of 1826," in *Private and Special Statutes of the Commonwealth of Massachusetts from May, 1822 to March, 1830* (Boston: Dutton and Wentworth, State Printers, 1837), c 182.

30. Quincy, *Municipal History*, pp. 106–7; Alexis de Tocqueville and Gustave Beaumont, *On the Penitentiary System in the United States*, ed. by Thorstein Sellin (Carbondale, Ill.: Southern Illinois Univ. Pr., 1964), p. 121.

31. Tocqueville and Beaumont, *On the Penitentiary System*, pp. 119–21; "The House of Reformation," *New England Magazine*, III (Nov. 1832), 386–87.

32. Negley K. Teeters, *They Were in Prison; A History of the Pennsylvania Prison Society, 1787–1937* (Philadelphia: John C. Winston Co., 1937), pp. 161–68; Pennsylvania, *Laws of 1826–27*, c XLVII.

33. Philadelphia House of Refuge, *An Address from the Managers of the House of Refuge to their fellow Citizens* (Philadelphia: D. & S. Neall, 1826), pp. 9–12.

34. Devoe, *Refuge System*, pp. 11, 28–29, 50–51.

35. Sir William Blackstone, *Commentaries on the Laws of England*, 4 vols. (Dublin: John Exshaw *et al.*, 1773), IV 23; *State v Guild*, 5 Halstead 163 (New Jersey State Law Reporter). Although the fact that the defendant was black may have affected the original decision, the appeal did establish a precedent for the application of the English Common Law to infants in American courts.

36. *Commonwealth v M'Keagy*, 1 Ashmead (1831), 248 (Pennsylvania State Law Reporter).

37. *Ex parte Crouse* 4 Wharton (1839), 9 (Pennsylvania State Law Reporter).

CHAPTER 4

1. Charles Dickens, *Oliver Twist* (New York: New American Library, 1961), pp. vi, 85–98; Joseph E. Carpenter, *Life and Work of Mary Carpenter* (London: Macmillan, 1879); Philip A. W. Collins, *Dickens and Education* (New York: St. Martin's Press, 1963); W. Walter Crotch, *Charles Dickens, Social Reformer: The Social Teachings of England's Greatest Novelist* (London: Chapman and Hall, 1913); Hnmphrey House, *The Dickens World* (London: Oxford Univ. Pr., 1941).

2. Mary Carpenter, *Reformatory Schools for the Children of the Perishing and Dangerous Classes, and for Juvenile Offenders* (London: C. Gilpin, 1851); Mary Carpenter, *Juvenile Delinquents; Their Condition and Treatment* (London: W. F. G. Cash, 1853); Dickens, *Oliver Twist*; Sir Llewellyn Woodward, *The Age of Re-*

form, 1815–1870 (Oxford: Oxford Univ. Press, 1962); Jerome Hamilton Buckley, *The Victorian Temper; A Study in Literary Culture* (Cambridge, Mass.: Harvard Univ. Pr., 1951).

3. Great Britain, 3 *Hansard's Parliamentary Debates,* XCIX (1848), 430.

4. McColgan, p. 219; J. E. Carpenter, pp. 31–44.

5. J. E. Carpenter, pp. 46–50; M. Carpenter, *Reformatory Schools,* pp. 111–117.

6. Quoted in J. E. Carpenter, p. 104; see also M. Carpenter, *Reformatory Schools,* pp. 118–19.

7. M. Carpenter, *Reformatory Schools,* pp. 121–48, 218, 261.

8. Henry Mayhew, *London Labour and the London Poor* (London: Griffin, Bohn and Co., 1964), IV, pp. 211, 273; W. A. Miles (ed.), *Poverty, Mendacity and Crime; or, The Facts, Examinations, &c. upon which the Report Was Founded, Presented to the House of Lords* (London: Shaw and Sons, 1839), pp. 87–93; Samuel Phillips Day, *Juvenile Crime; Its Causes, Character, and Cure* (London: J. F. Hope, 1858), pp. 36–46.

9. Quoted in Miles, p. 87.

10. Edmund Edward Antrobus, *The Prison and the School* (London: Staunton and Sons, 1853), p. 46; Miles, p. 93; Day, 242; Joseph Adshead, *Prisons and Prisoners* (London: Longmans, Brown, Green and Longman, 1845), p. 298; Samuel Thomas Biggs, *An Inquiry into the Extent and Cause of Juvenile Delinquency* (London: Charles Gilpin, 1849), p. 144; M. Carpenter, *Reformatory Schools,* 287–88; Miles, p. 91.

11. Agnes Freda Young and E. T. Ashton, *British Social Work in the Nineteenth Century* (London: Routledge and Kegan Paul, 1956), p. 163; Edouard Ducpetiaux, *Des Progrès et de l'état actuel de la réforme pénitentiaire et des institutions préventives, aux Etats-Unis, en France, en Suisse, en Angleterre et en Belgique. Appendice général aux ouvrages les plus récents sur la réforme des prisons* Bruxelles: Hauman, Cattori & Co., 1838), p. 305.

12. "Juvenile Offenders," *Law Times,* VIII (Oct. 24, 1846), 54; M. Carpenter, *Reformatory Schools,* p. 321; Barnard, p. 303; and Great Britain, Parliamentary Papers (*Sessional Papers,* Vol. XXIII), June 1853, "Report from the Select Committee on Criminal and Destitute Children: Together with the Proceedings of the Committee, Minutes of Evidence, and Appendix," pp. 58–59.

13. Great Britain, Parliamentary Papers (*Sessional Papers,* Vol. VII), June 1852, "Report from the Select Committee on Criminal and Destitute Juveniles; Together with the Proceedings of the Committee, Minutes of Evidence, Appendix and Index," pp. 32–33, and "Juvenile Offenders," *Law Times,* VI (Jan. 24, 1846), 335–36.

14. Young and Ashton, p. 165, and M. Carpenter, *Reformatory Schools,* pp. 226–27.

15. Great Britain, Parliamentary Papers (*Sessional Papers*, Vol. XXXI), 1837, "Third Report of the Commissioners on Criminal Law," p. 5, and Great Britain, *Statutes at Large*, 10 and 11 Vict., c 82 (1847); M. Carpenter, *Reformatory Schools*, pp. 290, 347–49, and J. Carpenter, p. 154.

16. Mary Carpenter, *Juvenile Delinquents: Their Condition and Treatment* (London: W. and F. G. Cash, 1853), pp. 180–81; Young and Ashton, p. 167; J. Carpenter, p. 157.

17. "Report from Select Committee on Criminal and Destitute Juveniles" (1852), p. 118.

18. "Report from Select Committee on Criminal and Destitute Juveniles" (1853), pp. iii–iv; Great Britain, 3 *Hansards' Parliamentary Debates* CXXIX (1853), 155, 1101–6.

19. M. Carpenter, *Juvenile Delinquents*, passim; J. E. Carpenter, p. 179; Great Britain, *Statutes at Large*, 17 and 18 Vict., c 86 (1854); "Juvenile Criminals," *North British Review*, X (Nov. 1848), 35.

20. Quoted in J. Carpenter, p. 254; J. Carpenter, pp. 207–209, 244–246; Charles A. Bennett, *Industrial Education up to 1870* (Peoria, Ill.: Manual Arts Press, 1926), pp. 321–232.

21. Mary Carpenter, *The Claims of the Ragged Schools to Pecuniary Educational Aid from the Annual Parliamentary Grant, as an Integral Part of the Educational Movement of the Country* (London: Partridge and Co., 1859), pp. 4–5.

22. M. Carpenter, *Ragged Schools*, pp. 6–9, and J. E. Carpenter, pp. 278–82.

23. Woodward, p. 483; J. E. Carpenter, p. 411; Great Britain, *Statutes at Large*, 29 and 30 Vict., c 118 (1866); Grace Abbott, *The Child and the State*, 2 vols. (Chicago: Univ. of Chicago Pr., 1938), II, 460.

CHAPTER 5

1. Jan De Liefde, *Six Months Among the Charities of Europe* (London: Alexander Strahan, 1866), pp. 12–81; Henry Barnard, *Reformatory Education: Papers on Preventive, Correctional and Reformatory Institutions and Agencies in Different Countries* (Hartford: F. C. Brownell, 1857), pp. 107–31; Mary Carpenter, *Juvenile Delinquents: Their Condition and Treatment* (London: W. F. G. Cash, 1853), pp. 258–97; Calvin W. Stowe, "Report on Elementary Public Instruction in Europe," *Reports on European Education*, ed. by Edgar W. Knight (New York: McGraw-Hill, 1930), pp. 262–67.

2. Barnard, *Reformatory Education*, p. 147; see above, Chapter 3.

3. Daniel T. McColgan, *Joseph Tuckerman; Pioneer in American Social Work* (Washington: Catholic Univ., 1940), pp. 97–150.

4. "Theodore Lyman," *American Journal of Education* (ed. by Henry Barnard), X (March 1861), 5–10.

5. Massachusetts General Court, Committee on Public Charitable In-

stitutions, *Investigation into the Management and Discipline of the State Reform School at Westborough* (Boston: A. J. Wright, State Printer, 1877), p. 780.

6. *American Journal of Education*, X, 10–14; Joseph A. Allen, *Westboro' State Reform School Reminiscences* (Boston: Lockwood, Brooks & Co., 1877); Charles A. Cummings, "Reformatory Institutions at Home and Abroad," *North American Review*, LXXXVI (Jan. 1858), 78; Alfred S. Roe, "Lyman School for Boys, Westborough, Massachusetts," *New England Magazine* XXVI (1902), 401–2; Massachusetts, *Acts and Resolves* (1847), c 165.

7. David M. Schneider, *The History of Public Welfare in New York State, 1609–1866* (Chicago: Univ. of Chicago Pr., 1938), pp. 325–27; Ronald E. Shaw, *Erie Water West: A History of the Erie Canal, 1792–1854* (Lexington: Univ. of Kentucky Pr., 1966), pp. 229–30; New York, *Laws of 1846*, c 143.

8. Massachusetts, *Acts and Resolves* (1854), c 52.

9. Samuel G. Howe, *A Letter to J. H. Wilkins, H. B. Rogers, and F. B. Fay, Commissioners of Massachusetts for the State Reform School for Girls* (Boston: Ticknor and Fields, 1854), pp. 3, 12–34.

10. Cummings, *North American Review*, LXXXVI, 77.

11. Ohio, *Laws of 1857*, p. 57.

12. U.S. Congress, House, *The Reformatory System in the United States*, Hse. Doc. No. 459, 56th Cong., 1st Sess. (1900), Barnard, *Reformatory Education*, p. 354.

CHAPTER 6

1. Quoted in Emma Brace, *The Life of Charles Loring Brace, Chiefly told in his own Letters* (New York: Charles Scribner's Sons, 1894), pp. 75–76.

2. Quoted in *ibid.*, p. 82.

3. Charles Loring Brace, "Child Helping in New York," *Journal of Social Science*, XVIII (May 1884), 289–305.

4. Miriam Langsam, *Children West: A History of the Placing-Out System of the New York Children's Aid Society, 1853–1890* (Madison: State Historical Society of Wisconsin for the Department of History, University of Wisconsin, 1964), pp. 33–44; Henry W. Thurston, *The Dependent Child: A Story of Changing Aims and Methods in the Care of Dependent Children* (New York: Columbia Univ. Pr., 1930), p. 92.

5. E. Brace, *C. L. Brace*, pp. 1–11.

6. *Ibid.*, pp. 30–34; *New York Tribune*, Aug. 14, 1890.

7. Frederick Law Olmsted to Charles Loring Brace, June 26, 1847; March 25, 1848, Box 2, Frederick Law Olmsted Papers, Manuscript Division, Library of Congress, Washington, D.C.

8. Quoted in E. Brace, *C. L. Brace*, pp. 100, 127.

9. *Ibid.*, p. 154; John Francis Richmond, *New York and its Institu-*

tions, 1609–1871 (New York: E. B. Treat, 1871), p. 478; Charles Dickens, *American Notes and Pictures from Italy* (London: Oxford Univ. Pr., 1957), pp. 100–103.

10. Richmond, *New York Institutions*, p. 478; Charles Loring Brace, *The Dangerous Classes of New York and Twenty Years Work Among Them* (New York: Wynkoop & Hallenbeck, 1872), p. 78; Thomas L. Harris, *Juvenile Depravity and Crime in our City* (New York: Charles B. Norton, 1850), p. 12, Appendix; *New York Tribune*, May 2, 1850.

11. Brace, *Dangerous Classes*, pp. 79–82; Langsam, *Children West*, pp. 2–3; *New York Times*, Jan. 23, 1852.

12. Brace, *Dangerous Classes*, pp. 84–85; E. Brace, *C. L. Brace*, pp. 156–57; Langsam, *Children West*, pp. 4–5.

13. *New York Times*, March 2, 1853; this circular may also be found in Brace, *Dangerous Classes*, pp. 90–92 and in E. Brace, *C. L. Brace*, pp. 489–92.

14. *New York Times*, May 2, 1853.

15. E. Brace, *C. L. Brace*, p. 160; Brace, *Dangerous Classes*, pp. 92–96, 134–42.

16. Charles Dawson Shanley, "Small Arabs of New York," *Atlantic*, XXIII (March 1869), 279; Children's Aid Society of New York (hereafter cited as CAS), *Second Annual Report* (1885); Irwin G. Wyllie, *The Self-Made Man in America* (New Brunswick, N.J.: Rutgers Univ. Pr., 1954), pp. 40–47; Elizabeth Oakes Smith, *The Newsboy* (New York: J. C. Derby, 1854), pp. 8–9, 33; Frank Gruber, *Horatio Alger, Jr.; A Biography and Bibliography* (West Los Angeles: Grover Jones Press, 1961), pp. 19–26; Brace, *Dangerous Classes*, pp. 98–99; for further discussion of Alger and the Newboys Lodging House, see below, Chapter 7.

17. Brace, *Dangerous Classes*, pp. 97–108.

18. *Ibid.*, pp. 100–5; CAS, *Second Annual Report*, pp. 13–15.

19. Brace, *Dangerous Classes*, pp. 302–9; CAS, *The Children's Aid Society of New York; Its History, Plan and Results, Compiled from the Writings of the Late Charles Loring Brace, the Founders of the Society, and from the Records of the Secretary's Office* (New York: Wynkoop & Hallenbeck, 1893), p. 19.

20. CAS, *The Crusade for Children: A Review of Child Life in New York During 75 Years, 1853–1928* (New York: Children's Aid Society, 1928), p. 24; CAS, *History*, pp. 18, 29.

21. Merle Curti, *The Social Ideas of American Educators: Report of the Commission on the Social Studies of the American Historical Association* (New York: Charles Scribner's Sons, 1935), p. 197.

22. Charles Loring Brace, *Home Life in Germany* (New York: Charles Scribner, 1856), p. 96.

23. Barbara Cross, *Horace Bushnell: Minister to a Changing America* (Chicago: Univ. of Chicago Pr., 1958), p. 67; Bernard Wishy, *The*

Child and the Republic: The Dawn of Modern American Child Nurture (Philadelphia: Univ. of Pennsylvania Pr., 1968), p. 22; Horace Bushnell, *Views of Christian Nurture and of Subjects Adjacent Thereto* (Hartford: Edwin Hunt, 1847), pp. 20–22, 185.

24. Bradford Kinney Peirce, *A Half-Century with Juvenile Delinquents or the House of Refuge and its Times* (New York: D. Appleton & Co., 1869), pp. 105, 218; CAS, *History*, p. 34.

25. *New York Times*, March 2, 1853; CAS, *History*, p. 34; Brace, *Journal of Social Science*, XVIII, 293.

26. E. Brace, *C. L. Brace*, Appendix B., pp. 492–501.

27. Charles Loring Brace to Whitelaw Reid, Feb. 12, 1879, Feb. 10, 1880, Box 8, Whitelaw Reid Papers, Manuscript Division, Library of Congress, Washington, D.C.; CAS, *Third Annual Report*, pp. 7–9; CAS, *History*, p. 34; Brace, *Dangerous Classes*, pp. 231–32; Brace, *Journal of Social Science*, XVIII, 293–94; Charles Loring Brace, "The Care of Poor and Vicious Children," *Journal of Social Science*, XI (May 1880), 93–98.

28. CAS, *Second Annual Report*, p. 43; CAS, *Third Annual Report*, p. 9.

29. CAS, *Second Annual Report*, pp. 5–7, 16–17; Brace, *Journal of Social Science*, XVIII, 294, 299–304; CAS, *Crusade*, p. 10; Brace, *Dangerous Classes*, p. 435; For a discussion of the finances of the Children's Aid Society, see Langsam, *Children West*, pp. 38–44.

30. *New York Times*, March 6, 1865; *New York Sun*, Feb. 28, 1860; *New York Tribune*, March 12, 1879.

31. Brace, *Dangerous Classes*, pp. 236–37; Brace, *Journal of Social Science*, XI, 95.

32. "Charities of New York," *Catholic World*, VIII (Nov. 1868), 282; "Public Charities," *Catholic World*, XVII (April 1873), 1–23; "Specimen Charities," *Catholic World*, XXI (June 1875), 302; Charles Loring Brace, "Pauperism," *North American Review*, CXX (April 1875), 330.

33. Langsam, *Children West*, p. 56; National Conference of Charities and Corrections, *Proceedings* (1875), p. 21 (hereafter cited as NCCP); Charles Loring Brace, "The Placing Out Plan for Homeless and Vagrant Children," NCCP (1876), pp. 135–44.

34. Brace, *Journal of Social Science*, XI, 93–98.

35. "Preventive Work Among Children," NCCP (1882), pp. 120–56.

36. *New York Tribune*, April 9, 1883; Brace, *Journal of Social Science*, XVIII, 289–305.

37. Hastings H. Hart, "Placing Out Children in the West," NCCP (1884), pp. 143–50.

38. U.S. Children's Bureau, *Foster Home Care for Dependent Children* (Washington, D.C.: Government Printing Office, 1924), p. 3.

39. A. E. Williams, *Barnardo of Stepney: The Father of Nobody's Children* (London: George Allen and Unwin, 1943), pp. 5–128; On-

tario Prison Reform Commission, *Report of the Commissioners Appointed to Inquire into the Prison and Reformatory System of Ontario* (Toronto: Printed by order of the Legislative Assembly, 1891), pp. 432–47.

40. U.S. Children's Bureau, *Laws Relating to Interstate Placement of Dependent Children*, compiled by Emelyn Foster Pick (Washington, D.C.; Government Printing Office, 1924).

41. Mary Bushnell Cheyney, *Life and Letters of Horace Bushnell* (New York: Charles Scribner's Sons, 1905), p. 79; quoted in E. Brace, *C. L. Brace*, p. 9; Theodore Parker, *A Sermon on the Dangerous Classes in Society* (Boston: C. and J. M. Spear, 1847), p. 35; Brace, *Dangerous Classes*, pp. 28–76; Charles Loring Brace, *The Best Method of Disposing of Our Pauper and Vagrant Children* (New York: Wynkoop, Hallenbeck and Thomas, 1859), pp. 3–16.

42. Brace, *Dangerous Classes*, pp. 440–41; Robert H. Bremner, *From the Depths: The Discovery of Poverty in the United States* (New York: New York Univ. Pr., 1956), p. 51.

43. Brace, *Best Method*, pp. 12–13.

44. Brace, *Journal of Social Science*, XI, 93–98.

CHAPTER 7

1. Mrs. James T. Fields, *James T. Fields: Biographical Notes and Personal Sketches* (Boston: Houghton Mifflin, 1881), pp. 223–26.

2. Albert E. Stone, Jr., *The Innocent Eye: Childhood in Mark Twain's Imagination* (New Haven: Yale Univ. Pr., 1961), p. 24; Jacob Blanck, "A Twentieth Century Look at Nineteenth Century Children's Books," in William Targ, ed., *Bibliophile in the Nursery: A Bookman's Treasury of Collectors' Lore on Old and Rare Children's Books* (Cleveland: World Publishing Co., 1957), pp. 439, 442, 448.

3. Alice M. Jordan, *From Rollo to Tom Sawyer and Other Papers* (Boston: The Horn Book, 1948), pp. 32–34, 40–46, 133; *Cambridge History of American Literature*, ed. by William Peterfield Trent and others, 3 vols. (New York: Macmillan, 1933), II, 403–5; see also Alice M. Jordan, "Magazines for Children," New York Public Library, *Bulletin*, LX (Nov.–Dec. 1956), 599–604.

4. Jay Martin, *Harvests of Change, American Literature, 1865–1914* (Englewood Cliffs, N.J.; Prentice-Hall, 1967), p. 184.

5. Gilliam Elise Avery, with the assistance of Angela Bull, *Nineteenth Century Children: Heroes and Heroines in English Children's Stories, 1790–1900* (London: Hodder and Stoughton, 1965), p. 65; Peter Coveney, *Poor Monkey: The Child in Literature* (London: Rockliff, 1957), p. 86; Jordon, *Rollo to Tom Sawyer*, pp. 128, 133.

6. Martin, p. 184; Richard Hofstadter, *Social Darwinism in American Thought*, rev. ed. (Boston: Beacon Press, 1964), p. 14; Sir Llewellyn Woodward, *The Age of Reform, 1815–1870* (Oxford: Oxford

Univ. Pr., 1962), pp. 147–53; Charles N. Glaab and A. Theodore Brown, *A History of Urban America* (New York: Macmillan, 1967), pp. 133–66.

7. Herbert R. Mayes, *Alger, a Biography without a Hero* (New York: Macy-Masius, 1928), pp. 28–36, 99–104; Frank Gruber, *Horatio Alger, Jr.: A Biography and Bibliography* (West Los Angeles: Grover Jones Press, 1961), pp. 12–25.

8. Horatio Alger, Jr., "Ragged Dick," in *Struggling Upward and Other Works* (New York: Cronon Publishers, 1945), pp. 154–55, 188, 218; Mayes, pp. 48, 117; see above, Chapter 6.

9. Mayes, pp. 38–48.

10. Henry M. Robinson, "Mr. Beadle's Books," *Bookman*, LXIX (March 1929), 20–24; Edmund Pearson, *Dime Novels; or, Following an Old Trail in Popular Literature* (Boston: Little, Brown, 1929), p. 92; Ralph Admari, "The House That Beadle Built," *American Book Collector*, V (Feb. 1934), 23.

11. Pearson, p. 37; "The Beadle Collection," New York Public Library, *Bulletin*, XXVI (July 1922), 558; Merle Curti, "Dime Novels and the American Tradition," *Yale Review*, n.s., XXVI (1936), 763; *Cambridge History of American Literature*, III, 67.

12. Mayes, p. 117; Stone, p. 27; Phillip D. Jordan, "The American Bad Boy," *Amateur Book Collector*, I (May 1951), 2–3.

13. T. S. Eliot, "Introduction," in Mark Twain [Samuel L. Clemens], *The Adventures of Huckleberry Finn* (New York: Chanticleer Press, 1950), p. vii; Martin, pp. 184–85; Mark Twain, *The Adventures of Tom Sawyer*, author's national edition (New York: Harper & Brothers, 1903), pp. 60–61, 67.

14. Mark Twain, *Tom Sawyer*, pp. 67, 315–20.

15. Mark Twain, *Huckleberry Finn*, pp. 15, 88, 214, 234.

16. William Graham Sumner, "What Our Boys Are Reading," *Scribner's Monthly*, XV (March 1878), 681–85.

17. Heywood Broun and Margaret Leech, *Anthony Comstock, Roundsman of the Lord* (New York: Literary Guild of America, 1927), pp. 82–85, 130–42, 143; Anthony Comstock, *Traps for the Young* (New York: Funk and Wagnalls, 1889), pp. ix, 12–15, 20–21, 24.

18. The use of "ideal" in opposition to "fantasy" is deliberate. In the "real" world of Comstock and Sumner's day men often made great sums of money by ignoring the tenets of the self-help cult, e.g. Jay Gould, Daniel Drew, Jim Fisk.

19. G. Stanley Hall, "Child Study as a Basis for Psychology and Psychological Teaching," in U.S., Commissioner of Education, *Annual Report, 1892–93* (Washington: Government Printing Office, 1895), p. 357; Hall, "The Study of Children," in *ibid.*, p. 366; Lawrence A. Cremin, *The Transformation of the School: Progressivism in American Education, 1876–1957* (New York: Alfred A. Knopf, 1961).

CHAPTER 8

1. Quoted in Charles N. Glaab, *The American City: A Documentary History* (Homewood, Illinois: The Dorsey Press, 1963), pp. 128, 270.
2. Adna F. Weber, *The Growth of Cities in the Nineteenth Century: A Study in Statistics* (New York: Macmillan Co., 1899; reprint Ithaca, N.Y.: Cornell Univ. Pr., 1963), pp. 173–74, 188, 198–99; *New York Times*, July 23, 1873.
3. *New York Times*, July 21, 1875.
4. *New York Times*, Aug. 14, 1890.
5. *New York Tribune*, Oct. 8, 1884; Frederick M. Thrasher, *The Gang: A Study of 1313 Gangs in Chicago* (Chicago: Univ. of Chicago Pr., 1936), pp. 17, 36.
6. Blake McKelvey, *The Urbanization of America* (New Brunswick, N.J.: Rutgers Univ. Pr., 1963), pp. 144–55; Robert H. Bremner, *From the Depths: The Discovery of Poverty in the United States* (New York: New York Univ. Pr., 1956), pp. 10, 38–54, 212.
7. Bremner, *From the Depths*, pp. 35–38; Roy Lubove, "The New York Association for Improving the Condition of the Poor: The Formative Years," *New-York Historical Society Quarterly*, XLIII (July 1959), 307–27; New York Association for Improving the Condition of the Poor (hereafter cited as AICP), *Annual Report* (1854), pp. 61–63.
8. George Paul Jacoby, *Catholic Child Care in Nineteenth Century New York* (Washington: Catholic University, 1941), pp. 65–67.
9. *New York Times*, April 30, 1873; *People* ex rel. *Splain* v *New York Juvenile Asylum*, 2 N.Y. Sup. Ct. 475 (1874).
10. William Pryor Letchworth, "Orphan Asylums and Other Institutions for the Care of Children," in New York State Board of Charities, *Ninth Annual Report* (1876), pp. 510, 514–16; John Francis Richmond, *New York and its Institutions, 1609–1871* (New York: E. B. Treat, 1871), pp. 328–30.
11. *New York Times*, Apr. 21, 1871; *New York Tribune*, July 7, 1879.
12. *New York Times*, May 18, Aug. 1, 1872; New York State Board of Charities, *Sixth Annual Report* (1872), pp. 61–63.
13. Thomas Matthew Bennett, "William Pryor Letchworth and His Work of Child-Saving" (unpublished Master's thesis, Ohio State University, 1967), pp. 9–11, 49–50; Josephus N. Larned, *The Life and Work of William Pryor Letchworth, Student and Minister of Public Benevolence* (New York: Houghton Mifflin, 1912), pp. 1–36; William Pryor Letchworth, *Industrial Training of Children in Houses of Refuge and Other Reformatory Schools* (Albany: The Argus Co., 1883), pp. 39–43: for a discussion of the *Rauhe Haus*, see above, Chapter 5.
14. *New York Tribune*, July 7, 1879, Apr. 9, Apr. 12, Apr. 17, 1882.

15. Homer Folks, *The Care of Destitute, Neglected, and Delinquent Children* (New York: Macmillan, 1902), p. 176; Jacoby, *Catholic Charities*, pp. 75–76; Helen Campbell, *Prisoners of Poverty: Women Wage-Workers, Their Trades and Their Lives* (Boston: Roberts Brothers, 1889), pp. 170–73; Society for the Prevention of Cruelty to Children (hereafter cited as SPCC), *Fifth Annual Report* (1879), pp. 7–8.
16. New York, *Laws of 1874*, c 116, *Laws of 1892*, c 217; SPCC, *Second Annual Report* (1877), pp. 40–41; SPCC, *Fifth Annual Report*, p. 9.
17. New York, *Laws of 1877*, c 428.
18. Edward P. Hutchinson, *Immigrants and Their Children, 1850–1950* (New York: John Wiley and Sons, 1956), p. 22; Charles N. Glaab and A. Theodore Brown, *A History of Urban America* (New York: Macmillan, 1967), pp. 138–39.
19. U.S., Congress, Senate, *Reports of the Immigration Commission*, Doc. No. 747, 61st Cong., 3rd Sess., 1911, I, 24–43, quoted in Edith Abbott, *Immigration: Select Documents and Case Records* (Chicago: Univ. of Chicago Pr., 1924), p. 543.
20. Glaab and Brown, p. 139; U.S. Congress, House, *Foreign Criminals and Paupers*, Rep. No. 359, 34th Cong., 1st Sess., 1856, pp. 16–17, quoted in Edith Abbott, *Historical Aspects of the Immigration Problem, Select Documents* (Chicago: Univ. of Chicago Pr., 1926), p. 621; Oscar Handlin, *The Uprooted* (Boston: Little, Brown, 1951), p. 146.
21. Hastings H. Hart, "Immigration and Crime," *American Journal of Sociology*, II (Nov. 1896), 369–71, E. E. Edmonson, "Juvenile Delinquency and Adult Crime," *Indiana University Studies*, VIII (March 1912), 37–38.
22. Robert H. Bremner, "The Children with the Organ Man," *American Quarterly*, VIII (Fall 1956), 277–82; Jeremy P. Felt, *Hostages of Fortune: Child Labor Reform in New York State* (Syracuse, N.Y.: Syracuse Univ. Pr., 1965), pp. 7–9, 19.
23. Frank D. Watson, *The Charity Organization Movement in the United States* (New York: Macmillan, 1922), pp. 276, 307.
24. Bremner, *From the Depths*, p. 51; Robert H. Bremner, *American Philanthropy* (Chicago: Univ. of Chicago Pr., 1960), pp. 98–104; Roy Lubove, *The Professional Altruist: The Emergence of Social Work as a Career, 1880–1930* (Cambridge, Mass.: Harvard Univ. Pr., 1965), pp. 2–20.
25. Bremner, *From the Depths*, p. 51; Felt, *Hostages of Fortune*, pp. 7–9, 19.

CHAPTER 9

1. Brockway's paper and an account of his life may be found in

Zebulon Brockway, *Fifty Years of Prison Service* (New York: Charities Publication Committee, 1912).

2. New York State Reformatory at Elmira, *Annual Report* (1894), p. 15 (hereafter cited as NYSRE).

3. See above, Chapter 3; Brockway, "The American Reformatory Prison System" *American Journal of Sociology*, XV (Jan. 1910), 456–71.

4. Orlando F. Lewis, *The Development of American Prisons and Prison Customs, 1776–1845, With Special Reference to Early Institutions in the State of New York* (Albany: Prison Association of New York, 1922; reprinted Montclair, N.J.: Peter Smith, 1967), pp. 13–17; Harry Elmer Barnes, "The Historical Origins of the Prison System in America," *Journal of the American Institute of Criminal Law and Criminology*, XII (May 1921), 44.

5. See above Chapters 2 and 3.

6. Brockway, *Fifty Years*, p. 134.

7. Brockway, *American Journal of Sociology*, XV, 454, 476.

8. NYSRE, *Annual Report* (1896), p. 7.

9. NYSRE, *Annual Report* (1894), p. 16.

10. Grace Abbott, *The Child and the State*, 2 vols. (Chicago: Univ. of Chicago Pr., 1938), II, 371–78.

11. John R. Commons, "The Junior Republic," *American Journal of Sociology*, III (Nov. 1897), 282–84; William R. George, *The Junior Republic; Its History and Ideals* (New York: D. Appleton and Co., 1912), pp. 5–7, 15.

12. Commons, *American Journal of Sociology*, III, 284–86; George, *Junior Republic*, pp. 17, 20.

13. J. W. Jenks, "The George Junior Republic," *Journal of Social Science*, XXXV (Dec. 1897), 65; Jeanne Robert, "A Republic for Boys and Girls—after Twenty Years," *Review of Reviews*, XLII (Dec. 1910), 707; George, *Junior Republic*, pp. 56–69.

14. Commons, *American Journal of Sociology*, III, 433.

15. T. M. Osborne, "The George Junior Republic," *Journal of Social Science*, XXXVI (Dec. 1898), 135–37; Commons, *American Journal of Sociology*, III, 433; George, *Citizens Made and Re-Made* (Boston: Houghton Mifflin, 1912), p. 169.

16. Robert, *Review of Reviews*, XLII, 710.

CHAPTER 10

1. Henry W. Thurston, "Ten Years of the Juvenile Court of Chicago," *Charities*, XXIII (Feb. 5, 1910), 661; *Juvenile Record*, II (Nov. 1900), 7–8.

2. Richard S. Tuthill, "Address," National Prison Association, Annual Congress, Proceedings (1902), p. 121; Thurston, p. 658.

3. Bessie Louise Pierce, *A History of Chicago*, Vol. III: *The Rise of a Modern City, 1871–1893* (New York: Alfred A. Knopf, 1957), pp. 20–47.

4. Jane Addams, *Twenty Years at Hull House* (New York: Macmillan, 1940), pp. 250–51.

5. Jane Addams, *The Spirit of Youth and the City Streets* (New York: Macmillan, 1930), pp. 67–69; Sara Nelson Franklin, "A Workshop of a Probation Officer," *Charities*, XI (Nov. 7, 1903), 414.

6. "A New View of the Juvenile Court," *Juvenile Record*, II (Feb. 1901), 13; Sophonisba Breckinridge and Edith Abbott, *The Delinquent Child and the Home* (New York: Charities Publication Committee, 1912), p. 1; Jane Addams, *My Friend, Julia Lathrop* (New York: Macmillan, 1935), p. 133.

7. "A New View of the Juvenile Court," *Juvenile Record*, II (Feb. 1901), 13; Breckinridge and Abbott, *Delinquent Child*, p. 4.

8. William T. Stead, *If Christ Came to Chicago* (Chicago: Laird and Lee, 1894), pp. 1, 386; Timothy D. Hurley, *Origins of the Illinois Juvenile Court Law; Juvenile Courts and What They Have Accomplished* (Chicago: Visitation and Aid Society, 1907), pp. 17, 71.

9. Quoted in Edith Abbott and Sophonisba Breckinridge, *Truancy and Non-Attendance in the Chicago Schools* (Chicago: Univ. of Chicago Pr., 1917), p. 55.

10. *The Child, the Clinic and the Court . . .* (New York: New Republic, 1925), pp. 292–93 (hereafter cited as CCC); Chicago Woman's Club, *Annals of the Chicago Woman's Club for the First Forty Years, 1876–1916*, compiled by Henriette Greenebaum Frank and Amalie Hofer Jerome (Chicago: Chicago Woman's Club, 1916), pp. 76, 125.

11. Quoted in Abbott and Breckinridge, *Truancy*, p. 71; *ibid.*, pp. 76, 85n, 86, 166.

12. Julia Lathrop, "The Development of the Probation System in a Large City," *Charities*, XIII (Jan. 7, 1905), 344–45; Addams, *Julia Lathrop*, p. 134; Cook County [Illinois] Grand Jury, *Report of Members of Cook County Grand Jury for May, 1898, on Method of Handling Boy Offenders by the City, County, and State* (Chicago: Rand, McNally, 1898), pp. 2–10.

13. CCC, p. 293; Chicago Woman's Club, p. 159. Cook County Grand Jury, pp. 15–16.

14. *Chicago Tribune*, Feb. 16, June 28, 1899; *Chicago Record*, Feb. 16, 20, July 1, 1899.

15. CCC, p. 294, pp. 324–25; Hurley, pp. 21–22; *Chicago Tribune*, Feb. 8, July 1, 1899; Hastings H. Hart, "The Juvenile Court—Its Uses and Limitations," National Prison Association, Annual Congress, *Proceedings* (1906), p. 245.

16. Illinois, *Laws of 1899*, p. 132. The complete text of the Illinois Juvenile Court Law of 1899 may be found conveniently in Grace Abbott, *The Child and the State* (Chicago: Univ. of Chicago Pr., 1938), II, 392–401.

17. Illinois, *Laws of 1899*, pp. 132–37.
18. Merritt W. Pickney, "The Juvenile Court," Chicago, Child Welfare Exhibit, *The Child in the City: A Series of Papers Presented at the Conference held during the Chicago Child Welfare Exhibit* (Chicago: Department of Social Investigation, Chicago School of Civics and Philanthropy, 1912), p. 316.
19. "Testimony of Judge Julian W. Mack," quoted in Breckinridge and Abbott, *Delinquent Child*, pp. 181–85; Sir William Holdsworth, *A History of English Law* (London: Methuen, 1936), I, 453–69, 475; Herbert H. Lou, *Juvenile Courts in the United States* (Chapel Hill, N.C.: Univ. of North Carolina Pr., 1947), pp. 4–5; Bernard Flexner, "The Juvenile Court—Its Legal Aspects," *Annals of the American Academy of Political and Social Science*, XXXVI (July 1910), 49; Frederick B. Sussman, *The Law of Juvenile Delinquency: The Laws of the Forty-eight States* (New York: Oceanna Publications, 1950), pp. 14–15; Grace Abbott, II, 330; Katherine F. Lenroot, "The Evolution of the Juvenile Court," *Annals of The American Academy of Political and Social Science*, CV (Jan. 1923), 213. Some states, like New York, provided for special chancery courts, but others gave equity jurisdiction to the regular courts. For a discussion see Roscoe Pound, *Organization of Courts* (Boston: Little, Brown, 1940), pp. 132–36.
20. Lou, pp. 4–5; *Commonwealth* v *Fisher*, 213 Pa. St. Rep. 48 (1906).
21. Lou, p. 7; Charles R. Henderson, "Juvenile Courts; Problems of Administration," *Charities*, XIII (Jan. 7, 1905), 340; Julian W. Mack, "The Law and the Child," *Survey*, XXIII (Feb. 5, 1910), 641; Lenroot, *Annals* . . . , CV, 213–15.
22. *Chicago Tribune*, June 26, 28, 1899; *Juvenile Record*, II (Dec. 1900), 4; Lathrop, 346.
23. *Hull House Bulletin*, III (Oct. 1898), 10; Addams, *Twenty Years*, pp. 323–24; Swarthmore College Peace Collection, Jane Addams MSS, scrap item or draft of an obituary notice (Jan. 1900); Lathrop, pp. 344–45.
24. Donald W. Moreland, "John Augustus and His Successors," National Probation Association, *Yearbook* (New York: National Probation Association, 1941), pp. 3–5; John Augustus, *John Augustus, First Probation Officer; Reprint of the Original Report of John Augustus Published in Boston in 1852, with an Introduction by Sheldon Glueck* (New York: National Probation Association, 1939), pp. 4–5, 13; *Boston Herald*, June 22, 1859; "John Augustus," DAB, I, 429.
25. Augustus, pp. 13–14, 33–34, 95–97; Moreland, pp. 15–18; Nicholas S. Timasheff, *One Hundred Years of Probation* (New York: Fordham Univ. Pr., 1941), p. 9; Massachusetts State Board of Charities, *Fifth Annual Report* (1868), quoted in Grace Abbott, II, 365–66; Massachusetts, *Acts and Resolves* (1869), c 453.

26. Massachusetts, *Acts and Resolves* (1870), c 359; Massachusetts State Board of Charities, *Eighth Annual Report* (1872), quoted in Grace Abbott, II, 369.

27. Ontario Prison Reform Commission, *Report on the Commissioners Appointed to Inquire into the Prison and Reformatory System of Ontario* (Toronto: Printed by order of the Legislative Assembly, 1891), pp. 230, 386–87; Grace Abbott, II, 330; Charles L. Chute, "The Development of Probation," National Probation Association, *Year Book* (New York; National Probation Association, 1941), p. 34.

28. *Chicago Tribune*, July 6, 1899; *Chicago Record*, July 11, 25, 1899.

29. Breckinridge and Abbott, *Delinquent Child*, p. 40; Illinois, *Laws of 1899*, p. 133.

30. Lathrop, pp. 345–46; Addams, *Twenty Years*, pp. 323–24; Tuthill, *Juvenile Record*, II (Dec. 1900), 5; Breckinridge and Abbott, *Delinquent Child*, p. 23n; Chicago Woman's Club, p. 229.

31. Tuthill, *Juvenile Record*, II (Dec. 1900), 4.

32. Breckinridge and Abbott, *Delinquent Child*, pp. 28–30, 35–38; Jane Addams, *A New Conscience and an Ancient Evil* (New York: Macmillan, 1912), p. 109.

33. "Testimony of Judge Merritt W. Pinckney (given before the Cook County Civil Service Commission, November 22, 23, 1911)," Appendix II, Breckinridge and Abbott, *Delinquent Child*, pp. 206–8.

34. Tuthill, *Juvenile Record*, II (Dec. 1900), 5; Homer Folks, "Juvenile Probation," National Conference of Charities and Corrections, *Proceedings* (1906), p. 119.

35. Bernard Flexner and Roger Baldwin, *Juvenile Courts and Probation* (New York: Century Co., 1914), p. 80; Roger Baldwin, quoted in Bernard Flexner, "The Juvenile Court as a Social Institution," *Survey*, XXIII (Feb. 5, 1910), 619; Lou, p. 143; Mary Richmond, *Social Diagnosis* (New York: Russell Sage, 1917), p. 44.

36. For a discussion of criminology and psychology, see below, Chapter 11; Tuthill, National Prison Association, Annual Congress, *Proceedings* (1902), 121; Flexner, *Survey*, XXIII (Feb. 5, 1910), 607; Lou, p. 113; Julian W. Mack, "The Juvenile Court," National Conference of Charities and Corrections, *Proceedings* (1906), 128; Hastings H. Hart, "The Juvenile Court," *Annals of the American Academy of Political and Social Sciences*, XXXVI (July 1910), 58.

37. Breckinridge and Abbott, *Delinquent Child*, p. 57; Julias W. Mayer, "The Child in the Large City," *Charities*, XI (Nov. 7, 1903), 418.

38. Mack, National Conference of Charities and Corrections, *Proceedings* (1906), 128; Lou, p. 113; Massachusetts, *Acts and Resolves* (1870), c 359; New York, *Laws of 1892*, c 217; "The Children's Court," *Charities*, X (Nov. 7, 1903), 395; Harvey Hurd, "The Juvenile Court Law," *Charities*, XIII (Jan. 7, 1905), 327; "A New View of the Juvenile Court," *Juvenile Record*, II (Feb. 1901), 13.

39. Tuthill, *Juvenile Record*, II (Dec. 1900), 5–6; Richard S. Tuthill, "The Necessity of a State Home for Delinquent Boys," *Juvenile Record*, II (Nov. 1901), 15–16.
40. Illinois, *Laws of 1899*, p. 132; *Juvenile Record*, II (March 1901), 16.
41. Illinois, *Revised Statutes* (1903), pp. 261, 265; New York, *Laws of 1892*, c 217.
42. Thomas D. Eliot, *The Juvenile Court and the Community* (New York: Macmillan, 1914), p. 3; "Dependent Children," *Charities*, IX (Nov. 1, 1902), 415; "Probation and Politics," *Survey*, XXVII (Mar. 30, 1912), 2003–4; "A Protest from Mr. Jenkins," *Charities*, IX (Sept. 20, 1902), 266–67; "Rejoinders from Chicago," *Charities*, IX (Sept. 20, 1902), 269.
43. Charles R. Henderson, "The Theory and Practice of Juvenile Courts," National Conference of Charities and Corrections, *Proceedings* (1904), p. 361; "Probation and Politics," *Survey*, XXVII (March 30, 1912), 2003–4.
44. Herbert W. Baker, "The Court and the Delinquent Child," *American Journal of Sociology*, XXVI (Sept. 1920), 177–78; Flexner, *Annals . . .*, XXXVI (July 1910), 55; Charles R. Henderson, "Juvenile Courts," *Charities*, XVI (Jan. 7, 1907), 340; Lou, pp. 24–25.

CHAPTER 11

1. Thomas Wilson, "Criminal Anthropology," *Annual Report of the Board of Regents of the Smithsonian Institution* (1890) (Washington: Government Printing Office, 1891), pp. 617–19.
2. Eugene M. Aaron, "Recent Researches in Criminology," *Scientific American Supplement*, XXXIII (June 18, 1892), 13727–28.
3. W. D. Morison, "Introduction," in Cesare Lombroso and William Ferrero, *The Female Offender* (London: T. Fisher Unwin, 1895), pp. xv–xvi; Maurice Parmlee, *The Principles of Anthropology and Sociology in Their Relations to Criminal Procedure* (New York: Macmillan, 1908), pp. 17, 24–32; Frances Anne Kellor, "Criminal Anthropology in Its Relation to Criminal Jurisprudence," *American Journal of Sociology*, IV (Jan. 1899), 516; C. Bernaldo DeQuiros, *Modern Theories of Crime* (Boston: Little, Brown, 1912), pp. 10–19.
4. Gabriel Tarde, *Penal Philosophy* (Boston: Little, Brown, 1912), pp. 259, 416; Kellor, *American Journal of Sociology*, IV, 518.
5. *Nouvelle mémoires de l'académie royale des sciences et belles-lettres de Bruxelles*, V (Dec. 1829), 25–38, VII (1831), 1–88; Adolphe Quételet, *Sur l'homme et le développement de ses facultés, ou essai de physique sociale* (Paris, 1835), p. 108, quoted in Frank H.

Hankins, "Adolphe Quetelet as Statistician," in *Studies in History, Economics and Public Law,* edited by the Faculty of Political Science of Columbia University, XXXI, No. 4 (New York: Columbia Univ. Pr., 1908), 530.

6. Auguste Comte, *The Positive Philosophy of Auguste Comte,* freely translated by Harriet Martineau, 3 vols. (London: Geo. Bell & Sons, 1896), I, 1–2; *Encyclopedia of the Social Sciences* (New York: Macmillan, 1935), IV, 151–52; L. Lévy-Bruhl, *The Philosophy of Auguste Comte,* translated by Kathleen de Beaumont-Klein (London: Iwan Sonnenschein, 1903), p. 239.

7. Luther L. Bernard and Jessie Bernard, *Origins of American Sociology: The Social Science Movement in the United States* (New York: Thomas Y. Crowell, 1943), p. 548; Frank J. Bruno, *Trends in Social Work as Reflected in the Proceedings of the National Conference of Social Work, 1874–1946* (New York: Columbia Univ. Pr., 1948), pp. 3–6.

8. For an extended analysis of the National Conference of Charities and Corrections see Bruno, *Trends in Social Work.* On the American Social Science see Bernard, *Origins of American Sociology.* See also *Proceedings* of the National Conference of Charities and Corrections and the *American Journal of Social Science.*

9. National Conference of Charities and Corrections, *Proceedings* (1885), pp. 228–40 (hereafter cited as NCCP).

10. NCCP (1886), p. 59; (1887), pp. 233–34; (1898), pp. 407, 411, 413.

11. Oscar C. McCullock, "The Tribe of Ismael—A Study in Social Degradation," NCCP (1888), pp. 154–59; Arthur E. Fink, *Causes of Crime: Biological Theories in the United States, 1800–1915* (New York: A. S. Barnes, 1962; first published Philadelphia: Univ. of Pennsylvania Pr., 1938), p. 179; Richard L. Dugdale, *The Jukes: A Study in Crime, Disease, and Heredity; Also Further Studies of Criminals,* 4th ed. (New York: G. P. Putnam's Sons, 1910), pp. 12, 65.

12. Robert E. L. Faris, "Evolution and American Sociology" in Stow Persons, ed., *Evolutionary Thought in America* (New Haven: Yale Univ. Pr., 1950), p. 163; John C. Burnham, *Lester Frank Ward in American Thought* (Washington, D.C.: Annals of American Sociology Public Affairs Press, 1956), pp. 1–22; see also Richard Hofstadter, *Social Darwinism in American Thought,* rev. ed. (Boston: Beacon Press, 1964), pp. 67–84.

13. Hofstadter, *Social Darwinism,* pp. 4–5, 37–44, 54–55.

14. *Ibid.,* p. 46; Samuel Chugerman, *Lester F. Ward, the American Aristotle* (Durham, N.C. Duke Univ. Pr., 1939), p. 201; Lester Frank Ward, *Dynamic Sociology* (New York: D. Appleton and Co., 1920), p. xxvi.

15. Albion W. Small, "Fifty Years of Sociology in the United States,"

American Journal of Sociology, XXI (May 1916), 769–70; Harry Elmer Barnes, *The History and Prospects of the Social Sciences* (New York: Alfred A. Knopf, 1925), pp. 763, 820.

16. Ralph E. Pumphrey and Muriel W. Pumphrey, eds., *The Heritage of American Social Work* (New York: Columbia Univ. Pr., 1961), pp. 202–3; Robert H. Bremner, *American Philanthropy* (Chicago: Univ. of Chicago Pr., 1960), p. 115; Roy Lubove, *The Professional Altruist: The Emergence of Social Work as a Career, 1880–1930* (Cambridge: Harvard Univ. Pr., 1965), p. 12.

17. Robert A. Woods and Albert J. Kennedy, *The Settlement Horizon* (New York: Russell Sage, 1922), pp. 22–27, 41–43; Arthur C. Holden, *The Settlement Idea: A Vision of Social Justice* (New York: Macmillan, 1922), p. 12.

18. Pumphrey and Pumphrey, p. 211; Louise C. Wade, *Graham Taylor: Pioneer for Social Justice, 1851–1938* (Chicago: Univ. of Chicago Pr., 1964), pp. 81, 162.

19. Jane Addams, "The Subtle Problems of Charity," *Atlantic Monthly*, LXII (Feb. 1899), 169, 170, 173, 177.

20. John C. Farrell, *Beloved Lady: A History of Jane Addams' Ideas on Reform and Peace* (Baltimore, Md.: The Johns Hopkins Pr., 1967), pp. 68–69.

21. Robert I. Watson, *The Great Psychologists from Aristotle to Freud* (Philadelphia: Lippincott, 1963), pp. 257, 317–42; Edward G. Boring, *A History of Experimental Psychology* (New York: D. Appleton Century, 1935), pp. 322, 377–79, 494–504.

22. Lorine Pruette, *G. Stanley Hall, a Biography of a Mind* (New York: D. Appleton and Co., 1926), pp. 83–101; Watson, pp. 68–69.

23. Watson, pp. 346–51; Boring, pp. 506–10.

24. Pruette, pp. 109–26; G. Stanley Hall, *Adolescence, Its Psychology and Its Relations to Psychology, Anthropology, Sociology, Sex, Crime Religion, and Education* (New York: D. Appleton and Co., 1922), pp. vii, 340, 342, 401, 405, 407.

25. Fink, p. 148; Wilson, p. 619.

26. Wilson, pp. 617–86; Robert Fletcher, "The New School of Criminal Anthropology," *American Anthropologist*, IV (July 1891), 201–36.

27. Aaron, *Scientific American Supplement*, XXXIII, 13727–29.

28. New York State Reformatory at Elmira, *Annual Report* (1895), p. 95.

29. August Drähms, *The Criminal, His Personnel and Environment: A Scientific Study* (New York: Macmillan, 1900), pp. vii–ix, xi–xiii, 59–219.

30. Frances A. Kellor, *Experimental Sociology* (New York: Macmillan Co., 1901), pp. vii, 12, 109.

31. G. Frank Lydston, *The Diseases of Society: The Vice and Crime Problem* (Philadelphia: Lippincott, 1904), pp. 27, 48, 78.

32. Kellor, *American Journal of Sociology*, IV, 519, 523.

33. George E. Dawson, "A Study of Youthful Degeneracy," *Pedagogical Seminary*, IV (Dec. 1896), 224–25, 235–37, 243–45, 256.
34. Maxmilian P. E. Groszmann, "Criminality in Children," *Arena*, XXII (Oct. 1899), 511, 521, 541, 646–47, 651; Dawson, *Pedagogical Seminary*, IV, 245.
35. Benjamin Reece, "Public Schools as Affecting Crime and Vice," *Popular Science Monthly*, XXVI (Jan. 1890), 321–23, 324, 327, 328.
36. A. W. Gould, "Education and Crime," *Popular Science Monthly*, XXXVII (June 1890), 214–16.
37. Enoch V. Stoddard, "Juvenile Delinquency and the Failures in Present Reformatory Methods," in New York State Board of Charities, *Thirty-first Annual Report* (1897), pp. 595, 601, 605.
38. U.S. Bureau of the Census, *Report on the Defective, Dependent and Delinquent Classes of the Population of the United States as Returned at the Tenth Census* (Washington: Government Printing Office, 1896), p. 551; U.S. Bureau of the Census, *Report on Crime, Pauperism and Benevolence at the Eleventh Census* (Washington: Government Printing Office, 1896), pp. 211–13, 522.
39. U.S. Bureau of the Census, *Defective, Dependent and Delinquent Classes*, p. ix; U.S. Bureau of the Census, *Crime, Pauperism and Benevolence*, p. 211.
40. U.S. Bureau of the Census, *Crime, Pauperism and Benevolence*, pp. 211–13; U.S. Bureau of Education, *Annual Report of the Commissioner of Education*, 2 vols. (1889–90), II, 1070–71.

CHAPTER 12

1. Ben Lindsey and Harvey J. O'Higgins, *The Beast* (New York: Doubleday, Page, 1910), pp. 75–87; Frances Anne Huber, "The Progressive Career of Ben B. Lindsey, 1900–1920," unpublished PhD. dissertation, University of Michigan, 1963, p. 440; Ben Lindsey, "Childhood and Crime," National Prison Association, Annual Congress, *Proceedings* (1905), pp. 171–72; Colorado, *Laws of 1899*, c 136.
2. Ben Lindsey and Rube Borough, *The Dangerous Life* (New York: Liveright, 1931), pp. 18, 28–30, 37–41, 42–45, 62–76, 82–86; Huber, pp. 16–21, 24–31, 39; Lindsey, *The Beast*, pp. 64–66, 74–75.
3. Lindsey, *The Beast*, pp. 79–82, 86–88; Ben Lindsey, "The Juvenile Court and Probation of Juvenile Offenders," Texas Society for the Friendless, *Bulletin* (Aug. 1906), n. p.; Denver, Colorado, Juvenile Court, *The Problem of the Children and How the State of Colorado Cares for Them* (Denver: Merchants Publishing Co., 1904), p. 35.
4. Lindsey, Tex. Soc. Friendless, *Bull.* (Aug. 1906); Ben Lindsey to Ames, Lindsey Papers, Manuscript Division, Library of Congress,

Box 80 (hereafter the Lindsey papers will be cited as LP); Lindsey to McPhee, Jan. 1902, Box 82, LP.

5. Lindsey, Tex. Soc. Friendless, *Bull.* (Aug. 1906); Lindsey to R. H. Malone, Sept. 18, 1902, Box 84, LP; Lindsey, "Some Experiences in the Juvenile Court of Denver," *Charities,* XI (Nov. 7, 1903), 405–7; Lindsey to James F. Hill, Jan. 17, 1903, Box 85, LP; Denver Jv. Ct., *Report* (1904), pp. 35, 72–74; *Juvenile Record,* II (April 1902), 14; Ella Castillo Bennett, "Juvenile Court of Denver," *Sunset,* XVI (March 1906), 462; Lindsey to R. L. Chambers, June 21, 1920, Box 83, LP; Lindsey to Sprague, April 19, 1902, Box 82, LP; Ben Lindsey, "The Reformation of Juvenile Delinquents through the Juvenile Court," National Conference of Charities and Corrections, *Proceedings* (1903), p. 218. (Hereafter the National Conference of Charities and Corrections will be cited as NCCP.)

6. Lindsey to Hall, Sept. 22, 1904, Box 2, LP.

7. Lindsey, *The Beast,* p. 96.

8. Lindsey to Ogden, Sept. 18, 1902, Box 84, LP; Lindsey to Chambers, June 17, 1902, Box 83, LP; Lindsey to Hurley, Jan. 17, 1902, Box 82, LP; Tuthill to Lindsey, Feb. 20, 1902, Box 82, LP.

9. Lindsey to C. Hill, July 20, 1902, Box 83, LP.

10. Lindsey to Armstrong, April 14, 1902, Box 82, LP; Lindsey, *The Beast,* pp. 98–110. "Wine Room" was a euphemism for house of prostitution.

11. Lindsey to Hurley, Sept. 20, 1902, Box 84, LP; Lindsey to J. F. Hill, Jan. 17, 1903, Box 85, LP; Colorado, *Laws of 1903,* c 85.

12. Hurley to Lindsey, Jan. 1, 1903, Box 1, LP; Colorado, *Laws of 1903,* c 85; Lindsey to J. F. Hill, Jan. 17, 1903, Box 85, LP.

13. See above, Chapter 9, for a discussion of the Illinois laws on juvenile courts; Colorado, *Laws of 1903,* c 85, c 94.

14. Charles L. Chute, "Fifty Years of the Juvenile Court," National Parole and Probation Association, *Yearbook* (1949), p. 5.

15. Lindsey to Chadsey, Sept. 25, 1909, Box 22, LP; Lindsey to J. F. Hill, Jan. 17, 1903, Box 85, LP; "Juvenile Delinquents," NCCP (1902), pp. 423, 436, 541.

16. Lindsey to Kellogg, May 9, 1907, Box 9, LP; NCCP (1902), p. 424; Lindsey to C. Hill, July 21, 1902, Box 83, LP.

17. Tex. Soc. Friend., *Bull.* (Aug. 1906); "Juvenile Courts," NCCP (1903), pp. 206–30; Lindsey, *Charities,* XI (Nov. 7, 1903), 403–13.

18. Ben Lindsey, "The Child and the State," California State Conference of Charities and Corrections, *Proceedings,* III (1904), 16, 24, 27.

19. Lindsey to Winship, Sept. 26, 1904, Box 2, LP; Lindsey to C. Hill, Sept. 27, 1904, Box 2, LP; Lindsey to Tolstoi, Sept. 27, 1904, Box 2, LP; Julia Lathrop to Lindsey, Sept. 15 [1904], Box 2, LP;

Thorndike to Lindsey, Sept. 28, 1904, Box 2, LP; Denver Jv. Ct., *Report* (1904).

20. NCCP (1905), pp. 150–51, 159–60; Lindsey to Hurley, March 8, 1905, Box 3, LP; Ben Lindsey, "The Boy and the Court: The Colorado Law and Its Administration," *Charities*, XIII (Jan. 7, 1905), 350–57.

21. Lindsey, *The Beast*, pp. 184–202, 294–97; Colorado, *Laws of 1907*, c 149.

22. Thomas D. Eliot, *The Juvenile Court and the Community* (New York: Macmillan, 1914), p. 3; Charles D. Hilles, "Juvenile Delinquency," *Charities*, X (June 6, 1903), 558 [Italics mine]; Lindsey to Cunningham, March 18, 1906, Box 9, LP; *Children's Courts*, 58 Cong. 2nd Sess. (1904), HR Doc. No. 701; George A. Stephens, *The Juvenile Court System of Kansas* (Topeka: Mail and Breeze Pub. Co., 1906), pp. 18–19; Lincoln Steffens, *The Autobiography of Lincoln Steffens* (New York: Harcourt, Brace, 1931); Lincoln Steffens, *Upbuilders* (New York: Doubleday, Page, 1909).

23. Helen Page Bates, "Digest of Statutes Relating to Juvenile Courts and Probation," *Charities*, XIII (Jan. 7, 1905), 331–33; Grace Abbott, *The Child and the State*, 2 vols. (Chicago: Univ. of Chicago Pr., 1938), II, 332; Francis H. Hiller, *Juvenile Court Laws of the United States: Topical Summary of Their Main Provisions* (New York: National Probation Association, 1933), pp. 9–12.

24. James A. Collins, "The Juvenile Court Movement in Indiana," *Indiana Magazine of History*, XXVII (March 1932), 1–2; "Indiana Juvenile Court Law," *Charities*, X (April 25, 1903), 405; *Juvenile Record*, II (June 1901), 14; *Juvenile Record*, II (Summer 1901), 6–7.

25. *Juvenile Record*, II (Summer 1901), 7, 11–12; "Children's Court," *Charities*, IX (Sept. 6, 1902), 204; New York, *Laws of 1901*, c 466; Bernard Flexner, "The Juvenile Court as a Social Institution," *Survey*, XXXIII (Feb. 5, 1910), 609, 612; Edwin Biorkman, "The New York Police Court," *Century*, LXV (Nov. 1902), 20–21; Frederick A. King, "Police Court Probation Work," *Charities*, IX (Sept. 20, 1902), 265.

26. Stephens, Kansas Juvenile Court, pp. 18–19; Massachusetts, *Acts and Resolves* (1906), c 413.

27. A. J. M'Kelway, "The Need of Reformatories and the Juvenile Court System in the South," American Prison Association, Annual Congress, *Proceedings* (1908), p. 55; Bates, *Charities*, XIII (Jan. 7, 1905), 333; "Juvenile Courts in New Orleans," *Charities*, XIV (May 20, 1905), 758.

28. Raymond W. Murray, *Delinquent Children and the Law: A Study of the Development of Legislation Concerning Delinquent Children in the District of Columbia with Special Reference to the Juvenile Court* (Washington: Catholic University, 1926), p. 21; Theodore Roosevelt, *The Works of Theodore Roosevelt*, XVII: *State Papers*

as Governor and President (New York: Charles Scribner's Sons, 1925), 266; U.S. Children's Bureau, *The Federal Courts and the Delinquent Child: A Study of the Methods of Dealing with Children Who Have Violated Federal Laws,* Compiled by Ruth Youngblood, Children's Bureau Pub. No. 103 (Washington: Government Printing Office, 1922), pp. 6–8; Abbott, II, 333.

29. Illinois, *Laws of 1907,* pp. 69–70, 70–78; Lindsey to Shirer, Sept. 10, 1907, Box 10, LP; Henry W. Thurston, "Ten Years of the Juvenile Court," *Survey,* XXIII (Feb. 5, 1910), 658, 662; Helen Rankin Jeter, *The Chicago Juvenile Court,* U.S. Children's Bureau Pub. No. 104 (Washington, D.C.: Government Printing Office, 1922), p. 9; Grace Abbott, "The Hull House Years," MSS in Elizabeth and Grace Abbott papers, Manuscript Division, University of Chicago Library.

30. Thurston, *Survey,* XXIII (Feb. 5, 1910), 663–64; U.S. Children's Bureau, *Chicago Juvenile Court,* p. 47; Jane Addams, *My Friend Julia Lathrop* (New York: Macmillan, 1935), pp. 140–41.

31. Addams, *Julia Lathrop,* p. 141; Healy to Lathrop, April 4, 1908, papers of Ethel Sturges Dummer, Women's Rights Collection; Women's Archives, Schlesinger Library, Radcliffe College, Cambridge, Mass.

32. William A. Healy, *The Individual Delinquent: A Textbook of Diagnosis and Prognosis for All Concerned in Understanding Offenders* (Boston: Little, Brown, 1915), 809, "Juvenile Protective League," Jan. 2, 1909, Folder 372, Dummer papers; *Chicago Record-Herald,* April 20, 1909: "William Healy," *Who's Who in America,* IX (1916–17), 1116; "William Healy," *American Men of Science,* 4th ed. (New York: Science Press, 1927), p. 426.

33. Healy, *Individual Delinquent;* William Healy, "Factors Other than Legal in Dealing with Criminal Cases," NCCP (1912), pp. 187–88.

34. Healy, *Individual Delinquent,* pp. 2, 14–16, 18, 22, 24–25, 33, 53–65, 145, 179–82, 209, 210.

35. William A. Healy and Augusta F. Bronner, "Youthful Offenders: A Comparative Study of Two Groups, Each of 1000 Young Recidivists," *American Journal of Sociology,* XXII (July 1916), 39, 41, 48, 52.

36. William A. Healy, *Mental Conflicts and Misconduct* (Boston: Little, Brown, 1917), pp. 2–3, 6, 7–8, 17, 19–20, 22–24, 30–31, 54, 71–72, 75–76, 316–17, 321, 325.

37. See above, Chapter 9; Arthur E. Fink, *Causes of Crime: Biological Theories in the United States, 1800–1915* (New York: A. S. Barnes, 1962), pp. viii–ix; Clarence P. Oberndorf, *A History of Psychoanalysis in America* (New York: Harper, 1964), pp. 55–56, 132; F. H. Matthews, "The Americanization of Sigmund Freud: Adaptation of Psychoanalysis before 1917," *Journal of American Studies,* I (April 1967), 40–42; David Rapaport, *The Influence of Freud on American Psychology* (Cleveland: World, 1968), p. 52.

A Note on Sources

A study of a subject as broad and diverse as this obviously cannot be based on a single collection or narrow range of sources. In this essay I cannot of course mention all of the materials consulted. The notes, however, provide a reasonably complete list. Of the manuscript collections the two most important for this study are the Records of the New York House of Refuge in the Manuscript Division of the Carnegie Library at Syracuse University, and the Benjamin Barr Lindsey Papers in the Manuscript Division of the Library of Congress. Other useful manuscript collections include the Papers of Edith and Grace Abbott at the University of Chicago, the Jane Addams Papers in the Swarthmore College Peace Collection at Swarthmore College, the Ellen Sturges Dummer Papers and the Miriam Van Waters Papers in the Women's Rights Collection of the Schlesinger Library at Radcliffe College, and the Records of the Massachusetts State Reform School for Boys at the Lyman School for Boys in Westborough, Massachusetts. Also useful because of correspondence with Charles Loring Brace are the papers of Frederick Law Olmsted and Whitelaw Reid in the Manuscript Division of the Library of Congress.

Much of the history of American society's response to juvenile delinquency is to be found in court cases and in session laws. Of the court cases the most important are *Commonwealth* v *Fisher* (213 Pa. St. Reports 48 [1903]); *Commonwealth* v *Green* (2 Pick [19 Mass.], 380 [1824]); *Commonwealth* v *M'Keagy* (1 Ashmead [Pa.], 248 [1831]); and *Ex parte Crouse* (4 Wharton [Pa.], 9 [1839]). The law which provided for the incorporation of the New York House of Refuge is C 146 in the New York Session Laws for 1824. The act establishing the Juvenile Court in Chicago is found on pages 132 to 137 in the Illinois Session Laws of 1899; it may also be found in Grace Abbott, *The Child and the State* (Chicago, 1938).

A number of documents pertaining to juvenile delinquency may be found in *The Child and the State*. Other collections of official documents and reports include Edith Abbott, *Immigration: Select Documents and Case Records* (Chicago, 1924); *Documents Relative to a House of Refuge* (published by the New York State Legislature in 1854); and Enoch Wines and Theodore Dwight, *Special Report on the Prisons and Reformatories of the United States and Canada* (New York, 1965). One of the most useful of official documents, because it includes verbatim transcripts of interviews with officials in American courts and juvenile reformatories, is the *Report of the Commissioners Appointed to Inquire into the Prison and Reformatory System of Ontario* (Toronto, 1891). Other official reports and records of great value for this study are the annual reports of the various institutions' studies. These are sometimes difficult to find in plain title edition, but most of them were also issued as state documents.

Newspapers were also very important for this study. Among the most significant were the *Boston Globe* for the trial of Jesse Pomeroy; the *Chicago Record* and the *Chicago Tribune* for the creation of the Chicago Juvenile Court; the *New York Spectator* for the establishment of the New York House of Refuge, and the *New York Times* and *New York Tribune* for illustrative material on the city of New York, particularly concerning the Children's Aid Society.

There is an abundance of material in various autobiographies, memoirs, and other personal printed documents. Among the most useful are Gustave de Beaumont and Alexis de Tocqueville, *On the Penitentiary System in the United States* . . . ed. by Thorstein Sellin (Carbondale, Ill., 1964); Charles Loring Brace, *The Dangerous Classes of New York and Twenty Years' Work Among Them* (New York, 1872); Emma Brace, *The Life of Charles Loring Brace Chiefly Told in His Own Letters* (New York, 1892); Zebulon Brockway, *Fifty Years of Prison Service* (New York, 1912); John Griscom, *A Year in Europe. Comprising a Journal of Observations in England, France, Switzerland, the North of Italy and Holland. In 1818 and 1819* (New York, 1910); Benjamin Barr Lindsey and Harvey J. O'Higgins, *The Beast* (New York, 1910); and Bradford Kinney Peirce, *A Half-Century with Juvenile Delinquents, or, The House of Refuge and Its Times* (New York, 1869).

There are hundreds of works which pertain to this study in one way or another, but those which deal directly with juvenile delinquency include Sophonisba Breckinridge and Edith Abbott, *The Delinquent Child and the Home* (New York, 1912); Mary Carpenter, *Juvenile Delinquents: Their Condition and Treatment* (London, 1853); Thomas Eliot, *The Juvenile Court and the Community* (New York, 1914); Bernard Flexner and Roger Baldwin, *Juvenile Courts and Probation* (New York, 1914); William Healy, *The Individual Delinquent: A Textbook of Diagnosis and Prognosis for All Concerned in Understanding Offenders* (Boston, 1915); Herbert H. Lou, *Juvenile Courts in the United States* (Chapel Hill, N.C., 1927); Robert S. Picket, *The House of Refuge: Origins of Juvenile Reform in New York State, 1815–1857* (Syracuse, 1969); and Anthony Platt, *The Child Savers* (Chicago, 1969).

Among the other works especially useful were Robert H. Bremner, *From the Depths: The Discovery of Poverty in the United States* (New York, 1956); Lawrence A. Cremin, *The Transformation of the School: Progressivism in American Education, 1876–1957* (New York, 1961); Kai Erickson, *Wayward Puritans: A Study in the Sociology of Deviance* (New York, 1966); Arthur Fink, *Causes of Crime, Biological Theories in the United States, 1800–1915* (New York, 1962); Mark Haller, *American Eugenics: Heredity and Social Thought, 1870–1930* (Ann Arbor, 1963); John Higham, *Strangers in the Land: Patterns of American Nativism 1860–1925* (New Brunswick, N.J., 1955); Roy Lubove, *The Professional Altruist: The Emergence of Social Work as a Career, 1880–1930* (Cambridge, Mass., 1965); Jay Martin, *Harvests of Change, American Literature, 1865–1914* (Englewood Cliffs, N.J., 1967); Charles Rosenberg, *The Trial of the Assassin Guiteau: Psychiatry and the Law in the Gilded Age* (Chicago, 1968); and Alice Felt Tyler, *Freedom's Ferment; Phases of American Social History to the Outbreak of the Civil War* (New York, 1962).

Those who wish a more complete bibliography may consult my dissertation, "Society Versus Its Children: Nineteenth-Century America's Response to the Challenge of Juvenile Delinquency," University of Texas, 1969, which is available from University Microfilms, Ann Arbor, Michigan.

Index